On Illusion

v	**Preface and Editorial**
1	**Baudrillard and the Ambiguities of Radical Illusion** Nicholas Zurbrugg
6	**Illusiontext** Goat Island
12	**Approaching the Real: Reality Effects and the Play of Fiction** Andrew Quick
23	**Presenting the Prima Donna: Black Femininity and Performance in Nineteenth-Century American Blackface Minstrelsy** Annemarie Bean
31	**Truthful Trickery: Shamanism, Acting and Reality** Etzel Cardeña and Jane Beard
40	**Come Back to Life: An Interview with André Stitt** Simon Herbert
46	**'... and so shall you seem to have cut your nose in sunder': Illusions of Power on the Elizabethan Stage and in the Elizabethan Market-place** Michael Mangan
58	**Rose English: A Perilous Profession** Lynn MacRitchie
71	**As If Dance Was Visible** André Lepecki
77	**Hotel Pro Forma: Exposing Reality as a Visual Illusion** Erik Exe Christoffersen
90	**The Ear of Man Hath Not Seen** Nicholas Till
94	**Five Microlectures** Matthew Goulish
100	**Book Reviews**
107	**Archive Review**
110	**Notes on Contributors**
	Prepared Pages
between pp. 30 & 31	'Waiting for Falling Rocks' Hans-Peter Litscher
between pp. 57 & 58	W.S.H. Rod Dickinson
between pp. 70 & 71	Eclat: Occupation des Lieux 1–10 Caroline Bergvall
between pp. 76 & 77	*Breast Heart* – a trailer for Rosita Clavel – a horse opera by Rose English and Ian Hill to be presented June 1997 Rose English and Martha Fleming

Performance Research
A Journal of Performing Arts

GENERAL EDITOR
Richard Gough
Artistic Director, Centre for Performance Research and Senior Research Fellow, University of Wales, Aberystwyth

JOINT EDITORS
Claire MacDonald
Senior Lecturer and Research Fellow, De Montfort University, Leicester, UK
Ric Allsopp
Founder of Writing Research Associates, Amsterdam, Netherlands and Research Fellow, Dartington College of Arts, Totnes, UK

CONSULTANT EDITOR
Talia Rodgers
Routledge, London, UK

ASSOCIATE EDITORS
Noel Witts
De Montfort University, Leicester, UK
Alan Read
Institute of Contemporary Arts, London, UK

CONTRIBUTING EDITORS
Awam Amkpa King Alfred's College, Winchester, UK
Günter Berghaus University of Bristol, UK
Johannes Birringer Northwestern University, Chicago, USA
Scott de Lahunta Writing Research Associates, Amsterdam, Netherlands
Josette Féral University of Quebec, Montreal, Canada
Nick Kaye University of Warwick, Coventry, UK
Andrea Phillips Freelance Writer and Editor, London, UK
Heike Roms Theatre Researcher, Cardiff, UK
Jatinder Verma Artistic Director, Tara Arts Group, London, UK
David Williams Victoria University, Melbourne, Australia
Nicholas Zurbrugg De Montfort University, Leicester, UK

EUROPEAN CORRESPONDENT EDITORS
Knut Ove Arntzen University of Bergen, Norway
Monna Dithmer Theatre Critic, Politiken, Denmark
Christine Gaigg Freelance Writer and Performer, Vienna, Austria
Emil Hvratin Director and Dramaturg, Ljubljana, Slovenia
Antonio Fernandez Lera Writer and Journalist, Madrid, Spain
Petr Oslzly Dramaturg and Cultural Advisor, Brno, Czech Republic

ADVISORY BOARD
John Ashford Director, The Place Theatre, London
Eugenio Barba Director, Nordisk Teaterlaboratorium, Holstebro, Denmark
Brian Catling Ruskin School of Drawing, Oxford University, UK
Enzo Cozzi Royal Holloway, University of London, UK
Susan Croft Manchester Metropolitan University, Crewe, UK
Norman Frisch Dramaturg and Producer, New York, USA
Peter Hulton Director, Arts Documentation Unit, Exeter, UK
Stephanie Jordan Roehampton Institute, London, UK
Alastair MacLennan University of Ulster, UK
Patrice Pavis University of Paris 8, France
Warner van Wely Performance Artist and Director, Amsterdam, Netherlands

ADMINISTRATOR
Clancy Pegg Cardiff, UK

Performance Research is an independent, peer reviewed journal published by Routledge for ARC, a division of the Centre for Performance Research Ltd, Cardiff, an educational charity limited by guarantee. Performance Research acknowledges support from The Arts Councils of England and Wales, De Montfort University and Dartington College of Arts.

Performance Research welcomes responses to the ideas and issues it raises and is keen to consider proposals for articles and submissions. Please address all correspondence to:

Clancy Pegg
Journal Administrator
Performance Research
CPR
Market Road
Canton
Cardiff CF5 1QE
Wales, UK

Tel.: +44 (0) 1 222 232997
Fax: +44 (0) 1 222 232997
Email: post@perfres.demon.co.uk

Performance Research is published three times a year by Routledge, 11 New Fetter Lane, London EC4P 4EE, UK
A full listing of Routledge journals is available by accessing http://www.routledge.com/routledge.html

Enquiries concerning subscriptions should be addressed to the Subscriptions Department, North Way, Andover, Hants SP10 5BE, UK
Tel.: +44 (0) 1264 342817   Fax: +44 (0) 1264 342807
For sample copies contact the Subscriptions Department or email: sample.journals@routledge.com

Except as otherwise permitted under the Copyright, Designs and Patents Act, 1988, this publication may only be reproduced, stored or transmitted, in any form or by any means, with the prior permission in writing of the Publishers or in the case of reprographic reproduction in accordance with the terms of licences issued by the Copyright Licensing Agency in the UK. US copyright law is applicable in the USA.

ISSN 1352–8165
© Routledge 1996

Transferred to Digital Printing 2004

Annual subscription rates:
UK/EC:	Institution £72	Personal £28
US:	Institution $108	Personal $42
Rest of World:	Institution £76	Personal £30

Members of the Centre for Performance Research (CPR) will receive Performance Research as part of their membership. For further information please contact:

Adam Hayward
Centre for Performance Research
8 Science Park, Aberystwyth
Ceredigion SY23 3AH

Tel.: + 44(0)1970 622133
Fax: + 44(0) 1970 622132
Email: cprwww@aber.ac.uk

Design: Secondary Modern
Typeset by Type Study, Scarborough, UK

FORTHCOMING ISSUES

Issues 2(1) and 2(2) of Performance Research will be entitled *Letters from Europe* and *Tourism and Identity* and will appear in the Spring and Summer of 1997.

Letters from Europe. Europe is a continent in transition. In the past five years twelve new states have emerged in a continent in which only five countries have had stable borders for more more than a hundred years. *Letters from Europe* will explore Europe's performance forms, the relationship of old and new, the minority theatres of Europe and the place of dissident theatres in Europe now through the framing device of the letter – letters from theatre makers, artists and critics will accompany in-depth articles and interviews on European performance today.

Tourism and Identity will be the first of two issues dedicated to the theme of 'Identity', to be followed by a later issue on 'Refuge'. The notions of performance and identity have lately become almost inseparable: the problem of identity, of our sense of self and other and of the identification with gender, class, race and culture has dominated most of recent performance practice, and the performative nature of identity is now a major concern of the current debate in cultural theory. This issue will look at the notion of identity and how it relates to performance in the context of tourism.

ESSAY COMPETITION

In order to encourage new writing and new writers Performance Research is establishing a yearly writing prize competition. The winning essay will be published annually in the Spring issue of the journal. The competition is open to anyone who has not published previously in a peer reviewed journal and is aimed at emerging writers, artists and graduates. Submissions can be made in the writer's preferred language.

Full details of the competition can be obtained from Clancy Pegg, Administrator, Performance Research, CPR, Market Road, Cardiff, CF5 1QE, UK. The closing date for the 1997 competition will be 1 September 1997.

The essay need not be linked to the journal's specific theme but should address contemporary practices or contemporary investigations of performance practice and its history. The essays will be judged by a select committee of members of the journal's Editorial and International Advisory Boards.

SUBMISSIONS

Performance Research is a peer reviewed arts journal published three times a year which addresses contemporary performance research and practice internationally. It aims to promote a cross-disciplinary exchange of ideas; making connections between theatre, dance, music, time-based and live art. The editors are interested in receiving submissions and proposals from artists, independent writers, critics and academics working in these fields and in other disciplines. We encourage proposals using visual, graphic and photographic forms, including photo essays, original artwork for the page of mixed media submissions as well as substantial articles and reviews. There is no payment for articles except in the case of commissions for which funding may be sought. It is the responsibility of authors to seek permissions for all visual material.

Proposals may be submitted on one sheet of A4 containing an abstract, proposed word count and description. Unsolicited articles may be submitted for consideration by email, on disk or double spaced in hard copy. Detailed guidelines for preparing text will be sent either on request or on acceptance for publication. Proposals are considered at least nine months before publication.
Proposals and articles, including book reviews, should be sent to:

Clancy Pegg, Administrator, Performance Research, CPR, Market Road, Cardiff, CF5 1QE, UK.
Email: post@perfres.demon.co.uk

Preface

As On Illusion goes to press the Higher Education Funding Council is finalizing its judgements about what constitutes valid academic research in British universities, and in relation to performance those judgements will have wide repercussions. Just as the academy has begun to take a serious interest in the kinds of art performance that until recently were seen as too marginal, too risky and too interdisciplinary to merit real attention, models of research and publication are becoming highly restrictive and standardized. The kind of informed and engaged criticism which we value in *Performance Research* – a criticism which combines eclecticism and critical independence with passion and urgency, and comes from artists, curators and freelance critics and writers as well as academic researchers – seems to us to sit uneasily in the emerging academic culture.

On Illusion completes the first volume of *Performance Research*, and its first year of publication. At this point the question of what constitutes research in relation to performance is one of several issues which stand out. It is evident that there is a continuing need for analytical and documentary research on work which is widely seen, reviewed and debated internationally, but which remains substantially undocumented. The many questions which are emerging from the profound shifts of culture, identity and place at the end of this millennium are also urgent. How the making of performance speaks to and of cultural change will be a theme underlying much of our second volume. Volume 2 will begin with a collection of 'Letters from Europe' (Spring 1997) marking voices and perspectives that reflect Europe through performance as a shifting and emergent identity.

We are now in the early stages of planning the first *Performance Research* conference, to be held in 1998, which will encourage young and/or new writers to present their work as well as create a platform for established artists and scholars.

There is a vitality and urgency about encountering performance at a time when its provenance has extended to the point where it seems to reflect some deep sense of cultural shift which has come through in the material we have read and published this year. We look forward with anticipation to what comes next.

Ric Allsopp, Richard Gough
and Claire MacDonald, Editors
(September 1996)

Editorial

The Polish theatre director Tadeusz Kantor ' after years of anti-illusionary work' stated that 'illusion shifts reality onto another track, the track of poetry' (Plesniarowicz 1994: 45). This track is earlier projected by Charles Olson in his discussion of an 'open field' poetics (Olson 1966: 16): 'the poet ... can go by no track other than the one the poem under hand declares, for itself.' I have always liked the ambiguity of this phrase 'the poem under hand declares' for its grasp of, the way it catches the meanings of 'under hand' as holding together images of control, craft and process with deception, artifice and risk. It is a phrase that aptly contains the mutual inseparability of illusion and the real within the project of performance; an image that echoes the various 'under hand' approaches to illusion that make up the conversation of this third issue of *Performance Research*. The conversations on illusion take two broad but not exclusive positions: illusion as magical trick or illusionist spectacle; and illusion as an approach to the problems of 'the real' and identity. As a whole they point towards radical uses of illusion as a means of framing performance work.

At the shrine of the Black Virgin of Guadalupe in Extrémadura you can ascend a broad stairway from behind the Chapel of the Virgin, that brings you to the '*camarín*', presided over in each corner by the waxen figures of Miriam, Judith, St Catherine and St Anne, almost lifelike in their flower-decked vitrines. The *camarín* forms an antechamber to the shrine of Our Lady of Silence. When enough visitors have climbed the stairway – pilgrims from the eastern bloc (it is 1987), local devotees, a man on his way home from work, cultural tourists – a monk appears from a small door concealed in the panelling and guides you into the shrine. Your attention is drawn to an enamelled panel between two openings that look down on to the nave of the chapel. It shows the miraculous episodes of the Black Virgin. The monk narrates each image in turn – the burial in Guadalupe of the statue in 711 after defeat by the Saracens; the rediscovery of the statue by a cowherd named Gil in 1326; the visitation of popes and kings to the shrine. The air of expectancy grows more tangible. As the final episode is completed the monk discreetly presses a lever which spins the Black Virgin into vision, turned like a page of the book she so oddly resembles. The inspiration – the literal intake of breath at this small disclosure – affects us all. For some it is a revelation, the culmination of an arduous journey, the possibility of a divine intervention within the everyday (an illness cured, a marriage saved, a trespass forgiven); for others it is a brief moment of theatre, or of storytelling, of showmanship which might recall Herbert Blau's comment that the 'illusion [is] so exhausted by history that it can barely reproduce itself' (Blau 1992: 27).

By way of beginning, these conversations are framed by Nicholas Zurbrugg's review article of Jean Baudrillard's recently published book *The Perfect Crime* (1996: 20–4), which begins with the epigraph: 'Given the mass of evidence, there is no plausible hypothesis but reality. Given the mass of evidence to the contrary, there is no solution but illusion.' Baudrillard argues that it is the 'proliferation of reality' produced by simulation, that is 'our true catastrophe'; and that illusion, not the real, opposes simulation. Only therefore through restoring the potency of illusion can the exponential curve of the real be exceeded. The Chicago-based perfomance group Goat Island, resident in the UK during the spring and summer of this year, have collectively contributed an 'Illusiontext' both as a form of active documentation of the processes of creating their new performance (*How Dear to Me the Hour When Daylight Dies*, May 1996) and as a testimony to the uses of illusion in exceeding the real – 'this performance will hurt'.

The hierarchy of western metaphysics has prioritized the real over illusion. The effects of this on notions of presence and absence within performance initiates Andrew Quick's discussion of the differing tensions between 'the operation[s] of representation, of repetition, of illusion' and the ontology and presence of 'the real' itself in performance. The now largely hidden work of the seminal English theatre company Impact Theatre (active 1976–86) is unearthed and reread through the work of Derrida, Lacan and Žižek and their deconstructions of 'the real'.

The performances of 'The Only Leon' – the 'most successful female impersonator in nineteenth-century blackface minstrelsy' – are reread by Annemarie Bean, in her article 'Presenting the Prima Donna', as constructing and securing, through gender transgression, both the identity of the dominant white male and black female sexuality. Such uses of illusion to mediate social desires through a 'performed cultural imaginary' are then taken up from a psychological perspective in Etzel Cardeña's 'Truthful Trickery: Shamanism, Acting and Reality'. The analogies between forms of shamanic performance and the methods of the western acting tradition allow us to question the usual distinctions between pretence and reality, appearance and substance. Illusion when used in particular performative ways can have concrete and real effects on the subject, not only therapeutically, but also as 'a jarring step' from illusion to a reality beyond the circumstances of the everyday.

Simon Herbert's interview with the Belfast performance artist André Stitt, whose work since 1976 has explored the extremities of life and art, describes this jarring step and the very real implications of the risk of illusion from the performer's viewpoint. The implications of such an intensified individual journey by the artist confront us with the nature of social responsibility, the possibilities of redemption and the edge between the illusion and reality of performance. The question of art and artifice – a debate resurrected by the impact and insistence of new media technologies – is identified by Baudrillard, in terms that evoke the work of André Stitt:

> True artifice is the artifice of the body in the throes of passion, the artifice of the sign of seduction, the artifice of ambivalence in gesture.
>
> (1993: 51)

Baudrillard argues that artifice as 'the power of illusion' is in no way concerned with what *generates* reality, but with what *alters* reality. The distinction is in trying to understand the uses of illusion rather than the meanings of illusion. As Michael Mangan points out in his article on Elizabethan uses of juggling and conjuring, northern renaissance culture displayed a nervousness of the 'juggler' and 'conjuror' – a nervousness that is still apparent. Operating on the margins and periphery of culture (which is the habitual place of performance) such 'jugglers and conjurors' enable us to experience an altered reality – a reality that might hold the possibility of a different future.

The staging of illusion is a problem that is taken up in Lynn MacRitchie's articles on the work of the British performance artist Rose English; in the performance writings of Caroline Bergvall, and in Exe Christoffersen's survey of a 'nomadic dramaturgy' in the work of the Danish theatre company Hotel Pro Forma.

Lynn MacRitchie guides us through the work of Rose English and particularly 'her deconstruction of the thaumaturgy – the wonderworking – of theatre'. Her rigorous examination of the terms and subtle distinctions that construct the conventions of theatre, has typified her work since the mid-1970s. English's interest in the ways in which theatre stages and spatializes the illusionary is echoed in the writings of Caroline Bergvall. The uses of illusion and the vestiges of the real, the identity or displacement of text with the spatiality of surface, are ideas that Bergvall addresses 'for the page' in the documentation of her recent (May 1996) text installation *Eclat: Occupation des Lieux, 1–10*. Here and in the 'live' performance of the text, the work keeps ironically pointing to the frequent ruptures between the play of illusory spatiality in the text, and the reading and consequent perception of the actual space of performance. The *trompe-l'oeil* as an imitation of nature which conjures up a world woven through with features of the real, as Exe Christoffersen puts it in his survey of the work of the Danish theatre company Hotel Pro Forma, 'points to the fact that limits exist while at the same time being a fiction and a passage to another fiction'. Their work since 1986 has explored not only the formal aspects of illusion, but also the status of marginality and ambiguity in audience–performer relationships. Christoffersen also reads the work through a notion of a 'nomadic' dramaturgy: a 'restless' non-linear dramaturgy somewhere between movement and being, format and identity.

Theatre and performance are forms that play within the ephemeral, the disappearing; forms that occupy a ludic space held in tension by momentary shifts between presence and absence. Baudrillard has elsewhere referred to the disappearance of the 'soul of art' – 'Art with its power of illusion, its capacity for negating reality, for setting up an "other scene" in opposition to reality' – and observes that *all* disappearing forms seek to duplicate themselves by simulation (1993: 14). In Baudrillard's terms the intensity and ubiquity of aesthetics produce a 'profusion of images' in which there is nothing to see but the grand illusion of the spectacle.

André Lepecki's reading of Kantor's 'room of memory' and his discussion of the invisibility of the dance is an example of recent work that is pointing towards the dematerialization of the 'object of performance'. It is not only the art object that is dematerializing. The ephemerality of performance itself becomes more and more the locus of critical thinking. The dematerialized trace and 'origin' of dance and its recollection in the act of writing bring to bear another contemporary theorization of the illusion/real as the 'spectacle' – the commodification of life – which increasingly erodes the realm of 'free' and 'unalienated experience'; or as Guy Debord (Plant 1992: 13) put it, 'the real consumer becomes a consumer of illusions. The commodity is this factually real illusion, and the spectacle is its general manifestation.'

Relations between the sonic and the visual occupy Nicholas Till in his review of the 1996 performances of Varèse's *Déserts* with accompanying film by Bill Viola; and Schubert's 'Winterreise' staged by Boltanski and Kalman.

The power of illusion is eating away at the edges and interstices of the 'real' as it is ordinarily constituted. It is perhaps these moments of illusion that allow us to move forward in the way suggested by Matthew Goulish in his *Five Microlectures*, through attention to the 'clearly shifting detail' of accumulating moments that begin to constitute a 'recognizable pattern'.

Ideas of artifice and fabrication, and how they allow us to visualize and construct our cultural imaginaries, characterize the artist's pages we have commissioned for this issue. Rod Dickinson's work *W.S.H.* explores questions of agency in the relation between art and fabrication, hoaxing and illusion, whilst the pages from Rose English act as a sort of 'premonition' for an as yet unrealized show. Playing somewhere in between artifice and reality, the Swiss theatre artist Hans-Peter Litscher pays homage to the illustrious Italian mountainscape painter Giovanni Sagatini in *Caduta Massi*.

There are book reviews by Claire MacDonald, cris cheek and Peter Hulton, and the conversations of the issue close with a review by Richard Gough of the recently opened archive in Krakow which houses the work of Tadeusz Kantor and his company Cricot 2.

The shrine at Guadalupe haunts a second more recent image. At the Stedelijk Museum in Amsterdam (it is 1993) you can ascend a broad stairway from the entrance hall and the garde-robe that will bring you to the Gary Hill exhibition, which starts in the main gallery on the first floor. In front and to your right you will see an installation *Crux* (1983–7) consisting of five video monitors 'mounted on the wall positioned to suggest the configuration of a cross as well as the elements of the human body, respecting its proportions, with head, two hands, and two feet. … A large, composite [moving] image, pieced together by the body's limbs, is presented on the monitors' (Stedelijk Museum 1993: 75). The place of the body, the torso itself, is absent, a void filled only with the imaginary implied by the five flickering 'vitrines'. Moving further into the gallery you will reach the darkened entrance to *Tall Ships* (1992). This oracular installation consists of 'a completely dark, ninety-foot long corridor-like space, [in which] sixteen black and white images of people, varying in ethnic origin, age and gender, are projected directly onto the walls. No border of light defines the frame of the images: only the figures themselves give off light into the space. The last projection is on the back wall, at the end of the corridor' (Stedelijk 1993: 98). In this silent space, peopled by the moving and projected ghosts of the familiar, the everyday, the narratives of each 'meeting' are constructed by each one of us alone, the revelation no longer attempts to speak collectively within the logic of theatre. For some it is a play of light, a technical demonstration, a silent slide-show in an age of movies and home video; for others these mute meetings are filled with unspoken conversations, with intense emotional impact, a displacement between virtual and real space that is intensified to such an extent that we find ourselves 'taking place', a transformation that turns inside ourselves.

Illusion lies in the space between these two images of Guadalupe and the Stedelijk. And so with 'nimble conveyance' I must declare that this particular 'under hand' process of trying to let the constellations of material in this issue find a form has been made possible only by the work and generosity of others, in particular the contributors, all those who have read and commented on submissions for us, and not least Clancy, Claire, Richard and Simon Josebury, to whom I offer the final lines of Wallace Stevens's 1937 meditation on the impossibility of grasping the real, 'The Man with the Blue Guitar':

> We shall forget by day, except
> The moments when we chose to play
> The imagined pine, the imagined jay.

Ric Allsopp, Issue Editor, *On Illusion*

REFERENCES

Baudrillard, Jean (1993) *The Transparency of Evil*, London: Verso.

Baudrillard, Jean (1996) *The Perfect Crime*, London: Verso.

Blau, Herbert (1992) *To All Appearances*, PAJ, Baltimore, MD: Johns Hopkins University Press.

Olson, Charles (1966) *Collected Writings*, ed. Robert Creeley, New York: New Directions.

Plant, Sadie (1992) *The Most Radical Gesture*, London: Routledge.

Plesniarowicz, Krzysztof (1994) *The Dead Memory Machine*, trans. William Brand, Krakow Cricoteka.

ALTERNATIVE VIEWS...

FOR THE CURIOUS...

An independent theatre organisation located in Wales and working internationally

For further information on the CPR range of projects and activities, see our World Wide Web site at: http://www.aber.ac.uk/~cprwww or contact us at:

Centre for Performance Research
8 Science Park, Aberystwyth
SY23 3AH, Wales, UK
Tel:+44 (0) 1970 622133
Fax:+44 (0) 1970 622132
E-Mail: cprwww@aber.ac.uk

Baudrillard and the Ambiguities of Radical Illusion

Nicholas Zurbrugg

Jean Baudrillard's *The Perfect Crime* is essentially a passionate defence of radical thought and, by extension, of the kind of radical writing that effects 'the resolution of the infelicity of meaning by the felicity of language' (1996: 120).

It is a book written by a performative writer, alarmed both by the pre-poetic register of rational thinking and by the post-poetic register of those information technologies which seemingly 'wipe out all the supernatural reflexes of thought extirpating all the magic from thought' (1996: 22). Put another way, *The Perfect Crime* articulates the anxieties of a verbal magician, intolerant towards the past, uncertain before the future.

Convinced that 'Analysis is, by definition, unhappy', whereas, 'language, for its part, is happy, even when referring to a world without illusion and without hope', Baudrillard speculates:

> That might even be the definition of a radical thinking: a happy form and an intelligence without hope.... What counts is the poetic singularity of the analysis ... not the wretched critical objectivity of ideas ... better a despairing analysis in felicitous language than an optimistic analysis in an infelicitous language that is maddeningly tedious and demoralizingly platitudinous, as is most often the case ... among those who speak only of the transcending and transforming of the world when they are incapable of transfiguring their own language.
> (1996: 119–20)

How do writers transfigure their own language? Updating the old maxim that 'It don't mean a thing if it ain't got swing', Baudrillard argues that 'by its very form', transfigured language 'appeals to the spiritual and material imagination of sounds and rhythm, to the dispersal of meaning in the event of language', propelled by what he calls a 'passion for artifice, for illusion', for 'undoing ... meaning', and for 'letting the imposture of the world show through' (1996: 121).

When writing really swings, one might say, it becomes an event, and as such transmutes what Baudrillard takes to be the inadequate illusions of reason into the felicitous illusions of the supernatural and of magic. But how exactly is this done? Some thirty years ago, William Burroughs's *Nova Express* (1964) evoked this kind of cabalistic alchemy with the haunting imperative:

> *Partisans of all nations, open fire – tilt – blast – pound – stab – strafe – kill – ... – This is war to extermination – Shift linguals – Cut word lines – Vibrate tourists – Free doorways – Photo falling – Word falling – Break through in grey room – Calling Partisans of all nations – Towers, open fire –*
> (Burroughs 1968: 62)

For his part, Baudrillard appeals to his peers with the encouraging words: 'Thinkers, one more effort!' (1996: 113), recommending:

> Cipher, do not decipher. Work over the illusion. Create illusion to create an event. Make enigmatic what is clear, render unintelligible what is only too intelligible, make the event itself

unreadable. Accentuate the false transparency of the world to spread a terroristic confusion about it, or the germs or viruses of a radical illusion – in other words, a radical disillusioning of the real. Viral, pernicious thought, corrosive of meaning, generative of an erotic perception of reality's turmoil.

(1996: 121)

What exactly does Baudrillard understand by the event of language? Such events, it seems, are distinguished above all by their 'suddenness', and by their 'non-anteriority' as an 'emergence from the void' (1996: 68). Breaking 'with all previous causality',

> The event of language is what makes it re-emerge miraculously every day, as a finished form, outside of all previous significations. Photography, too, is the art of dissociating the object from any previous existence and capturing its probability of disappearing in the moment that follows. In the end we prefer the *ab nihilo*, prefer what derives its magic from the arbitrary, from the absences of causes and history. Nothing gives greater pleasure than what emerges or disappears at a stroke, than emptiness succeeding plenitude. Illusion is made up of this magic portion, this accursed share which creates a kind of absolute surplus-value by subtraction of causes or by dissolution of effects and causes.

(1996: 68–9)

As a process born of 'the poetic imagination' the event of radical thought, radical language or radical photography is distinct, first, from 'analytic thought' – which for Baudrillard always 'has an origin and a history' (1996: 66) – and, second, from the 'classical and "rational"' orders of thought that he associates with the Enlightenment's project of modernity, with their hypotheses of 'an evolution and a progress of living forms' (1996: 67). In this respect, it is 'unintelligible' because 'without historical continuity'; and as such, a source of protection from the tri-part perils of being, of mortality and of determinacy.

> Born at a stroke, it is not susceptible of having an end set to it, we are protected from its end by this non-meaning which takes the force of poetic illusion. Illusion, being pre-eminently the art of appearing, of emerging from nothing, protects us from being. And being also pre-eminently the art of disappearing, it protects us from death. The world is protected from its end by its diabolic indeterminacy. By contrast, all that is determinate is condemned to be exterminated.

(1996: 66–7)

Ironically, Baudrillard's concept of a poetic event without origins, history, determinacy or mortality reiterates the ideals of innumerable culturally modernist and postmodern visionaries, to speak only of its most recent precursors. One thinks, for example, of Walter Pater's advocacy of a pre-Baudrillardian 'passion for artifice' in *Studies of the Renaissance* (1873). Here Pater insists that the artist and writer should 'burn always with this hard gem-like flame' rather than 'form habits . . . relative to a stereotyped world' (Pater 1981: 631). Explaining that only 'High passions give one this quickened sense of life, ecstasy', Pater specifies:

> Only, be sure it is passion, that it does yield you this fruit of a quickened, multiplied consciousness. Of this wisdom, the poetic passion, the desire of beauty, the love of art for art's sake has most; for art comes to you professing frankly to give nothing but the highest quality to your moments as they pass, and simply for those moments' sake.

(Pater 1981: 632)

Alternatively, one thinks of Burroughs's definition of immortality as a condition informed by 'increased flexibility, capacity for change' (Burroughs 1985: 135), and by the potential mutation that he associates with 'training for space conditions' (1985: 136), within a domain in which 'you must leave the old verbal garbage behind' (1985: 137). For Burroughs,

> Artists and creative thinkers . . . are providing us with the only maps for space travel. *We are not setting out to explore static pre-existing data.* We are setting out to *create* new worlds, new beings, new modes of consciousness.

(1985: 102)

If Baudrillard's final comments to the first section of *The Perfect Crime* suggest that he shares Burroughs's commitment to innovative art, insofar as he claims that 'Thought has to be exceptional, anticipatory and at the margin' (1996: 117), Baudrillard's general critique of 'static pre-existing data' and the 'stereotyped world' culminates in double derision; first, for the 'absurdity' of those 'progressive ideologies' which deny that 'man is an ambiguous, untameable animal' and 'attempt to extirpate evil from him in order to turn him into a rational being' (1996: 169), and second, for those progressive artists who aspire to create new worlds, beings or modes of consciousness.

Contending that 'We cannot project more order or disorder into the world than there is' and that 'We cannot transform it more than it transforms itself', Baudrillard opens fire upon both philosophic and poetic idealism.

> All the philosophies of change, the revolutionary, nihilistic, futuristic utopias, all this poetics of subversion and transgression so characteristic of modernity, will appear naive when compared with the instability and natural reversibility of the world. Not only transgression, but even destruction is beyond our reach.
>
> (1996: 13)

It is perhaps for this reason that Baudrillard celebrates the work of Andy Warhol as an exemplary 'challenge to the very notion of art and aesthetics' (1996: 92), or as what one might think of as the work of an artist all dressed up to kill every trace of ideological and aesthetic ambition, but with nowhere to go, and apparently evincing 'the minimum pretension to being, the minimum strategy of means and ends' (1996: 90).

> Warhol starts out from any old image, eliminates its imaginary dimension and makes it a pure visual product... Warhol's images... are products of the elevation of the image to pure figuration, without the least transfiguration. Not transcendence any longer, but the... sign which, losing all natural signification, shines forth in the void with the full gleam of its artificial light.
>
> (1996: 88)

Bearing in mind that Baudrillard celebrates 'An irony which plays not on negation but on empty positivity' and reveres 'the splendour of the void', arguing that 'Irony is the only spiritual form in the modern world' (1996: 84), it is not surprising that he defines Warhol's 'ecstatic, insignificant iconry' (1996: 88) in terms of a distinctively non-sacral aura – 'that fetishistic aura which attaches to the singularity of the void' (1996: 91). For Baudrillard, Warhol's work radiates a peculiarly descendental anti-mysticism.

As the lines below indicate, Baudrillard prefaces his sense of the inevitable vacuity of contemporary, technologically mediated, revelation with a brief definition of conventional mysticism. In other words, if progressive thinkers 'explore the wretchedness of others to prove our existence *a contrario*' (1996: 158), his argument tends to first outline and then outlaw the values of others, in order to prove our wretchedness '*a contrario*'.

> In the mystical vision, the illumination of the slightest detail comes from the divine intuition which lights it, the sense of transcendence which inhabits it. For us, by contrast, the stupefying exactness of the world comes from the sense of an essence fleeing it, a truth which no longer inhabits it. It comes from a minutely detailed perception of the simulacrum and, more precisely, of the media and industrial simulacrum. Such is Warhol... at once both our new mystic and the absolute anti-mystic, in the sense that every detail of the world, every image, remains initiatory, but initiatory into nothing at all.
>
> (1996: 89)

But why should media and industrial culture culminate in 'nothing at all'? Why should techno-culture impose a 'state of pure operational intelligence'? Why should those who 'persuade us that technology will inevitably produce good' champion the 'radical disillusioning of thought' (1996: 22)? Anticipating such questions, perhaps, and reflecting that '*the failure of an attempt at annihilation is, necessarily, vital and positive*' (1996: 172), Baudrillard predicts the way in which his scathing account of techno-culture prompts reconsideration of such exceptions to his rules as the American artists John Giorno and Bill Viola.

Discussing his performance as Joe in the La Mama Experimental Theatre's January 1995 production of Beckett's *Eh Joe* in New York, in which his offstage gestures were projected live by video on to a wall-sized screen in the theatre, before an audience hearing the play's monologue by individual radio-headsets, New York poet John Giorno argues that in this production, as in any other high-tech or low-tech performance,

> The one ingredient that makes performance successful . . . is the amount of energy that a person gives from their heart to the audience. It can be done any way – Diana Ross does it in her way, or a poet or an actor can do it in their way. When you understand those things, it's understanding a concept experientially in a visceral way.
> (Giorno 1996)

Asked whether he felt this blown-up video image was more impactful than Warhol's monumental portraits, Giorno (who slept in Warhol's film *Sleep*), suggested both were 'equally strong', explaining:

> Apparently they've rediscovered Andy Warhol's screen tests from the early 1950s, including mine, and someone who saw it in a show in San Francisco . . . was saying how powerful it was. Take anybody's head and show it from chin to forehead, and it's probably powerful!
> (Giorno 1996)

In Giorno's terms, the 'visceral' impact of his own technologically mediated 'eyes . . . fifty feet apart . . . tears three feet wide, going down the screen!' generated all the intensity that Baudrillard associates with the creative 'event', and when shown in Italy –'it's quite a sad play – a tragic play . . . and you know – Italians and tears!' – proved 'a huge, huge success in Rome!' (Giorno 1996).

For his part, Los Angeles video artist Bill Viola similarly asserts his 'great faith in the inherent power of images', despite 'the onslaught of media images that incessantly confront us and skew our perceptions' (Viola 1995: 251). For Viola, 'One of the most interesting aspects of the recording media is how they tell us so much about the way we perceive the world', offering us 'surrogate sensory perceptual systems' (1995: 65), which re-establish our links with past cultures, past questions, and past insights.

> The new technologies of image-making are by necessity bringing us back to fundamental questions, whether we want to face them or not. . . . Spend time with a video camera and you will confront some of the primary issues: What is this fleeting image called life? . . . And why are the essential elements of life change, movement, and transformation, but not stability, immobility, and constancy?
> (1995: 257)

While Viola and Baudrillard ask near-identical questions, their answers could not be more different. For Baudrillard, consideration of techno-culture demonstrates that 'there is no point taking refuge in the defence of values, even critical ones' (1996: 75), and confirms that 'we no longer know what to do with the real world' because 'the real . . . has been "laid off" ' (1996: 51), just as 'the machinery of thought . . . is laid off' (1996: 33) and 'every natural desire, is laid off' (1996: 144). For Viola, utilization of techno-culture reveals that 'questions of form . . . and the "how" of image-making drop away', as 'You realize that the real work for this time is not abstract, theoretical, and speculative – it is urgent, moral, and practical' (1995: 257).

On occasion, however, Baudrillard hesitatingly hints that his superficial cynicism conceals more profound afterthoughts. For example, prompted by Heidegger's suggestion that ' "When we look into the ambiguous essence of technology, we behold . . . the stellar course of the mystery" ' , Baudrillard seems to concede that techno-culture may sometimes evince unexpected spiritual and ironic depths, observing:

> The Japanese sense the presence of a divinity in every industrial object. For us, that sacred presence has been reduced to a tiny ironic glimmer, a nuance of play and distantiation. Though this is, none the less, a spiritual form, behind which lurks the evil genius of technology which sees to itself that the mystery of the world is well-guarded. The Evil Spirit keeps watch beneath artefacts and, of all our artificial productions, one might say what Canetti says of animals: that behind each of them there is hidden someone thumbing his nose at us.
> (1996: 84)

One discovers the same speculation in Baudrillard's concluding meditation upon Borges's story of the 'mirror people', which prompts his suggestion that behind every reflection or representation 'a defeated enemy lies concealed'; a defeated 'singularity', which 'will one day rebel'. But at this point Baudrillard's prophecies grind to a halt: 'What will come of this victory? No one knows' (1996: 171). In much the same way, Baudrillard ponders: 'As for art . . . There must surely be some meaning to it . . . but we can't see what it is' (1996: 147).

Can't see? Or won't see? As his sympathetic references to other artists and writers such as Hopper, Warhol, Borges, Brecht, Canetti, Heidegger, Jarry, Nabokov and so on indicate, Baudrillard, like Viola, situates himself among a distinguished lineage of fellow-spirits. Like Viola, Baudrillard may well eventually concede that the best of contemporary art, like his art, like any exceptional art, attains comparable 'poetic singularity' (1996: 120), and that, 'As we take the first steps into data space . . . Fascinating relationships between ancient and modern technologies become evident' (Viola 1995: 106).

Explicitly denying and implicitly exemplifying these fascinating relationships, Baudrillard's *The Perfect Crime* draws them, paws them, irresistibly, inevitably, inexorably, to our attention. And what more could one for ask than that?

REFERENCES

Baudrillard, Jean (1996) *The Perfect Crime*, trans. Chris Turner, London: Verso.

Burroughs, William (1968) *Nova Express*, London: Panther.

——(1985) *The Adding Machine: Collected Essays*, London: John Calder.

Giorno, John (1996) Unpublished interview with the author.

Pater, Walter (1981) Extract from 'Conclusion', *Studies in the History of the Renaissance*, in Gordon S. Haight (ed.) *The Portable Victorian Reader*, Harmondsworth: Penguin.

Viola, Bill (1995) *Reasons for Knocking at an Empty House, Writings 1973–1994*, Cambridge, MA: MIT Press.

Illusiontext

Goat Island

A. BETTER *Bryan Saner*

I heard an interview with a Nazi death camp survivor who after fifty years of healing and counselling and processing still wept with his memories and confessed to his rabbi, saying: 'It's not going to get any better than this, is it.'

I saw an old beer advertisement. Several young men were frying the fish they just caught on an open fire in the mountains. They were reaching for beers out of a large cooler filled with ice. One man said, 'It just doesn't get any better than this does it.'

B. PUPPET SHOW / 1 *Lin Hixson*

When I was 9, I received a puppet theatre for Christmas. It was too big for my bedroom so it ended up in my brother's room. Consequently, he began to perform puppet shows for me by hiding behind the yellow castle with its red and blue Bavarian patterns.

Three hinged panels formed the castle theatre. The main stage was an open-air rectangle cut into the centre panel and framed by scarlet curtains. In height it was just the size of my brother's head if you included his neck. In width, he could fit two hands with his fingers spread. The two side panels adjusted to provide his secret chamber.

Of course the task was never to see hand or head of my brother, but only the adventures of the king and queen or the lion and the mouse. The beginning of his plays usually went well; the king and queen danced; the lion bit the mouse's head. But soon my brother's foot would creep out off to the side, looming larger than the full figure of the queen. The top of his head would appear bobbing visibly with the king as he waltzed. Sometimes the sleeve of his shirt became the bottom of the mouse's body. And then finally, when tired, he'd sit up, his big head taking up the whole rectangle and becoming the godzilla backdrop to the lives of these smaller beings.

I grew to love these breakdowns; these scenes filled with the tension of his imminent arrival. How long would the fantastic world of the miniature people and animals last before they were disrupted by my brother's head ? When would the lion become the lion-sleeve, or the queen become the queen-ear?

C. THE FUTURE *Adrian Blundell*

It seemed obvious to me when I was younger. We were living at the end of one age and the beginning of another. I knew as I sat in the classroom that things would be different from now on, computers would change everything. Peter and I could see, as we half-listened to him explain that after all was said about hormones, fluids and tissues that it was most of all . . . fun (I would keep my virginity for another four years), that there would be no need for most of the labour currently undertaken, in a very short time.

We envisioned a larger class of English people who would have time and money, provided by a government elected by an educated people, to make up ways to live a life.

I see now that the way forward was not that of no work for many because most prefer to study and play. But no work for the many because work is a precious and scarce commodity to be parcelled for the desperate.

D. BLOODSHIRT CONSTRUCTION (AFTER MELVILLE) *Antonio Poppe*

To construct the bloodshirt
with my bloodshot eyes
after diving and coming up again
like a great whale going down stairs five miles or more.

Being Dishonoured 1: All of us have said that if any harm came to Memory, and there were not at least 600 bloodshot eyes lying at the foot of Memory's stairway, we would be dishonoured.

Being Dishonoured 2: all of us have said that if any harm came to memory, and there were not at least 600 bloodshot eyes lying at the foot of Memory's stairway, we would dive like a great whale going down stairs five miles or more ... the last act is bloody.

A first motion
Proliferating inside an eyebath full of red
Breaking open without batting an eyelid
Oral rumours and sounds of docile closure during the movement
Sudden attention
Sudden closure and then to blink touching the blood with my eyelash
Improvising each blink
Linked from one red to another
Arrival
At a disturbing sound from a different tradition ...
For example, *palpebra*, that means eyelid in Portuguese
Because we all like to use certain words for the sound they make in our mouth and
Ears
Eye-drops

E. PRESSURE *Karen Christopher*

In Goat Island's piece *It's Shifting, Hank*, a great deal of tension builds up before a final climactic scene in which two men stick their heads into big buckets of water. They are on their hands and knees and they dunk their heads into the water after taking big breaths. One man is pulled out of the water by a third man after a certain amount of time has passed. There is nothing holding either of these men down under water, and yet the audience is under great pressure at this point. Audience members have said that they felt the men might drown if they were not pulled out in time, even though one of the men pulls his head out without assistance. The events that lead up to this point put pressure on this action. Directly before this, the cast of four performs the gruelling physical task of crawling backwards, face down, on elbows and toes. The four do this until they drop, and the task is repeated for a longer than comfortable period of time. The crawling action causes the climate of pressure. The audience assigns this pressure to the next action they see, that of the two men sticking their heads into buckets of water.

• *How Dear to Me the Hour When Daylight Dies*, Goat Island, 1996. Photo: Alan Crumlish.

F. WHAT WE SEE *Matthew Goulish*

In 1929, the philosopher Alfred North Whitehead attempted to make adjustments to the world of Isaac Newton. Where Newton's world of 1687 was one of actions and reactions, Whitehead's world of 1929 was one of organism and process. In his book *Process and Reality*, in Part I, 'The Speculative Scheme', in Chapter I, 'Speculative Philosophy', in Section II under the heading *Defects of Insight and Language*, Whitehead states that: 1. the sole justification for any thought – any thought at all – is the elucidation of experience; and, 2. the starting-point for any thought – any thought at all – is the analytic observation of components of experience. Since this starting-point cannot arrive without sense perception, Whitehead continues by examining what it is that we see.

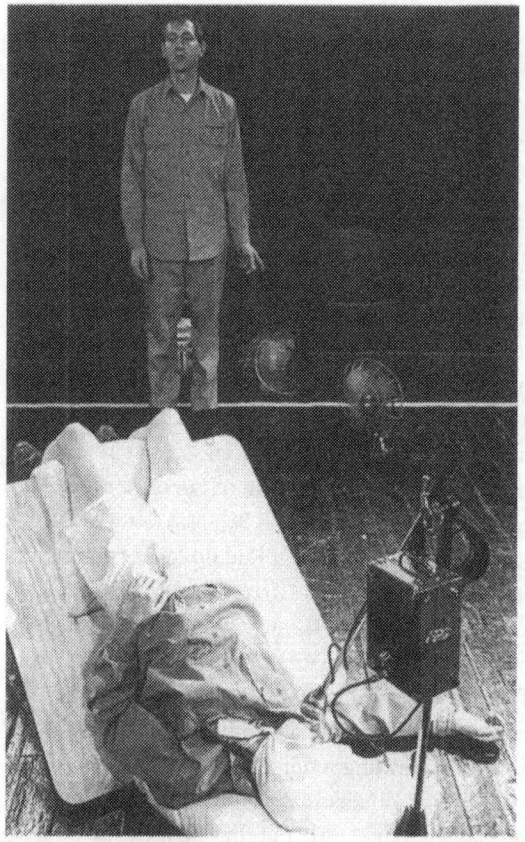

• *How Dear to Me the Hour When Daylight Dies*, Goat Island, 1996. Photo: Alan Crumlish.

In his book *Process and Reality*, in Part II, 'Discussions and Applications', in Chapter II, 'The Extensive Continuum', in Section IV on the world of 1929 as distinct from the world of 1687, Whitehead defines an event – any event at all – as follows: the actual world is built up of actual occasions. Whatever things there are, in any sense of 'existence', are derived by abstraction from actual occasions interrelated in some determinate fashion I shall call an 'event'. This brings us to what we see.

What we see is never more than the evidence of an event – an event which, along with its myriad composition of occasions, we can never entirely know, but only begin to guess at. For example: when we see five neat rows of casserole dishes lying on the ocean floor, we can only guess that we see them because they are the result of an event which includes the occasion of the *Titanic* striking the iceberg. And: when we see Mike Walker, America's Fattest Man, lying immobilized at 1,187 pounds in the middle of Kansas, which is in the middle of the United States, we can only guess that we see him as a result of an event which included the occasions of the US war in Korea, which lasted from 1948 to 1953, left 54,000 Americans, 200,000 Chinese and 2 million Koreans dead, and left Mike Walker with an insatiable appetite.

E. FINGER *Karen Christopher*

In Goat Island's piece *Can't Take Johnny to the Funeral*, when I hold my first finger pointing straight up and it describes a circle in the air, my hand swivelling at the wrist, I am thinking of a woman I once knew who had to leave her children in the custody of the state. I am not doing an imitation of her or of anything. The gesture comes from a gesture I made spontaneously once while describing the way my own mother listened to a particular 45 record over and over again. One woman told me that when she saw this gesture in the performance, she saw a woman waiting for her man to come home from war, another saw her 2-year-old winding up to wreak havoc. These things were really seen by these women, and other people saw their own images too. Because of what led to this moment, what came after, each person's reference points, and my own intentions and those of Goat Island, the moment does not look the same to everyone. It is not as simple as a magician pulling a coin out of a person's ear, but it is no less a collaboration between the performer and the spectator. The moment occurs with the involvement of all parties.

D. IN MEMORY OF GILLES DELEUZE *Antonio Poppe*

A journey created from one instant to the next. That is how I travelled with him, within a flow of rhythm, moving like a bee, motionless at great pace, being moved in the direction of life, never looking back, never regretting, vibrating, leaping, encountering, melding. Now – what happened behind the sockets of my eyes?! – touching them from inside. Where did I stop, what could I do, what have I become capable of ? Words inside, I can use them, he gave me words in motion and with them a will to will my own will. No more no less than freedom, an open space for me to work upon. To be moved by joy, to laugh and smile unravelling the face, kissing in public as a weapon in the middle of aberrant movements, the slightest caress full of gaiety and how important it is to dance, to go along like a dancer, imperceptible, as if walking still by still, stretching the neck like Buster Keaton in a sudden turning upon itself, he knew that 'his face was his torture and his source' (Giorgio Agamben). It's matter of rising forth – *being such as it is* – such that it always matters – such as it is choosing – such as it desires – such as it is not indifferent – such as it is taking place – being such singularity that left the world of guilt and justice. Takeoff, make eye-to-eye contact with the world like Jiulietta Masina, 'a kaleidoscope forming a new combination every time, deep attention, and then, sudden closure', binding people to each other by a look that is immediately transformed into a motion, walk out, map out life through becoming everything you love,

the freedom of varying in an infinite number of ways. 'As a matter of fact, the only creatures that seem to survive are those that give themselves away in a flash and sparkle and gay flicker of joyful life; those that go glittering abroad with a bit of splendour' (D. H. Lawrence). Life and work are the same thing, one being that wants to become 'such as it is', to live in a Spinozist manner, 'composed of an infinite number of particles; it is the relation of motion and rest, of speeds and slowness between particles, that define a body, the singularity of a body. A body affects other bodies, or is affected by … it is this capacity for affecting and being affected that also defines a body in its singularity.' As Buster Keaton in the way he melds with everything around, every time composing a new relation with a machine a crowd a ship a rotating wheel a monkey a train, and picking up speeds along the way by being a very special kind of dancer in the middle of the world. If one could map their movements, their own generations, and the connections of the figures they trace, something very similar to a Paul Klee drawing would appear. An exemplary life.

C. THE NEWT *Adrian Blundell*

On the day that Pete and I were dredging the pond under the footbridge for newts, Martin was not there. His method was to stare through the reflections on the surface of the water, identify the shadow of the sitting newt, and creep it into a clear glass jar using his spare hand as decoy. Martin hunted like a heron. Pete and I would dredge using butterfly nets on a cane. The dredging method meant that a newt would be carried into the net along with everything else on the bottom of the pond; dead leaves, twigs and black sulphurous mud. Most drags would yield sticklebacks or mosquito larvae. The newt would wriggle and squirm smoothly through your fingers. They have sleek smooth bodies, like a mermaid. Your heart would stop if you held it in your hand. Then I saw one writhing in the mud. 'I've got one.' My hand closed around it before it squirmed free. I could feel a strong and eely body snaking against my flesh. It was sharp, not smooth, and it bit me and I knew. A nausea wave swept through me as I visualized it. Nasty jaws and pointy claws. I let it fall. I tasted a spoonful of sick in the back of my throat.

Later that day at the pool we circled, diving for pennies, arm-bands, a discarded Band-Aid or whatever we could see through the cloudy chlorine water with no goggles. We went to the deep end. The bottom was three or four strong pulls. Pressure pushed on your ears. From the surface we could see the unusual lumpish object, but once you got down there it seemed to become invisible. Refraction and a slim depth of field hid it from us for long enough that it took several breathless drops to locate. I was the best swimmer. The first dive, I touched it. 'It feels like wax.' The next dive my hand closed around it and I carried it to the surface. 'I've got it.' A closer look; another wave of nausea and a mouthful of bitter vomit to be swallowed or spat into the pool. I dropped a child-size turd and watched it sink back to the bottom.

B. PUPPET SHOW / 2 *Lin Hixson*

Basil ran into the toyroom and we followed. Out the windows, the night lights of Fribourg flickered. It was an evening in late July, and our sojourn in Switzerland was about to end. We had just finished performing *It's Shifting, Hank*, and this 7-year-old boy was staging a puppet show for us on the evening of our day off. We gathered around the 5-foot puppet stage. Adrian, our 18-year-old translator, perched on his knees next to the theatre. A green puppet appeared in a purple dress with gold trim.

'Bon soir, Mesdames et Messieurs,' said the queen.
'Good evening, ladies and gentlemen,' Adrian translated.
'Bienvenue au théâtre du marionettes,' she said, spreading her arms.
'Welcome to the puppet show,' said Adrian.
'Ne parlez pas pendant cette performance.'
'No talking during the performance.'
'Ne fumez pas dans le théâtre.'
'There is no smoking allowed in the theatre.'

Suddenly, behind the queen, an arm rose, its hand covered with a yellow furry lion. The startled queen lurched for a moment, then rocketed through the air towards the audience, striking my neighbour in the eye. 'Ow!' yelled the startled spectator.

After a moment, the lion spoke, 'Cette performance va faire mal.'
Adrian translated, 'The performance will hurt.'

A. MIRROR *Bryan Saner*

On my grandfather's 90th birthday I called him up and asked how he was. 'I'm fine,' he said, 'but my body doesn't work like it did when I was 70.'

There is a monk in Manhattan who is marketing the Virtual Mirror. It is a mirror that doesn't reverse your image. (Technically speaking it may not be a *mirror*, since by its nature the not-virtual mirror does reverse the image; as in a dance when two people *mirror* movement when facing each other – one person raises the right hand, the other raises the left.) Looking into this mirror you see yourself as others see you, from another point of view. The monk believes that this mirror more truthfully reflects your inner self, your emotional status, your internal light, your soul. It is very difficult to shave with this mirror, however.

Over the years I've come to believe that there is another reality. My grandfather talks comfortably about going home when he dies. I wake up from my dreaming and turn on the artificial light in the bathroom. The sink looks odd to me ... unreal, a cheap imitation of the real sink that exists in the other. Or perhaps it is an object that has no purpose in the other. And what am I doing here ... with this body? But here I am, and by the time I have finished shaving everything seems normal.

Illusiontext by Goat Island (1996)

TDR

The Journal of Performance Studies

Edited by Richard Schechner

Art   Activism   Experimentation
Theatre   Dance   Performance Art
Performances   Books   Spectacles
Theory   History   Analysis
Politics   Play   Ritual

Public Burnings and Hangings in Colonial New York
Mark Fearnow

Cross-Dressing Performances on the Chinese Stage
Chou Huiling

Reza Abdoh: Interviews, Essays, and Performance Texts
Sabrina Artel
John Bell
Josette Feral

Fluxus Feminus
Kathy O'Dell

Experimental Sound & Radio
Guest Editor
Allen S. Weiss

Read it.

Write it.

Participate in it.

Browse The MIT Press online catalog on the World Wide Web: http://www-mitpress.mit.edu

Send letters and submissions to:
Mariellen R. Sandford
Associate Editor
TDR
721 Broadway, 6th Fl.
New York, NY 10003

Published quarterly by The MIT Press. ISSN 1054-2043

1996 Rates:
Individual $34.00.
Institution $95.00.
Student & Retired $20.00.
Outside USA add $16 postage and handling. Canadians add additional 7% GST. Prices are subject to change without notice. Prepayment is required. Send check drawn against a US bank in US funds, American Express, MasterCard or VISA number to:

MIT Press Journals
55 Hayward Street
Cambridge, MA 02142
TEL: 617-253-2889
FAX: 617-577-1545
journals-orders@mit.edu

Approaching the Real: Reality Effects and the Play of Fiction

Andrew Quick

Re-presentation: theatre does not show 'things in themselves', nor does it represent them, it shows a representation, shows itself to be a fiction; it is less engaged in setting forth things or the image of things than it is in setting up a machine.

(Derrida 1981: 238)

The stage, the place where art comes closest to life.
Dreams of effective language.
The temptations to go from this imitation of
life to life itself.

(Artaud 1974: 167)

BORDERING REALITY

Ian Hinchcliffe, in the catalogue celebrating/commemorating ten years of the National Review of Live Art (NRLA), outlines what he perceives to be some of the characteristics of performance art. In reaction to the 'obmutescent blandness of the eighties' when performance art 'cleaned up its act', Hinchcliffe asserts that performance art 'should be about flesh and blood, a big lump of throbbing adrenaline, swishing there with and touching the beholder's tripes' (Hinchcliffe 1990: 6). This invocation of a visceral reality which is situated in the body (of performer and spectator) is similarly expressed by Simon Jones on the next page of the catalogue. In 'Thirteen fragments for a manifesto of performance' he invokes a purity in the performance relation which, evading the operation of critique and signification, begins to assert its ontology: 'This is its nature: oscillation between intensities: a pure effect, unique to performance: indeed an effect of purity in ambivalence, blurred vision, cacophony and confusion (say, confluence: flowing together/with)' (Jones 1990: 7). The statements by these writers repeat and (both in meaning and form) allude to Antonin Artaud's clamour for a theatre which 'is a passionate overflowing/ a frightful transfer of forces/ from body to body'. A transfer which Artaud claims 'can never be produced twice' (Artaud 1989: 99–200). What links these assertions is the possibility and necessity of a practice that appears to resist the operation of representation, of repetition, of illusion, while somehow being or presenting 'the real' itself.

In certain critical discourses, often produced by the artists themselves, performance art has been differentiated from theatre through an emphasis on prevalent reality-effects: the focus on the body, history and personality of the individual performer; the use of objects that relate to the performer or the space of the event, which signify through use in real-time actions or through symbolic interaction rather than through the frame of narratives or fictions; actions that take place in real time; actions that take place where time is a fundamental element, where duration is the locus of experience; events that are constructed through processes that are spontaneous, aleatory, transitory and accidental. Perhaps what begins to mark out performance art in relation to other performance genres is its attempt to destabilize those frameworks that operate to transform the event into an object: to resist or undermine the apparatuses which both inculcate the representational order and render the performance event commodifiable: to emphasize, or rather work through, the 'presentness' of performance itself.

Nick Kaye in his book *Postmodernism and Performance*, in which he contrasts the modernist (contradictory) pursuit of value and purity against the disruptive forces of the 'postmodern' work that seeks to distort or negate such foundational structures, argues that 'the emergence of strategies which look specifically toward performance can be read as a final move toward an unravelling of the discrete or bounded work of art' (Kaye 1994: 32). Such strategies, which operate through the modalities of performance, or at least eventhood, Kaye outlines, fundamentally disrupt and expose the contradiction at the locus of the modernist project: the emphasis on an interior 'life' or 'essence' somehow embodied in a work of art which is at the same time constructed and framed by notions of value and convention and the specificities of historical conditions. The disturbance of the modernist aesthetic is achieved through an emphasis on the act of speculation which is either incorporated into or demanded (through the drawing of attention to specific material contexts) by the work of art. The taking into account and use of the specificities of place, duration and the cultural context of the spectator or witness are seen to undo the teleological drive behind modernist practice/critique.

It is possible to see that the demand for the work of art to have integrity, as expressed by modernist critics such as Clement Greenberg and Michael Fried, is a reiteration (or part of a continuum in Enlightenment aesthetics) of Kant's theory of aesthetics which was put forward in his *Third Critique*. Derrida in *The Truth in Painting* (Derrida 1987) interrogates Kant's idea of art achieving the state of integrity, characterized by the term the *ergon*, by emphasizing the disruptive qualities of that which frames the work of art, what Derrida defines as the *parergon*. The idea of art achieving some sort of autonomy is always undone by the (unavoidable) processes of framing; including the 'classical' frame that encases the picture and also contextualizations that occur as a result of the spectator/viewer/witness standing before a work of art. These processes of framing, which always include temporal, ethical and contemplative dynamics, prohibit the idea of pure perception. In this sense the frame can neither contain everything within it, nor permit an absolute scrutiny, nor can it prevent other contexts (forces) from infecting the art work from the outside thus destroying any claim to an autonomy or 'wholeness'. The promise made by Cezanne that 'I owe you the truth in painting and I will tell it to you' (Derrida 1987: 2) is revealed to be unrealizable. Derrida works over the foundational premise proffered in a version of aesthetics which asserts that it can, somehow, represent 'the truth' through the operation either of mimesis (classicism/realism) or idealism (romanticism). In effect Derrida's argument, if we see the term 'theatricality' as a version of 'framing', challenges Fried's idea that an art work can free itself from 'theatrical' contextualization. That even within the exemplars of modernism, Cezanne being one of its major figures, the desire for such autonomy is subject to a profound failure. This, of course, might account for the force of Fried's statement in defence of the autonomous status of art when he argued 'Art degenerates as it approaches the condition of theatre' (Fried 1968: 141). It does, and if Derrida is correct this process of degeneration is inscribed into the ontology of art and cannot be avoided.

Some definitions of performance art or performance practices, as I have indicated, point to the possibility of inscribing a notion of a primordial reality within the eventhood of performance: of a real which might evade the operation of the frame. The problem with such writing on performance art is that it begins to intimate that a reality, the real, is existent in/as the event: that eventhood itself might be truthful, the *ergon*. The promise then becomes, to rewrite Cezanne, 'I owe you the truth in eventhood and I will tell it to you.' Consider the last section of an article entitled 'Beating the live art trail', published in *Performance*, written by Rob La Frenais, where the difference between the frame(s) of theatricality and the seemingly borderless being of performance is marked out:

> Each of the four members had been blindfolded, each experimented upon, bathed in the glow of monitors. They were beginning to stop 'performing'. Yet, there was still a kind of hidden, unspoken barrier around them and their area. It was only when they got to Brighton, UK that things started to change for them. In the polytechnic gallery, where I visited, right at the end of the whole eight days, they had transformed their space into a working environment.

In his commentary on an installation by Hidden Grin performed in Nottingham and Brighton, UK in 1984, La Frenais outlines the slow progression towards the real that the performers undergo through the duration (eight days) of the event. An initial encounter with the piece in Nottingham provokes the following response, 'They were beginning to stop "performing". Yet, there was still a kind of hidden, unspoken barrier around them and their area.' La Frenais invokes the theatrical frame, 'the hidden, unspoken barrier', which blocks the real interaction between their actions/practices in space and time and the practices of spectating. By the end of the eight days the piece has undergone a profound change. Performers become 'technicians' who acknowledged 'the presence of the public when they walked in'. These are the technicians of the real who move around 'the space in "real time" not acted time. When something was about to happen they said so.' The closing section of the article presents the journey's end, the transformation from the theatre to performance art:

> They had made the trip, from eight days previous in Nottingham to Brighton, along the trail from mannerism to ... what? Whatever it was they were there, not in some method actor's imaginary space. Welcome to performance art, Hidden Grin.
> (La Frenais 1986: 10)

'Thereness' or 'presentness' is implicated as the term that might fill the empty space (in La Frenais's text) that opens out at the end point between mannerism (theatre?) and performance ('... what'/'Whatever'). Here the barrier or frame is finally dissolved to present/expose the real: a real which is beyond the reach of the symbolic (language) and even the imaginary (the unconscious). I must assume it is La Frenais's intention to render the arrival into performance art as being outside the order of language since he cannot find a word or phrase to describe it. A similar observation is made by Mark Gaynor in his article 'A question of difference', written in response to the Platform Discussion at the eighth National Review of Live Art in 1987. At the end of the article he attempts to mark out the difference between Live Art and theatre through the former's emphasis on a real or reality. He writes: 'Perhaps then, one definition of live art is an art that takes into account and tries to understand the contextual relationship between the artist and the spectator through the exposition of *actual experience*' (my emphasis). Gaynor in his invocation of an 'actual experience' places its source in the space or relationship between artist and spectator, between watched and watcher, which appears to avoid the theatrical frame with its emphasis on skill (training), technology (mediation) and narrative (fiction). What this 'actual experience' is remains undefined within his argument. Perhaps the indefinable nature of such experience haunts his closing line when he claims, 'It's so difficult to talk about something when there is no consensus on what that something is' (Gaynor 1988: 31).

This analysis infers that there might be a real beyond language, exterior to the operation of signification, which is, somehow, still known or at least felt in the subject's encounter with it. This is the knowledge or feeling that induces La Frenais's declaration of welcome at Hidden Grin's arrival at a sort of pure presentness and begins to explain Gaynor's difficulty in his encounter with difference. The problem is that such writing, in erasing the frame, the parergon, instils or at least promises an autonomy in the event which, in a state of pure presence, avoids the operation of signification. The conclusion, then, becomes that the event is unspeakable: felt, perhaps, but beyond the order of symbolization; that what might return with such a perception of performance is the idea of the *ergon*. In this article I wish to tease out some of the assumptions that might lie behind the various notions of the real and reality with specific reference to Lacan's writing on the real and its relationship to the construction of subjectivity. With specific reference to Impact Theatre* and the later work of two of its founder members, Claire MacDonald and Pete Brooks, I intend to argue that the representation of the real is an impossible endeavour; that the failing attempt at the real's representation is necessary both to the idea of replete subjectivity and to the sense of the loss the subject feels of this ideal state.

* Impact Theatre was formed in 1978 and toured in the UK and Europe until 1985. Its importance to and influence on contemporary experimental theatre in Britain cannot be underestimated although the company's work received very little critical/academic attention at the time.

Many of its group members are currently practising performance.

THE REAL AND REALITY

It is difficult to ascertain what actual, real, or reality such writing is attempting to refer to or articulate. Lacan's writing on 'the Real' and 'reality' and the differentiations that he makes between these terms are a useful starting-point in the following attempt to mark out what distinguishes certain experimenting practices in the theatre from a particular narrative on performance art: useful because his writing on the real and reality begins a process of untangling concepts which are, more often than not, placed as truths in certain critical discourses. For Lacan, reality is socially constructed and it is reality which is inculcated through the operation of language. Our experience of the world, what we are, what we see, is prescribed by language and its structures. In *Seminar 1*, Lacan describes language 'as a network, a net over the entirety of things, over the totality of the real' (Lacan 1988: 262). Language is the regulatory system by which reality is comprehended as a concrete form manifested, in his terms, as the symbolic.

Lacan appears to locate an order ('the totality of the real') prior to or beyond the system(s) of language and its 'network'; a real which avoids the dynamics through which reality is constructed. In an earlier section in *Seminar 1* he attempts the following definition of this version of the real: 'the real, or what is perceived as such, is what resists symbolisation absolutely' (Lacan 1988: 66). This is the state of 'whatever' La Frenais refers to in his writing on Hidden Grin: a 'whatever' that cannot be marked by or positioned within the linguistic frame. It may also be the 'actual experience' in Gaynor's attempt to locate an ontology in his version of 'Live Art'. The real, in Lacanian analysis, although ineffable and beyond symbolization, is revealed to haunt the symbolic order. In fact, as Fred Botting forcibly argues in his article 'Culture, subjectivity and the real; or, psychoanalysis reading postmodernity', the real is 'the site of loss and anxiety, associated with mourning and psychosis'. Botting also points out that this loss demands, within the language system, the return of 'symbolic authority, for the erection of the signifier or paternal metaphor to regulate and repair the unity of the symbolic framework' (Botting 1995: 89). The real is something which is 'known' by the subject but lost in the process of becoming a subject. This loss is felt by the subject and experienced as trauma.

The real as Slavoj Zizek puts it, is 'the fullness of inert presence, positivity' (Zizek 1989: 169). In this sense the real is founded on the absence of absence or as Lacan states the 'lack of lack'. It is lack, absence and difference, Lacan argues, that constitute the order of language, forming the structures of symbolization. If we return to Lacan's idea of reality we find that subjectivity (identity) is formed from a contradiction within the language system. The subject is constructed as a subject through the operation of language: through the recognition of an Other that embodies and instils difference as the locus of any signifying system. The subject is thus formed from an attempt (in language) to shore up the symbolic framework (constructed through difference) and yet is haunted by the loss of unity that occurred before such frameworks came into operation. This loss is felt, for example, through the loss of the Other, as in the death of the loved object, which necessitates the ritual of mourning. The ritual of mourning is itself a signifying process or activity that attempts to recover the signifying system, by which subjectivity is constructed, which is destabilized by such loss. It is the sense of this loss that opens out a space or a void in reality, in its network of signification, which acts to undo any attempt of closure, of destabilizing any action that attempts to secure the operation of signification.

In short Lacan indicates that the real cannot be reached since it always escapes symbolization. The real is the point of origin that is for ever lost and trauma marks this loss. In other words the unsymbolizable excess of the real disturbs the structures put into place by the imaginary and symbolic economies. The real is felt in the attempt to recover from this loss, to fill the hole left by the encounter with it. The real is felt at the very point where language attempts to secure the foundations where reality can be marked out, where the exterior – the materiality of things – is held in place for the subject.

Lacan's observations on the real point to its capacity to haunt signification and play a dynamic role in the creation of identity but also allude to the impossibility of its representation (although representation would appear to rely on the encounter with the real). I would like to propose that this contradiction (constructed and negotiated as/through performance) is evinced in the work of particular practitioners within the theatrical framework: a contradiction which might be seen to differentiate this work from the more idealistic, or romantic, tendency evinced in particular discursive narratives that describe performance art as somehow presenting the real itself. I do not intend to imply that all the practices which have been defined or described as performance art or live art can be framed in relation to the real. It is interesting that much writing on British performance in the 1980s and 1990s, as I have outlined, constantly uses the notion of the real/reality as a metaphor to differentiate it from other forms and practices which are often described as being theatrical or illusionary. What I wish to emphasize is that the reading or contextualization of these genres of performance (whether they are defined as experimental theatre, performance art, or live art) which defines and frames them in relation to a pure (idealized) presentation of the real or reality is severely limited and may, indeed, be unwittingly contradictory.

Claire MacDonald's introduction to her text *Storms from Paradise* (MacDonald 1992) outlines the distinction (and importance) of the real and the representational in the following way. Describing her work with Impact Theatre she observes that the performance work

> was characterized by a sense of high fiction combined by a sense of a visceral 'realness' in which the experience of the performers was always marked, as we performed on sets filled with freezing water or sand or became exhausted in the extreme physicality of the action.
>
> (MacDonald 1992: 161)

This emphasis on the combination of 'high fiction' and 'realness' is used to identify the work of Impact and the juxtaposition between the two landscapes/territories (symbolic and real) intimates the basis for examining this work's distinctive quality. MacDonald's statement above is very similar to her description of Impact that appears in the National Review of Live Art's *Commissioned Articles* (1990). Interestingly there is an important difference in the above description which was published two years later. In 1990 the real is described as 'the palpably real' whereas in the text above, by placing the real in inverted commas, she indicates that realness is either an effect of/in the theatre and is not necessarily representable (as pure presence) within its framework or that it is (at least) a contestable concept. Counter to the sense of purity implied by the terminology of the 'actual' or 'the real' which some artists and critics foreground as being the basis or locus of a performance art practice, the work of Impact Theatre is situated within the theatrical frame and is, I maintain, witness to the effects of the real shadowing representation and representation shadowing the real.

As I outlined earlier, the problem of the real and how it might be located and defined is not necessarily clarified by the juxtaposition of the actual and fictional: the blocking together of real-time actions with/against fictional (representational) ones. In MacDonald's initial statement, the real, she claims, is presentable in the physical actions of the performers, in the physical environments they perform in. In her later examination of Impact the relationship between fiction and visceral reality is expressed as being more fragile although her phrase 'combination' still suggests that they are distinct territories/realms that have to be placed together (in juxtaposition). I wonder if the two dynamics or orders are ever separated in the way she implies. Returning to and reflecting back upon Derrida's analysis of the parergon and the ergon put into question the idea that the two orders, real and representational (or in Lacanian terms, real and symbolic) can be presented and more importantly perceived and experienced as different realms. As Derrida argues, the frame which attempts to establish the autonomy of the art object is, in fact, the 'corrupting' surface which destabilizes this very endeavour. Is it then possible, within the theatre space, for the fictional (symbolic) frame(work) to disappear through the force of the encounter with the real whether this real be physical excess or non-fictional or non-narrative real-time actions? The encounter between the fictional and the real might pose the same question: does the real, whatever it might be, disappear when faced with the force of the fictional? At best there might be a flickering between these two states, although within the theatrical space it is difficult to conceive of the representational apparatus 'giving way' utterly to the real: of its complete disappearance when faced with the 'noise' of the real. This may be as much a consequence of the practices of spectating, which, as I have already indicated, work over and disrupt the art work's possible autonomous status. It is not as if the audience can ever forget the material context of their participation: of being spectators (with)in the theatre and its concomitant representational apparatus. Consequently it might be more useful to see physical actions whether they be visceral or real time as effects, generated by the encounter with the real, felt as trauma or loss, which are scored across and into the shifting fictional or narrative frames which exist within the theatre space and machine: effects which vitiate the theatrical representational apparatus. Of course this encounter might not be real itself but performed as if it was a 'genuine' (whatever that might be) encounter with the real.

THE LOST REFERENT OF THE REAL

It is possible to view Impact's work as an investigation of the loss (and its effects) of the referent that supports the representational system. The referent might be considered as either the real itself (the origin, in Lacanian terms) or the Logos (the Word of God, in Derridean terms) that shores up the signifying system. Pieces such as *Dammerungstrasse 55* (1981), *Useful Vices* (1982), *No Weapons For Mourning* (1982), *A Place in Europe* (1983), *Songs of the Clay People* (1983) and *The Carrier Frequency* (1984) frequently allude to this sense of loss and enact the attempted recovery from it by and through the processes and procedures of mourning and its associated ritual practices. The failures of these attempts at recovering and rebuilding the symbolic order within their pieces usually herald periods of extreme physical activity often incorporating repetitive actions and gestures. These extreme physical actions can be seen, although such a view might be criticized as being too 'neat', to enact or to mirror the experience of trauma produced by the recognition and effect of the failure of the symbolic order and its impact on the subject as put forward by Lacan in his writing. Perhaps the clearest example of this examination of loss, can be found in *The Carrier Frequency* which Impact created in collaboration with the novelist Russell Hoban in 1984.

In this piece five figures occupy a partly submerged world: concrete platforms rise up out of a pool of black water in a circular set which is backed by sheets of industrial plastic. As the action unfolds it becomes clear that these figures are the ancestors of the survivors of a nuclear war, the remnants of a civilization which harks back to the utopia (life before the bomb) that is mythologized in a language and a ritual practice that do not appear able to withstand the experience of their present predicament. The structures of language and ritual practices which promise stability are enacted as being inconstant and highly motile. The spoken text, written by Hoban, is constructed out of a sort of linguistic detritus formed from the attempt to remember a way of speaking before the nuclear catastrophe and its aftermath, the post-holocaust world which its fictional figures strive to survive in and make sense of. As a result language is portrayed as a material that is always mutating and reconfiguring, where a grounded meaning becomes impossible.

The live speech, spoken on stage through head-set microphones, attempts to reconstruct a logos that will give purpose to existence. This logosphere (world of language) constructs itself around a post-nuclear deity 'Erny Warling'. A mutation of 'early warning', part of the technosphere built to protect humanity, Erny Warling becomes the central figure in a linguistic maelstrom in which meaning, through hysteresis, exists as a half-life: a presence that decays through the processes of its own vigorous assertion. The mutation of the name carries within itself a devastating ambiguity where 'warn' slides into 'war' which dislocates the protective essence of the word. Language becomes, as Barthes observes, 'a vast and perpetual conflict of paranoias'. Erny Warling is like Barthes's 'final figure' invented through the remnants of language, the fictions, jargons and slangs, 'which brand the adversary with a half-scientific, half-ethical name' (Barthes 1979: 28). Erny, the figures on stage claim, is their saviour, 'Erny saveya Erny savus allya', who warns off and offers protection from the enemy; the 'fuckin megatons' and the 'boomboom hardstuff'. Erny Warling becomes the locus in a linguistic hierarchy to which all the

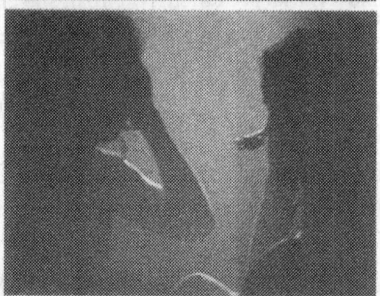

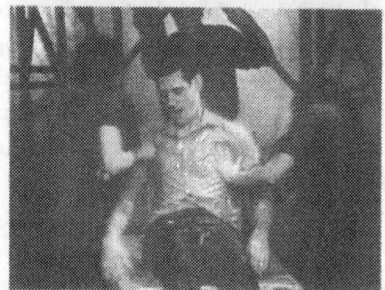

• *The Carrier Frequency*: Impact Theatre/Russell Hoban (1984).
Photo: Steve Littman/Kent Institute of Art & Design

mechanisms of language and meaning should adhere.

The figures in *The Carrier Frequency* re-create a deistic order to overcome despair, to give hope, in the ruins of their existence. The identity of a God (Erny Warling) as the ultimate foundation relocates the essential structure to which the interplay of language and meaning refers. Such a structure, as Deleuze observes in *The Logic of Sense*, predicts a hierarchy where the identity of the world exists in relation to God 'as the ambient environment', the identity of the individual 'as a well founded agency' with the 'identity of bodies as the base' (Deleuze 1990: 292). This structure is supported, Deleuze argues, by the 'identity of language as the power denoting everything else'. According to Deleuze the death of God, as described by Nietzsche, fractures this system, which results in the 'destruction of the world, the dissolution of the person, the disintegration of bodies', and the shifting function of 'language which now expresses only intensities' (Deleuze 1990: 292). A similar process of dissolution is enacted both in physical and linguistic terms in the stage action in *The Carrier Frequency*. Erny exists as a deity that has already failed the figures on stage and the repeated mythologization of his exculpable stature is unable to withstand the living presence of the speakers. They finally have to admit his defeat and his death: 'You know hes dead doanshiteme' (Hoban 1984).

The death of God, of 'Erny Warling', induces the collapse of the signifying system. The figures attempt to locate a reality in the void left by Erny's disappearance. Complex assemblages are re-enacted as grotesque rituals around a discarded table covered in a shred of white plastic: carrying, rescuing, resuscitation, washing, worship and resurrection. Signification haunts their actions as the figures attempt to relocate the myths of origin and the symbolic actions which would restore symbolic authority. The comprehension that such an act of restoration is impossible results in the breakdown of ritualistic enactments and instils a destructive sequence of fragmented attempts to recover from the sense of the loss of the figure that inculcated the symbolic system: that made sense of a world-order for the figures in the piece. The search for the lost referent, now unrecoverable, is halted only through the performers' physical exhaustion. In this case there is no return to a symbolic authority and the piece plays out the failure of the paternal metaphor (Erny Warling) to restore any unity to the symbolic framework: the only rest from this collapse is the corporeal limit (a real of sorts) – the physical exhaustion of the performers.

The limit(ation) of the symbolic framework is constantly invoked in Impact's work. Consequently the spoken language of the pieces is often constructed out of combinations of French and German or a deliberate nonsense ('cod' language) that mirror the structures of these other European languages. There is an absence of symbolic authority that would create the (infra)structures through which the processes of signification could cohere, which might hold the system together. The collaging of the multiple texts and fictional references has a similar effect. Impact's performances often appeared to be constructed as 'dream spaces' (MacDonald 1992: 161) where different genres of narrative, detective, film, science-fiction and the gothic, are imbricated and/or blocked together to produce an experience in which multiple interpretations compete with each other and which disrupts any narrative closure. These fictional or narrative genres are utilized in an attempt to recover and to secure a signifying system which would return the figures on stage to the unity of the symbolic framework based on the lost referent: the mythology of the real.

REAL ENCOUNTERS: SUBJECTIVITY AND THE PLAY OF FICTION.

Fiction and narrative (telling stories), in the work of Impact, are revealed as structures in which identities attempt to manifest themselves and become coherent: a process which is both vigorously played out and revealed to be doomed to failure. The primordial presence of Hinchcliffe's 'flesh and blood', in which the real and identity would be fully embodied, is perceived as a sought-for yet inaccessible state. Tim Etchells in his essay 'Diverse assembly: some trends in recent performance' describes the fluctuating 'nature' of identity put forward (staged) within certain practices of experimentation. Arguing that 'identity on-stage is now rarely a fixed point', Etchells outlines a notion of identity that refutes or negates any possibility of its ontological status or at least challenges the idea that Being might have a base or stable structure. In other words he describes how identity is performed or played out which, whilst revealing a fixed idea of Being as an impossibility, might also be seen to describe such fluctuation as the ontology of Being itself. He writes, 'More often, through actions, choreographies, or even speech the performers are seen as sharing a constituency of texts in which their own part or parts must be worked out, or in which their role is ever fluid – subject to play and change' (Etchells 1994: 108). What Etchells alludes to in this statement is the absence of a proper locus of the self, whether they be performer or spectator, thus disrupting the notion of the subject's autonomous place. The play of fiction then becomes one of the tactical intrusions or manoeuvres within the representational apparatus of the theatre-machine, a play which is seen as an always failing attempt at the recovery of the real.

Tim Etchells in his outlining of the dynamics and 'conventions' of experimentation in performance invokes the real, described as 'a text-beneath-the-text, a sea of real presence, or of real-time work from which fiction can occasionally rise', as one of its identifying features (Etchells 1994: 108). The vertical metaphor operating in Etchells's definition of the real may suggest that it is the ground (the truth) which forms the foundation for the fictional operation, 'from which fiction can occasionally arise'. In spite of this Etchells may be making a helpful distinction between the real and the fictional which reconstructs the idea of a real in performance in fictional or at least in representational terms. By describing the real as a 'text-beneath-the-text' Etchells indicates its representational 'nature'. That within the theatrical machine the frame of representation will always mark that which might be designated as the real. The real is determined in relation to (the lack of) definition where performers are dispossessed (of meaning) through the activities of 'waiting, watching, setting up materials for another section or resting'. The effect of this dispossession is to create spaces or gaps in which any fictional or rhythmic continuum might be disrupted. What Etchells seems to indicate here is not a real of inert presence but one where a singular definitive comprehension of an event or occurrence is put into flux: that the syntax of meaning production is rendered inoperable. As such the real is perceived as a tangible dynamic, as an effect, within the scene of performance and not as a transcendental entity or realm somehow conjured up in certain extreme (or enervated) performance conditions. As in the writing of Lacan, the real is thus seen in terms of the gap, the space, the aporia, in the representational apparatus.

The real, however it might be perceived or described, is seen by both MacDonald and Etchells as that which disrupts narrative closure. At the same time, the emphasis on fiction points to its potential and the possibility of creating utopias, of its potential to construct something, if not tangible then imaginable, in the playing space of the real. As MacDonald writes of her piece *Storms from Paradise*, the two characters embrace 'a tradition of telling tales, tall stories, sports to pass away dead time, dead lives, dead relationships, to imagine models and imaginary worlds other than this, a tradition of creating and destroying utopias' (MacDonald 1992: 161). In 'A few notes about procedure' Etchells designates a similar role to the operation of narrative. In writing about Forced Entertainment's piece *Club of No Regrets*, which he directed, Etchells describes how it is constructed from the 'shards' of familiar and recognizable fictional genres; that these elements hint at narrative while creating patterns more pertinent to that of 'music' or 'meditative space'. The quest, he states, and I assume this is as much for the audience as the performers, 'is to get the stories that we do know to *yield* us the space beyond stories' (my emphasis) (Etchells 1993: 3).

An Imitation of Life, written by MacDonald and directed by Brooks in 1986, might be seen as an embodiment of the attempt to locate such a space. Here the fictional place is a hotel room in which two figures narrate various stories which constantly retell versions of their lives and an imaginary city being excavated and reconstructed. The piece has consistent characters named Adele, Bishop and Judith, although there are only two performers on the stage. The activity of story-telling, in which the two characters compete for the narrative coherence of their histories and dreams of the future, puts into question the stability of narrative itself. Narrative is performed as landscape in which possibility and versions of the past are explored and in which the instability of identity is played out.

The director, Pete Brooks, as if to disrupt any possibility of fictional coherence, inserts a series of movement sections in which the characters on stage, Adele and Bishop, physically attempt to establish and maintain the power relationships which had previously been explored through the scripted text. The two figures perform a fragile violent dance, of hits and slaps to the face, which flicker between being a sexual game and an aggressive fight. The sequence ends with the man cowering and submissive, the woman upright but exhausted. This sudden leap or jump from the relatively closed narrative structure created through the spoken text and overt characterization to the more abstract qualities of dance and physical action (still part of the signifying system) has the effect of putting these very structures into question. Interestingly, this blocking together of two very different and possibly contradictory performance conventions means that both performance languages become unstable. The characters' attempt at arriving at some sort of stability in terms of their relationships with each other and themselves is enmeshed in the endeavour to find a stability within a fictional or narrative context of representation itself. The attempt at fixing or locating fictional closure is thus equated with the fixing of identity – of being able to tell the story of the self.

The final section of the piece closes with a recognition of the potential of the power of the imagination: that Bishop's notion of the ideal city, uncorrupted by the limitation of subjectivity (of the failure of imagination), might be a realizable. This potential is articulated as a dream, as a 'fancy', but at the same time it hints at a faith in the possibility of creating a utopia; although such faith exists in the attempt at/of creation rather than its outcome:

> Later – much later, a traveller in that country is to report a strange sensation. That in part of the desert, near the delta he felt he was walking among ancient buildings, not ruins but tall buildings. From the middle of this place he could almost fancy himself in a bustling city, but from further away he could see nothing. From the sand he picks up a fragment of paper, and fragments of bone, cloth and stone. From the fragments he begins to construct a memory of what might be to come, a perfectly proportioned, exact, a representation, an imitation, a model if you like – a model city.
>
> (MacDonald 1987: 21)

This is no longer Bishop's ideal city but a traveller's, an anonymous figure, through which the whole process of building an imaginary world will begin again. Bishop's act of creation in the metaphysical space of the imagination (which is, it is implied, akin to the theatre space) has failed. This is signalled in the woman's previous utterance to the speech above in which she remarks: 'And so he leaves. Things look different now – he sees himself dirty and surrounded by rubble. What was once a metaphysical space is now a dirty and empty city, Bishop strikes out, with his plans for his ideal city ... he leaves, and leaves the city alone' (MacDonald 1987: 21). MacDonald implicates the representational machine, the theatre, in the playing space of this 'closure', in these final words.

The perfect model, 'a representation, an imitation', is discernible (but impossible to create) in the detritus, the texts, the narratives and fictions, that remain as part of the world's debris. It is from out of this rubble, the 'fragment of paper, and fragments of bone, cloth and stone', that the representational apparatus is constructed, by a subject, in order to create the model in which life itself might be reflected. These fragments are decaying signs, shards which invoke the lost unity of form. They mark the promise of representation, of imitation, of the possibility of structure and meaning while at the same time, since their presence is based on the absence of the totality of form, they reveal the failure of representation at the centre of this promise: the failure to represent reality fully. This is the impossible potential of representation, of the symbolic order, which drives narrative, which instils the signifying system and yet which implicates the limit of the representational apparatus and its ultimate failure to represent exactly: in other words, the very failure, at the locus of representation, the failure of the symbolic to recover the real which renders it only an imitation of life.

REFERENCES

Artaud, Antonin (1974) 'Documents relating to The Theatre and its Double', in *Collected Works*, Volume 4, London: John Calder.

——(1989) *Artaud on Theatre*, ed. Claude Schumacher, London: Methuen.

Barthes, Roland (1979) *The Pleasure of the Text*, London: Cape.

Botting, Fred (1995) 'Culture, subjectivity and the real: or, Psychoanalysis reading postmodernity', in Barbara Adam and Stuart Allan (eds) *Theorizing Culture: An Interdisciplinary Critique After Postmodernism*, London: UCL Press, 87–99.

Deleuze, Gilles (1990) *The Logic of Sense*, London: Athlone.

Derrida, Jacques (1981) *Dissemination*, London: Athlone.

——(1987) *The Truth in Painting*, Chicago: Chicago University Press.

Etchells, Tim (1993) 'A few thoughts about procedure...', programme note for *Club of No Regrets*, Sheffield.

——(1994) 'Diverse assembly: some trends in recent performance', in Theodore Shank (ed.) *Contemporary British Theatre*, London: Macmillan, 107–22.

Fried, Michael (1968) 'Art and objecthood', in Gregory Battock (ed.) *Minimal Art: A Critical Anthology*, New York: Dutton, 116–47.

Gaynor, Mark (1988) 'A question of difference', *Performance* 56–7: 10.

Hinchcliffe, Ian (1990) 'Performance art? Fizzling or thriving? I dunno', in *Commissioned Articles: National Review of Live Art 1990*, Glasgow: NRLA, 6.

Hoban, Russell (1984) *The Carrier Frequency*, unpublished performance text.

Jones, Simon (1990) 'Thirteen fragments for a manifesto of performance', in *Commissioned Articles: National Review of Live Art 1990*, Glasgow: NRLA, 7.

Kaye, Nick (1994) *Postmodernism and Performance*, London: Macmillan.

Lacan, Jacques (1988) *The Seminar of Jacques Lacan 1*, Cambridge: Cambridge University Press.

La Frenais, Rob (1986) 'Beating the live art trail', *Performance* 38: 10.

MacDonald, Claire (1987) *An Imitation of Life*, unpublished performance text.

——(1992) 'Storms from Paradise', in Deborah Levy (ed.) *Walks on Water*, London: Methuen, 159–81.

Žižek, Slavoj (1989) *The Sublime Object of Ideology*, London: Verso.

Presenting the Prima Donna

Black Femininity and Performance in Nineteenth-Century American Blackface Minstrelsy

Annemarie Bean

NINETEENTH-CENTURY CULTURAL IMAGINARY AND BLACK FEMININITY

Ralph Ellison insightfully identified nineteenth-century blackface minstrelsy as a theatrical venue where Americans enacted a unique performance of desires. The minstrel stage, Ellison noted in his essay 'Change the joke and slip the yoke', is where 'private is public and the public private, where black is white and white black, where the immoral becomes moral, and the moral is anything that makes one feel good' (1972: 49–50). Performed primarily in northern, urban venues to white male audiences, early minstrelsy situated itself in the South, giving a symbolic significance to a contained universe located on the plantation which also allowed a permissible attitude of 'anything goes'. Nationalism was on the rise in 1850s America, an age of abolitionist and women's movements, and minstrelsy kept at bay an urban culture demanding that men give up their individual identity to the mega-identity of the city. Based in a hyper-nostalgic state, minstrelsy was where the plantation culture of the South existed as a performed cultural imaginary of the urban displaced white man.

Integral to early blackface minstrelsy were negative interpretations of the life-style of African-Americans; blacks were crippled (as in the cripple jump of 'Jim Crow'), passive and, ultimately, feminized. Meaning on the minstrelsy stage was a negotiated code where the audience relied on performances, such as that of the female impersonator, grounded in passivity, eroticism and femininity to define their anxious time. It is the portrayals of femininity in its most elaborate form – that of a blacked-up, cross-dressed white male minstrel as a female impersonator portraying an ultra-feminine light-skinned black woman – that I will consider in this paper. In an early essay on gender impersonation, Laurence Senelick notes that the word 'impersonator' was coined in the 1850s (Senelick 1982: 32) – coinciding with the rise of blackface minstrelsy. One reading of this theatrical paralleling is that the primary object of early minstrelsy, the South (as performed by the minstrels), maintained a fixed object for the collective libido of a displaced (by urbanity and its related issues of capitalism and immigration) male audience. Additionally, beyond the practical demand of dramatic necessity, minstrelsy in America recognized that the search for a secured white masculine identity required that a fantasy of a living black female be performed, and thus came the advent of the role of the mulatta female impersonator as an integral part of the minstrelsy. Through the blackened-up female impersonator, black female sexuality was saved from disappearance and contained by the white male body at the same time.

MINSTRELSY SONGS AND THE 'DARK TRIANGLE'

The founding of blackface minstrelsy is most often credited to Thomas D. ('Daddy') Rice in 1828 (Toll 1974: 25-64). Group minstrelsy, which included several musicians/dancers, was founded by the Virginia Minstrels in the early 1840s (Nathan 1977: 123-34). A fundamental element of the minstrelsy performance, from early minstrelsy in the 1820s through 1900, was the minstrelsy song. The music was what the audience could take away with them, and what, in many ways, has continued in American patriotic consciousness through songs such as 'Oh, Susanna' (1849) and 'The Yellow Rose of Texas' (1858). The two central themes of minstrelsy songs were usually around two characters: the ethnic male Other (be he black, Irish, German, Jewish, Native American, or Chinese) and the black woman (Toll 1974: 160–94). Ultimately, it was the lyrics of the minstrelsy songs that established the types of people portrayed by the minstrels. In 1846, Dan Emmett and Frank Brower of the Virginia Minstrels developed a scene around a song about a Southern mulatta widely popular in Boston, 'Lucy Long'. The Virginia Minstrels, according to the historian Hans Nathan, did not don female costumes as they performed the song, but this act is considered the first female impersonation role of minstrelsy, named the 'wench performance' (Nathan 1977: 131). In *Love and Theft* (1993), Eric Lott notes that no one has been able to prove that the early 'wench' actually sang in the sketches which included her as a character; rather, she became the 'lyric and theatrical object of the song' (see illustration below) and of the entire theatre arena in the early minstrel show (160). Borrowing from the style of the English stage, Emmett and Brower punctuated the song about the attractive mulatta Lucy Long with dialogue:

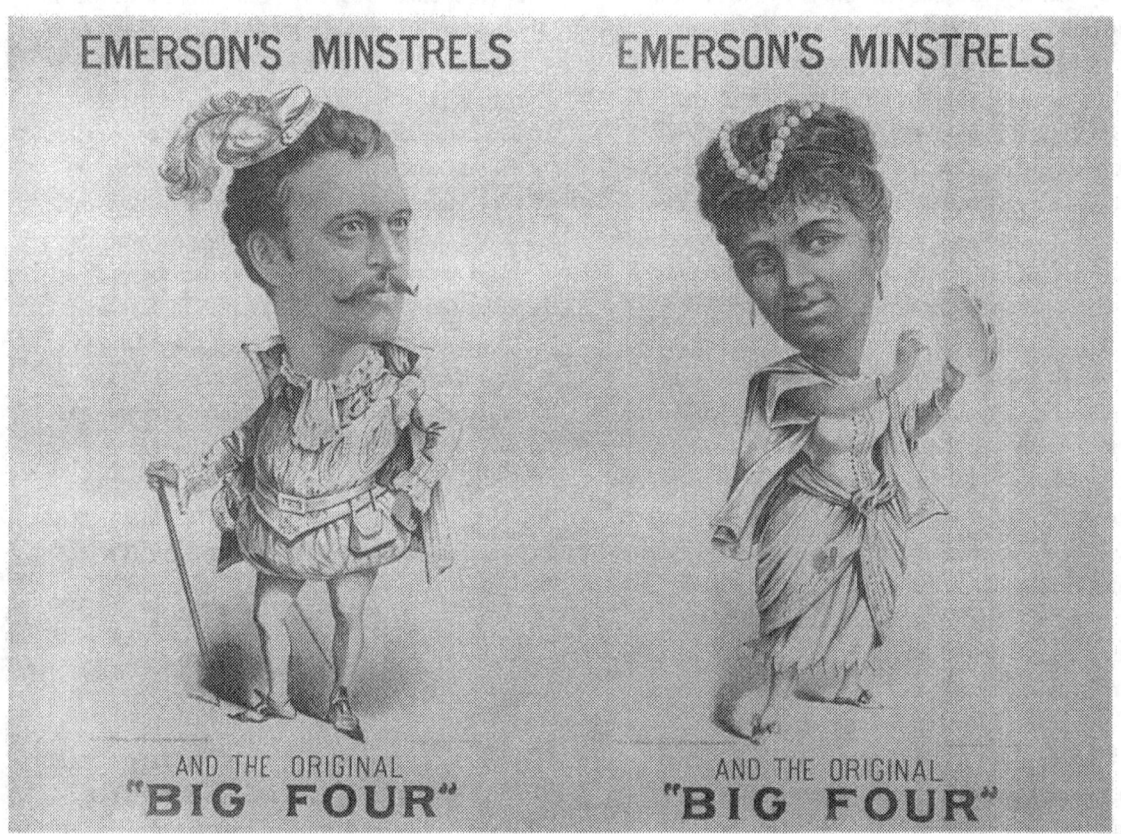

• Emerson's Minstrels and the Original 'Big Four', c. 1860. Courtesy of the Harvard Theater Collection, the Houghton Library.

Chorus [both singing]:
Take your time Miss Lucy
Take your time Miss Lucy Long
Rock de cradle Lucy
Take your time my dear.
[Dialogue.]
Frank. I trade her off for bean soup.
Dan. Well, you is hungryest nigger eber I saw. You'r neber satisfied widout your tinken bout bean soup all de time.

(Nathan 1977: 131)

Not atypical of the genre, the song tells us that Lucy Long's illustrated worth, if she forsakes love by reprimanding her suitor, is less than an edible commodity, food. In this and in the many versions of 'Lucy Long' which flourished in the 1840s and 1850s, the character of Lucy was portrayed in the scene by a white male minstrel in blackface, such as George Christy or Dan Gardner (Nathan 1977: 131; Paskman and Spaeth 1928: 92). It seems probable that the cross-dressing of the role led 'Miss Lucy Long' to become the most popular minstrel show hit from 1843 to 1852 (Winans 1976: 81). The mulatta Lucy Long, and other characters like her in songs such as 'Maggie May', 'Ada with the Golden Hair', 'Laura', 'The Coal Black Rose' (*St James* 1868); 'The Virginia Rosebud', 'Miss Lucy Neal', 'Dinah's Wedding Day', 'Mary Blaine', 'Buffalo Gals', 'Lucinda Snow' and 'Nelly Was a Lady' (Winans 1976: 81) were comic roles in narrative performances of minstrelsy songs. These songs always cast black women as lovers, wives, property, and objects of desire. For instance, the song 'Lucy Long' portrayed her as a woman so assured of her value as a sexual object that she needed to be reminded that she had the status of property, not personhood. The on-stage mulatta, a character identifiable as neither black nor white, and who was pretty (transcending the accepted equivalence of black as ugly), was nevertheless reinscribed as being black and owned. Therefore, the popularity of 'Lucy Long' was not related to its unique musical contribution, according to the music historian Robert Winans, who found the melody simplistic and repetitious (1976: 83), but was probably based on this triumph over unclear social definitions contained within the cross-dressed mulatta body, thriving on the comedic tension of the cross-dressing of the role. I believe the impetus and the popularity of the song lies in the audience's desire to put Lucy Long in her place – she is property and should not be particular about her lovers. Indeed, early minstrelsy was founded in songs which commodified the sexual being of black and mulatta women, often involving a mulatta wench and two darker-skinned men rivalling for her attention – named the 'dark triangle' in one minstrelsy book (Paskman and Spaeth 1928: 91).

The black woman was staged as utilizing her power over black men, but in reality, as all the members of the 'dark triangle' were white men, the social drama played out on the minstrel stage was similar to that of a plantation 'romance' perpetuated by sentiments like the ones below:

The Negro slave woman was an absolute dependent; dependent upon white men who dominated the little isolated world of the plantation. The black woman as other women subject or economically dependent upon controlling males made use of such powers as nature had given her for her personal aggrandizement. Was the white man or the black woman the aggressor?

(Johnston 1937: 1)

I believe that the use of mulatta and black women as comic material on the ante-bellum American minstrelsy stage was another example of society's exploration into its own interculturalness. As Hazel Carby has pointed out in the case of literature, the two functional discourses around the mulatta in the nineteenth century were to use her as a 'vehicle for an exploration of the relationship between the races and, at the same time, an expression of [that] relationship' (1987: 89). The minstrelsy mulatta personified her audience's conflicting sentiments during the Jacksonian age, when white men felt assaulted by urbanity as well as abolitionist and women's movements. In the same *body*, the mulatta *embodied* the *potential* for sexual and racial transgression and the fact that miscegenation had occurred and would continue to occur. Add to this the doubled sexual transgression of cross-dressing, and the blackfaced female impersonator gave the audience a titillation possibly unequalled on the American popular stage. Female impersonation in blackface minstrelsy began with the wench character because it was a portrayal based on the white population's characterization of black women as using 'such powers as nature had given' to obtain a better life for themselves.

EVOLUTION OF FEMALE IMPERSONATION

In the period after the Civil War female impersonation split into two characterizations: the comic 'Funny Old Gal' role and the prima donna. Both characterizations would remain in white minstrelsy until its absorption into vaudeville at the turn of the century. Most major companies had female impersonators by the mid-1850s; they were as integral as the endmen and Interlocutor.* Female impersonators noted in Paskman and Spaeth's 1928 minstrelsy book *Gentlemen, Be Seated!* are George Holland, M. S. Pike, Henry Wood, Charlie Backus, William Henry Rice, Lew Dockstader, and Willis P. Sweatman (Paskman and Spaeth 1928: 92). Female impersonators were often used to illustrate comic songs (Winans 1976: 81–3), and given the large physiques and noted comic talents of some of these minstrels, it can be inferred that many of the men listed above played the low-comedy 'Funny Old Gal' role (see illustration). The early 'Funny Old Gal' recalled the performance tradition of the comic Dame role in burlesque. Deeply rooted in American burlesque was a blatant ridicule for Shakespeare. In a response against Shakespearean tradition and general anti-Enlightenment disdain there developed the beginnings of 'legitimate burlesque' which was often produced in the same houses as white minstrelsy, and several minstrels worked both in burlesque and minstrelsy (Hutton 1891: 157). For instance, George Holland, who later perfected a minstrelsy afterpiece featuring 'Ms. Araminta Belinda Caudle Toodles' (Paskman and Spaeth 1928: 92), began his New York career portraying both the First Grave-Digger and Ophelia in John Poole's send-up of *Hamlet* in 1828 (Hutton 1891: 157). The 'prima donna' role probably emerged from burlesque performance tradition as well. The male soprano with an androgynous name reached his apex of popularity about the same time that biological women accessed the post-Civil War American popular stage in leg shows, ballet extravaganzas like *The Black Crook*, and English burlesque as introduced to America by Lydia Thompson and her British Blondes (Senelick 1993: 90). Additionally, Laurence Senelick notes that 'glamour drag' had performance roots in circus and equestrian transvestite performance in the nineteenth century, as well as in British public school drama and American collegiate theatrical groups such as Harvard's Hasty Pudding Club. In any event, it seems certain that the advent of the

* The endmen were Tambo (who played the banjo) and Bones (who played the fiddle). The Interlocutor was the straight man of the group.

• John F. Byrnes and Miss Helene, *c.* 1870. Courtesy of the Harvard Theater Collection, the Houghton Library.

prima donna in the 1860s would provide minstrelsy spectators with visual pleasure that rivalled the 'new' presence of biological women on stage.

Beginning in the 1870s, the prima donna female impersonators of the minstrel stage eclipsed the minstrel companies with which they were associated; the emotional responses of their audiences are legendary. As Toll recounts in *Blacking Up*, prima donnas had their wardrobes detailed in newspapers and were interviewed extensively (1974: 144) . Toll interprets the popularity of the prima donna as an indicator of cultural anxiety (1974: 141):

> Men in the audience probably were titillated by the alluring stage characters whom they were momentarily drawn to … [w]omen were probably intrigued by the impeccable grace and femininity of the beautiful illusionists.

Eric Lott sees the prima donnas as theatrical achievements of the 'sexually variable' (1993: 161). According to Lott, the blackfaced minstrel and the white spectator were engaged in a conversion from 'sexual defensiveness into same-sex desire' (1993: 161–2). Undoubtedly this type of desire was occurring, but I am more inclined towards Laurence Senelick's reading of the prima donna as popular because, in part, 'the audience could savor sexually provocative behavior because it had ostensibly been neutralized by the transvestitism' (1993: 93). Judith Butler moves in this direction when she discusses the way 'the performative act reestablishes the system of compulsory heterosexuality [by] reproduc[ing] and conceal[ing . . .] through the cultivation of bodies into discrete sexes with "natural" appearances and "natural" heterosexual dispositions' (1990: 275). Toll also sees the prima donna as the feminized version of the '"blackface" fool who educated audiences while also reassuring them that he was their inferior. Neither man nor woman, the female impersonator threatened no one' (1974: 144). Marjorie Garber furthers this reading: '"Black" (or "Negro") was as much in quotation and under erasure as "woman" in the white minstrel show: a black-impersonating female impersonator summed up and disempowered (or emasculated) [several] threatening forces at once' (Garber 1993: 277).

Though masculinity was perceived to be threatened by dark-skinned women, the white male audience members and the performers were also titillated and comforted by the prima donna, for she was, for the American culture at that time, the quintessential whore. The well-dressed mulatta female impersonator represented both the possibility of sexual and racial transgression (she is accessible) and the fact that it has happened (in the offspring of a white father and black mother), while at the same time containing the limits of those transgressions in the white male body. The prima donna required the mulatta to forgo her position as the 'lyrical and theatrical object' in minstrelsy to a superior position – that of a highly stylized and costumed near-white woman amidst the 'second part' or 'afterpiece' of the minstrel show, after the songs and dances featured in the 'first part' consisting of jokes and stories. The star prima donnas were the men with singular names – 'Eugene', 'Ricardo', 'Stuart', and 'The Only Leon'. One such prima donna, 'Eugene' (D'Ameli, 1836–1907) was a minstrel declaimed for his 'delineations of female characters [that] were so finished, so true to life' (Rice 1911: 344). 'Eugene' began with Wood's Minstrels, where he was joined by George Christy in 1853, and ended his career thirty years later with the Leon and Cushman Company in 1883. 'Ricardo' was born Foley McKeever in Ireland and worked with several well-known minstrel groups, including Kelly and Leon. 'Stuart' was known as the Male Patti*, after the Black Patti, and was rescued from a life as mail clerk by Tom Heath of McIntyre and Heath's Minstrels in 1887 (Rice 1911: 344).

* Black Patti was the stage name of the African-American soprano singing sensation Sissieretta Jones (see Watkins 1994: 150–1).

THE ONLY LEON

> In a fine but pleasing voice he commenced conversation on his art and his wardrobe, which he makes an essential element. With real feminine pride he showed the dress he wore at the performance last evening. It was not of stage material, but, like every article of his wardrobe, was genuine stuff.
> (*New York Clipper*, 31 December 1881)

The most successful female impersonator in nineteenth-century blackface minstrelsy was 'The Only Leon', also known as Francis Leon (see illustration below). The article from which the above excerpt was taken appeared during the zenith of Francis Leon's career. Born around 1840, the evolution of Patrick Francis Glassey into Francis Leon began with his notable gift of a boy soprano voice that never altered. Leon began working in blackface minstrelsy at the age of 14 with Wood's Minstrels. After studying ballet and voice for eight years, he formed Kelly and Leon's Minstrels with Edwin Kelly, an Irish immigrant (see illustration over page). The Kelly and Leon troupe refitted an old New York City chapel in 1866 and played the space for three years (Wittke 1930: 221–2). They then toured England and pleased the Prince of Wales so much he 'evinc[ed] his delight with applause' (*New York Clipper*, 1881). Leon flourished beyond the collapse of Kelly and Leon's Minstrels to continue on to Australia (Wittke 1930: 222). By 1882, aligned with Haverly's Minstrels, Leon was the profession's highest paid performer. His success spawned so many impersonators of 'Leon, The Female Impersonator' that he copyrighted his performance name as 'The Only Leon' (Senelick 1993: 85).

Robert Toll (1974: 142) gives the most detailed compilation of accounts regarding Leon:

> Leon is the best male female actor known to the stage. He does it with such dignity, modesty, and refinement that it is truly art.
>
> He is more womanly in his by-play and mannerisms, than the most charming female imaginable.
>
> Heaps of boys in my locality don't believe yet it's a man in spite of my saying it was.
>
> Leon's charms could cause 'to make a fool of a man if he wasn't sure.'

The 1881 *Clipper* account (subtitled 'Leon, The Lovely – The Great Female Impersonator and His Life and Wardrobe') splits its column space between biographical background of Leon and the particularities of his costume. The details of expenditure, no doubt fed to the reporter by proud Leon himself, included all manner of disclosure: 'The reporter blushingly asked Leon if he wore underskirts, and in reply the artist produced several of those garments in spotless white, and trimmed with costly embroidery.' The evocation of art, purity, authenticity and illusion all seem to function in the mythical world that surrounded Leon. The male audience members elevated Leon's artistry beyond the public status of women, which Robert Toll and Marjorie Garber indicate bespeaks the 'inferior' position in the social hierarchy biological women had on the minstrel stage. Leon played both white and mulatta women (one memorable poster has him costumed as the actress Sarah Bernhardt and creole Rose Michon) throughout his career. His portrayals were seen as highly respectable in their sexually charged, but controlled, titillation. Eric Lott notes that the game of 'gender guessing' (a term quoted from Lillian Schissel) raised the stakes of sexual identity roles in the assumed femininity of the performer Leon and the masculinity of the male audience member (1993: 166). The female audience

• The Only Leon, c. 1880. Courtesy of the Museum of the City of New York.

members' accounts are less plentiful than the men's, and I did not find primary source substantiation of Toll's and others' conclusions that women primarily enjoyed Leon's performances because they could observe, close-up, the latest fashions. It does appear by all accounts that 'Leon's performances can, without any reservation or qualification, be placed under the category of "truly wonderful"' (*New York Clipper* 1881) in the performance history of American minstrelsy in his ability to accomplish a theatrical body that transcended the limits of his, and his audience's, white maleness. But an examination of Leon's career reveals one surprising aspect – there is no report of his death. Marjorie Garber addresses the point as typical of highly stylized drag performers: with Leon's death a mystery, and his life one of carefully mediated disclosure, the realm of the unconscious which Leon occupied is masked or veiled, thereby containing its power in literalization (1993: 356). What is a mystery, beyond the death of Leon, is if there was an oppositional consciousness functioning with Leon. As the son of Irish immigrants, Leon was certainly aware that his inherited persona, as Irish, was ridiculed by minstrels in their quest to entertain through caricature: Irishmen on the minstrel stage 'had brogues, drank whisky, partied, and fought' (Toll 1974: 169). I would like to postulate that by performing as a female, Leon possibly could be performing subversion of his Irish identity. In *Bodies That Matter* (1993), Judith Butler astutely clarifies her previously muted point in *Gender Trouble* that 'there is no necessary relation between drag and subversion, and that drag may well be used in the service of both the denaturalization and reidealization of hyperbolic heterosexual gender norms' (1993: 125). However, Leon's perfectionism in performing femininity could be seen as a performative response to minstrelsy's manipulation of ethnic stereotypes, such as that of his fellow Irishmen. Leon's possible combating of the theatrical perpetuation of a derogatory view of the Irish by becoming a skilled gender transgressor intrigues

• Kelly and Leon's Minstrels, 1878. Courtesy of the Harvard Theater Collection, the Houghton Library.

me as it indicates the ambivalent, inherently political act of drag when the transgression also involves race.

CONTINUUM

In looking back on nineteenth-century blackface minstrelsy, I foreground one of many moments in American history when white men feared the limitlessness of expansion. In his illuminating book on the Jacksonian period, Alexander Saxton accounts for the permissiveness in gender transgression through cross-dressing and lyrics redolent with masturbation and homosexuality as based in the urban and frontier anxieties of the white male. And, as blackface minstrelsy was the staging for this era of conquering (Mexicans and Native Americans) and journeying (westward and, for immigrants, across oceans), it is fitting that the practice of minstrelsy – and the coinciding theatrical material based on re-staging the other, be it black, female, Irish, German, Jewish, or a combination – served as an instrument of establishing limits in an age of limitlessness. It is not surprising, therefore, that the legacy that minstrelsy has left theatrically continues to require that the woman onstage – especially the black woman – carry the fantasies of the social order. The American popular entertainment black woman was established by cross-dressed white male minstrels, and it is indeed ironic that the transgressions of race and gender of these white men contained limits on performed black femininity maintained in popular entertainment ever since.

REFERENCES

Butler, Judith (1990) 'Performative acts and gender constitution', in Sue-Ellen Case (ed.) *Performing Feminisms: Feminist Critical Theory and Theatre*, Baltimore, MD: Johns Hopkins University Press.

——(1993) *Bodies That Matter: On the Discursive Limits of 'Sex'*, New York: Routledge.

Carby, Hazel (1987) *Reconstructing Womanhood*, New York: Oxford University Press.

Ellison, Ralph (1972) 'Change the joke and slip the yoke', in *Shadow and Act*, New York: Vintage.

Garber, Marjorie (1993) *Vested Interests: Cross-Dressing and Cultural Anxiety*, New York: HarperPerennial.

Hutton, Laurence (1891) *Curiosities of the American Stage*, New York: Harper & Brothers.

Johnston, James Hugo (1937) 'Miscegenation in the antebellum South', PhD dissertation, University of Chicago.

Lott, Eric (1993) *Love and Theft: Blackface Minstrelsy and the American Working Class*, New York: Oxford University Press.

Nathan, Hans (1977) *Dan Emmett and the Rise of Early Negro Minstrelsy*, Norman, OK: University of Oklahoma.

New York Clipper, The (1881) 'Leon, The Female Impersonator', 31 December.

Paskman, Dailey and Spaeth, Sigmund (1928) *'Gentlemen, Be Seated!': A Parade of the Old-Time Minstrels*, Garden City, NY: Doubleday, Doran.

Rice, Edward Le Roy (1911) *Monarchs of Minstrelsy*, New York: Kenny.

St. James Hall Veritable and Legitimate Christy Minstrels Christmas Annual (1868) London: J. E. Adlard.

Saxton, Alexander (1990) *The Rise and Fall of the White Republic*, London: Verso.

Senelick, Laurence (1982) 'The evolution of the male impersonator on the nineteenth-century popular stage', *Essays in Theatre* 1, 1: 30–44.

——(1993) 'Boys and girls together: subculture origins of glamour drag and male impersonation on the nineteenth-century stage', in L. Ferris (ed.) *Crossing the Stage: Controversies on Cross-Dressing*, London: Routledge.

Toll, Robert C. (1974) *Blacking Up: The Minstrel Show in Nineteenth-Century America*, New York: Oxford University Press.

Watkins, M. (1994) *On the Real Side*, New York.

Winans, Robert B. (1976) 'The folk, the stage, and the five-string banjo in the nineteenth century', *Journal of American Folklore* 89 (354): 407–37.

Wittke, Carl (1930) *Tambo and Bones: A History of the American Minstrel Stage*, Durham, NC: Duke University Press.

Between pp. 30 & 31 • Caduta Massi/'Watch for Falling Rocks'; Homage to Stephan Mahler and Giovanni Segantini; presented by Hans Peter Litscher in Frankfurt (Theater am Turm, 1994) and Munich (Haus der Kunst, 1995). Pic: Brigitte Enguerand.

Truthful Trickery: Shamanism, Acting and Reality

Etzel Cardeña and Jane Beard

Hay un juicioso consejo de la Kabala: No hay que jugar al espectro, porque se llega a serlo. (The Kabala has wise advice: Do not pretend to be a spectre, because you may become one.) (Ruben Darío)

ACTING AND SHAMANISM

Acting and shamanism are sometimes discussed together under the umbrella of self-deception, fakery, or feigning, as forms of illusion that, at best, provide rest or escape from reality. But are acting and shamanism just eccentricities through which trained liars and fakers artfully express their deceit and, sometimes, even earn a meagre living? Or do they show us that the distinctions between pretence and reality, appearance and substance, are far more ambiguous and tentative than the dictionary would have it? To paraphrase the Kabala dictum quoted by Darío, can actors not only pretend to be but actually become spectres?

Besides the sceptical reactions that acting and shamanism evoke, there are other reasons to discuss them together in a paper on illusion. Shamanism has been considered a probable source for eastern and western performance in general, and it is known that specific performance techniques such as ventriloquism are used by shamans to indicate the presence of spirits. Leaving aside the somewhat academic issue of the origins of different performance traditions, it is undeniable that ritual, shamanism and performance have been variously linked throughout history and remain in a dialectic relationship (Schechner 1988).

Shamans are required to be performers of the first order, to enact struggles with spiritual forces or magical flights to other realities, to sing, dance and compose poetry. It is likely that at least some performance practices became separate specializations of the original shamanic role as technician of the sacred/ healer/ performer/ psychologist. Shamanic philosophy, motifs and techniques have continued affecting contemporary performance, music and the visual arts (Cardeña 1987; Tucker 1992).

But even 'traditional' theatre shares certain common elements with shamanism. After all, attending to a play typically involves, Brecht notwithstanding, an imaginal adventure in which we are asked to suspend our usual orientation to the surrounding reality and become engaged in a reality with different parameters than the one outside of the stage. For example, in *The Tempest* or *King Lear*, we are asked to participate in a journey with some similarities to the Balinese Barong ritual (Belo 1960) in which evil struggles with good. While these performances are not geared to expose and solve the psychological or philosophical problems of any particular individual in the audience, they allow the audience to obtain a glimpse of the conditions that underlie their everyday concerns. Our external circumstances are different from those of Prospero or Lear, yet we have to endure many affronts and injustices and, somehow, make enough sense of it all to continue living. For the extent of the performance we engage in an imaginal journey, not to the 'upper' or 'lower' worlds of shamanic cosmology, but to a different province from which we can retrieve insight, compassion and entertainment. That these journeys are often puerile, as Peter Brook has incisively commented, does not eliminate the extraordinary potential of the stage, both for the performer and the observer.

ILLUSION

The Merriam Webster's Collegiate Dictionary, tenth edition, defines illusion as 'the action of deceiving ... the state or fact of being intellectually deceived or misled ... a misleading image presented to the vision' (1994: 578). The determination is categorical: illusion is false, antithetical to some implied truth. Before discussing the ontological status of illusion, we have to make some distinctions. Optical illusions will serve as a good starting-point. Let's take a Hermann grid illusion (see illustration), in which dark spots are observed in the intersections of white horizontal and vertical stripes. Perception textbooks tell us that the optical illusion is produced by centre/surround antagonism of

• Hermann grid illusion

retinal cells (Sekuler and Blake 1985: 75). Indeed, from the perspective of a light meter, the apparent darker spots at the intersection of the lines are illusory. From a third-person (or measuring instrument) perspective, the reality is that there are no darker intersections. From a first-person, experiential account, however, they are there whether the observer knows perceptual theory or not. Conceivably, someone could use those 'non-existent' darker intersections to send a specific message, thus blurring the distinction between the observed and the real. When the ground for the illusion is the experiencer him/herself, there is an even greater potential to blur this distinction. We will discuss illusion, acting and shamanism from first- and third-person perspectives throughout the remainder of this paper.

Four categories of illusions are particularly relevant for this discussion: intentional versus accidental, self-directed versus other-directed, illusions that make the objectively real not seem so, and those that make the objectively unreal seem real. We will briefly define these dimensions and then retell a story that illustrates some of them. Most illusions in shamanic and acting performance intentionally seek to affect the thoughts, feelings, or perceptions of the audience, but sometimes a gesture or a behaviour will provoke an unintended effect on the observer. The gesture that a traditional shaman may make in brushing away a mosquito may be seen as a struggle with unseen forces, a struggle which may be experienced at that point by the observer. An actor's irritating contact lens may be interpreted as the emotional tears of a committed performance, thus producing a real emotional effect on the audience.

Illusions can be self-directed as when a shaman or an actor purposefully uses props or a costume to produce a change in behaviour and self-concept. They can be other-directed. Some healers may claim to be fully taken by their experience while they are just 'going through the motions'. But in many, perhaps most, cases self- and other-directed illusion occur simultaneously. The reactions of the audience (see below) may further enhance the performer's own conviction or the shaman's prestige and efficacy. Finally, although illusion is usually understood as making something unreal seem real, the converse effect can be created. Some years ago an Italian company toured a piece in which an actor opened a trunk and started tossing out life-size puppets. After two or three had been tossed out, the next one suddenly jumped out by itself and, after a brief gasp, it became obvious that the audience had been 'tricked' into believing the actor was a puppet.

The story of Quesalid, a reluctant and sceptic Kwakiutl shaman, as described by Lévi-Strauss (1969) from ethnographic work by Franz Boas, illustrates the complex interactions of various aspects of illusion. Shamanism includes a number of tricks of the trade including sleights-of-hand, ventriloquism, using informants to obtain information about the patient surreptitiously, and the prototypical 'sucking' cure (Eliade 1972). Despite Quesalid's doubts about the validity of shamanic healing, he learned the tricks of the trade, especially the sucking technique that has been described as far apart as the Americas, Siberia and Africa. This technique involves preparing a piece of down that the healer later extracts from her own mouth after she has 'sucked' the disease/ sorcery/ bad medicine from the patient's body. The shaman prominently displays this object – which usually contains organic material such as hair and blood – to the patient and observers before disposing of it and, consequently, of the disease. Quesalid had been taught well. He produced a foul object smeared with his own blood (obtained covertly by making his gums or tongue bleed slightly) that represented the malignancy of the patient. Despite Quesalid's own scepticism about this sleight-of-hand, he eventually found out that his services were sought after because other healers who were not as well versed in this technique proved less effective than he. To a degree, Quesalid's illusion-for-others became an illusion-for-himself, as he reluctantly became persuaded that this illusory cure of illness had concrete and real effects.

From a third-person perspective, it should be concluded that Quesalid and other healers engage in deception and, perhaps, in self-deception, as Warner (1980) maintains, but there are some valid alternative perspectives. Among them is the interpretation that the healer gives concrete form and shape to a vague, ungraspable disease, and that by this and other means the expectations of a possible cure are enhanced. Strengthening of expectations, expression of emotions and labelling of the ailment, are among the factors that facilitate a cure, whether in a pre-industrial society or in a modern hospital (Frank 1973).

The healer's own perspective, may be that the sleight-of-hand is actually the enactment of a spiritual struggle through which the healer is able to overcome a noxious influence on the patient's welfare (Turner 1964). It is not surprising that Victor Turner was not able to persuade any of the Ndembu healers he studied that they were engaging in deception. It is also significant for the topic of acting that he concluded: 'whatever efficacy the rite possesses – and it does have ameliorative effects on patients ... resides in the degree of skill wielded by the doctor in each instance of its performance' (1964: 240). While Quesalid and other traditional healers may not be conversant with Aristotle's explanation of the therapeutic effect of tragedy through catharsis, they still recognize that a performed illusion may achieve more than mere expressionless words.

ACTING AND ILLUSION

The word 'acting' is paradoxical. While its connotations include artistic feigning, simulation, representation, or impersonation (Kirby 1972), the word itself merely refers to making or doing an action or 'playing', as 'acting' is used in French (*jeu*) and German (*spiel*). It is also paradoxical that although acting is seen as faking, many performers engage in this practice specifically because it gives them a greater sense of 'authenticity' than most other activities. From a third-person perspective – without room for a dynamic, narrative account of the self – this does not make sense; in terms of experience it does.

Performance can be defined as a series of purposeful, intentional acts, rather than as a form of deception (see Hanna 1979). Although it goes against the beliefs we hold about the extent to which we are fully conscious and free agents, some spiritual traditions and findings in psychology agree that much of what we do is an automatic reaction of which we are only imperfectly and transitorily aware. Research has shown that ordinary consciousness, which we typically take as providing an accurate account of reality, is in fact a reconstruction of continuously changing shifts between perceptions, fantasies, repetitive thoughts and so on (Klinger 1978; Tart 1986). Were this not the case, focusing our attention for a certain amount of time on an event would not be as difficult as any meditation practice shows it to be. One of the first paradoxes we encounter in a discussion of illusion and acting is that what we define as being 'authentic' or 'real' is, in many instances, a collection of automatic, semi-conscious behaviours, thoughts and experiences, many of which are intended to deflect or misrepresent a given state of affairs. Psychodynamic theory describes many of these strategies as defence mechanisms, other theories speak of social roles, Hinduism would call it 'the veil of maya'. It is not surprising that the metaphor of a mask has been used by many theoreticians to refer to our ordinary personality (Monte 1991). Paradoxically, performers use actual masks to explore aspects of themselves that are covered by social and personal conventions.

But there is more to acting than the intentionality of an act. Another basic aspect is that these intentional acts are constrained by set parameters: the circumstances given by the script or improvisation, the lines to be delivered and responded to, the time and space framework provided by the stage and the length of the play, the established relationship with the audience. The adoption of these parameters is perhaps the major difference between acting and other potentially fully conscious acts. While these constraints would seem to limit the agency of the actor, they can have the opposite effect. With all of the given circumstances in place, an actor need not worry about distractions, maintaining a self-image, or coming up with activities to fill the existential void. Instead, the performer can choose to commit fully to a chosen intention and to actions and reactions as they unfold. Billie Whitelaw, one of Samuel Beckett's foremost interpreters, once commented that the extraordinarily structured direction in his play *Rockaby* had given her the unusual freedom to explore the resonances of her performance deeply because she did not have to worry about specific actions or inflections, which Beckett had marked literally to the second.

Actors can, of course, be less than fully committed to the action and to the moment. They may be preoccupied by, among other things, anticipating a particular action before it occurs or by trying to please what they imagine to be the wishes of the audience. This type of imperfect, uncommitted acting is perhaps the common staple of most of our theatres. Unsuccessful acting may be also manifested in unintentional, incongruous behaviours. Even without the help of physiological measures or a probe of the actor's mind, we may recognize that the tone, the posture, or some other feature is absent or not quite in synchrony with the rest of the actor's behaviours. A study by Gosselin, Kirouac and Dor (1995) with conservatory actors gives a good example of this. These actors provided samples of various emotions, some of them were felt, some of them were not. While the unfelt samples generally had all of the facial actions of the emotion portrayed, they were not in synchrony, in contrast with natural displays of emotions or the actors' own felt portrayals. A fully realized performance involves the organic integration of experience, physiology, cognition and behaviour, whereas less realized acting may miss an element or lack proper harmony among various somatic and psychological components. Sometimes this type of acting may be very 'showy', but it may be perceived by the actor or the audience as 'empty' acting. None the less, in the study by Gosselin and collaborators, naive raters could not distinguish very well between the felt and unfelt manifestations, which probably explains why so much bad acting goes unremarked.

A different disconnection can occur when the actor experiences an event but a body indicator is incongruous with the report of that experience. Besides the earnest but untalented actors that we all know, psychologists have found a group of individuals labelled repressors who honestly claim to be calm while talking, for instance, about their parents, while their electrodermal responses manifest great arousal (Weinberger 1990).

The previous are examples in which the initial illusion of acting does not transcend its initial status. By far the most interesting case, however, is that in which an actor creates an illusion that becomes real for self and for the audience. As compared with a magician who manipulates a number of special objects that help create an illusion, the actor's main and sometimes only instrument is herself. For analytical purposes we will divide this discussion into bodily and mental strategies, but a successful actor will not unintentionally disconnect behaviours and mental strategies during a performance.

One of the simplest but still effective strategies to induce the experience of an emotion is to shape one's face and body to conform to the natural expression of emotions. While intuitively this has been known for a long time, not until recently has research shown that manipulating facial muscles and bodily postures can give rise to the emotions with which they are associated (Duclos *et al.* 1989; Ekman *et al.* 1983). It is noteworthy that the study by Ekman and collaborators found that directly changing facial expressions without any association to emotional labels and thoughts was more effective than thinking about personal memories associated with those emotions. This result helps explain why Stanislavski's own work developed from a very 'internalized' method to a growing stress on 'externalized' physical actions.

Psychology has recently rediscovered the relationship between expressions, postures and emotion that interested Darwin and others, but performers have known about it all along. During the nineteenth century, the voice professor Delsarte (cf. Shawn 1974) provided a taxonomy of facial expressions, body postures and gestures, and supplied a more integrated view of emotions, thoughts and behaviours than psychology had until recently.

When discussing character structure, the director Michael Chekhov (1984) worked with the actor's imagination and, very directly, with the body. For instance, one of his exercises used facial expressions and gestures to imitate the character's face, characteristic movements and gestures (1984: 71). In the field of psychology, a striking example of the blurring between illusion and reality is described in a study by Lanzetta, Cartwright-Smith and Kleck (1976). They asked their participants intentionally to conceal or exaggerate their reaction to painful shocks of varying intensity. Measurements of their experience and physiology (i.e. skin conductivity) of pain showed that concealing their expression of pain decreased the objective and subjective reactions to pain, whilst exaggerating the pain increased those reactions: a perfect example of an initial deception becoming something else. Although academics have usually studied one psychological indicator at a time, the simultaneous combination and interaction of facial expression, posture, breathing, and so forth, should produce stronger and more reliable experiences of an emotion than changing a single element (Bloch *et al.* 1987). Instead of assuming that an emotion is only/or first either a cognitive appraisal, a conscious felt experience, or a physiological reaction, we would do much better by defining emotions as integrative events that involve these factors in complex interactive relations (Carlson and Hatfield 1992; Lewis *et al.* 1990).

Using mental strategies to evoke an emotion provides a different route from shaping the face or the body. For example, deceit has been successfully employed to bring about real changes in physiology and experience. Valins (1966, in Carlson and Hatfield 1992) showed that male undergraduates based their ratings of how attractive they found

Playboy's centrefold on false physiological feedback they received. A later study by Hirschman (1975, in Carlson and Hatfield 1992) accounted for this finding by showing that false feedback can produce physiological changes in the direction of the feedback.

The study of hypnosis, whose modern history started by most accounts with the very dramatic performances of Mesmer, is a particularly relevant area in the consideration of illusion and performance. Not surprisingly, hypnosis has been analysed in dramaturgical terms (Coe and Sarbin 1991). A number of hypnotic inductions also use 'tricks' such as reinterpreting naturally occurring bodily reactions (for example, the eyes becoming strained after focusing them for a number of minutes) as the effects of the hypnotist's suggestions. This reinterpretation may change the individual's expectations, and focus of attention, in a similar way to the 'magical' information that shamans and other healers provide. Hypnotic phenomena are based on the specific suggestions given. For instance, raising the participants' beliefs that a hypnotic procedure will enhance memory will produce that effect, whilst telling the participants that the procedure will impair memory will produce the opposite effect (Orne 1959). Suggestions thus help not only to define but also to shape experience and behaviour.

Many individuals who respond strongly to hypnotic suggestions have a history of 'imaginative involvements', including participation in theatrical and other artistic activities (Hilgard 1979), and share some characteristics with shamans (Cardeña 1996). One of the most interesting hypnotic phenomena involves the suggestion of hallucinations, either to experience stimuli that are not present, or not to experience stimuli that are present. Hypnotic suggestions can, for instance, ameliorate pain, or create the negative hallucination that a stimulus is not really present. This and other strategies do not produce responses that are equivalent to the total absence of a stimulus (Spanos 1986), but they affect experience and the underlying brain processes in the direction of the suggestion given. From a first-person perspective, an honest account of pain decrease *is* an amelioration of pain, whether obtained by hypnotic suggestions or another form of illusion. As with acting, a clear intention by the person in the hypnotic condition to commit himself to the task (in this case to follow suggestions without being distracted by extraneous concerns) is necessary for a successful hypnotic performance.

Some studies also show that cortical responses to stimuli (event-related potentials) in individuals who are very susceptible to hypnosis are concordant with suggestions to 'hallucinate' either the absence of the stimulus or its increase (e.g. Spiegel *et al.*1985). In the case of individuals with dissociative identity disorder or 'multiple personality', this effect seems to depend on the type of identity that the person exhibits at the moment (Cardeña *et al.*1989).

Recent research on emotional expression and on hypnosis confirms that no single route is ideal for everyone. Some individuals are more responsive to their facial expression than others (Duclos *et al.* 1989), some use specific imagery to achieve sensory alterations while for others pure intention without imagery is the preferred strategy (Miller and Bowers 1993), some prefer practices that alter consciousness through the vigorous use of the body, others prefer to become absorbed in the inner theatre of imaginal experiences (Cardeña 1996). The ability to evoke particular emotions in an audience seems to depend on the ability to feel an emotion strongly, be able to express it, and be unresponsive to the incompatible emotions of others (Hatfield, Cacioppo and Rapson 1994).

However, sole concentration on body mechanics or inner experiences to elicit an emotion mechanically is unlikely to sustain the complexity of an actual performance. The actor needs to have a strategy that will keep her fully engaged throughout the scene or the play. Stanislavski provided a good route-map with his consideration of objectives and his method of physical actions. Especially in the latter part of his work he explored the actor's commitment to specific physical actions given the circumstances of the character, the play and the ongoing interactions with other actors. These actions are not just mechanical movements but integrated behavioural and experiential events that involve a very clear intention, motivated by a very precise reason. While physical actions may bring about particular emotions, energy levels, etc., their primary purpose is to give a moment-to-moment direction and focus to what the actor does. Stanislavski also stated that emotions could not be tapped directly, at least not in a consistent way.

Grotowski has recently clarified his lineage with Stanislavski and made a distinction between mechanical behaviours and physical actions. The latter involve a specific, dynamic intention that has a precise motivation and a clear way to achieve that intention (Richards 1995: 30).

Physical actions, intentions, or objectives provide a framework that maintains the attention of actors focused on the present moment in which they need to achieve their purpose. The intention or objective revolves around the purpose of the character placed in a given set of circumstances, and in interaction with the intentions and obstacles of the other characters. The intention should be general enough to allow for a real-time reaction to what the other actors provide, yet distinct enough to maintain the committed attention of the actor. Although Schechner (1988) distinguishes what he calls ecstatic non-self experiences in some non-Western traditions from character possession in the Stanislavskian tradition, they can both be subsumed under the umbrella of full, deliberate intent. They are distinguished in that the parameters and given circumstances for a character are circumscribed by the text and the given circumstances and actions of the other characters, whereas ritualistic performances may be focused on a sequence of physical actions and/or openness to spontaneous physical impulses. The importance of intention and its link with shamanism has also been discussed in the context of the visual arts (Sinclair 1991).

Another important consideration is the effect of the performer's intention on the audience. In many rituals, in ritually based performances and in some contemporary projects such as Grotowski's paratheatrical activities, there is no distinction between performer and audience, or that distinction is mild, so the previous considerations would apply to all participants. But even in performances in which there is a strong distinction between performer and audience, the audience can react strongly. In those events, the level of involvement, intention and presence of the individuals is mediated by individual variations of what the hypnosis field calls imaginative involvement or the capacity to become fully absorbed in the event, by the implicit and explicit knowledge of the roles and activities to be carried out in a particular context (cf. Cardeña and Spiegel 1991; Shor 1959), and by the ability to read and react to emotional expressions (Hatfield, Cacioppo and Rapson 1994).

The effect of a shamanic or theatrical performance will evidently depend on the artistic and psychological characteristics of members of the audience, but it is also equally evident that performance is an interactive event. The reaction of an audience will depend on the empathic response of its members. Hoffman (1984) has argued that there are various modes of empathy, from basic responses such as mimicry, to more sophisticated cognitive processes such as sympathizing with the plight of another. An initial mode of empathy may occur in the infant's imitation of the facial expressions of the care-taker, imitation that activates facial muscles which then generate a particular emotional response, an argument consistent with the evidence reviewed above.

A more esoteric mechanism has also been proposed. Stanislavski wrote that an actor could sometimes feel direct 'energy' links with the audience, an assertion that has found echo in reports by some modern actors (Bates 1988) and in descriptions of shamanic rituals (Katz 1982). These experiences are also reflected in our language; for instance, in our expression about an 'electrifying' performance. Whether these experiences of 'energy' are metaphors for sensory and emotional responses, or they describe other processes remains an open question.

Such focus and direction of physical and psychological process, underpinned by an intention that has to react to moment-to-moment changes in self and others, is rare in contexts other than acting. These factors explain why acting can be imbued with greater reality than most events outside of performance. While western performance is not ordinarily analysed in these terms, other traditions discuss the integration of physical, psychological and spiritual processes within a performance (cf. Zarrilli 1993). Stanislavski advised actors to act 'as if' the circumstances of the character and the play were real. The magic of it all is that, if they indeed manage to fully engage in acting 'as if' these events were happening, their experience and their body, and that of the audience, will create real and intense events from that original illusion. If the performer's intention is imperfectly or incompletely realized, the audience will remain more a detached observer than a full participant, its own potentials unfulfilled. In this case, the illusion of the performance remains just an illusion. But when intention is impeccable and the performers achieve moment-to-moment presence, they and the audience take a jarring step from illusion to reality. That such a reality is bound by a certain context and lasts only for some minutes or hours is quite inconsequential. All events are transient. Paraphrasing what Havelock Ellis said about dreaming, truthful acting is only real while it lasts, but the same can be said of life.

REFERENCES

Bates, B. (1988) *The Way of the Actor*, Boston, MA: Shambala.

Belo, Jane (1960) *Trance in Bali*, New York: Columbia University Press.

Bloch, Susana, Orthous, Pedro and Santibaxez, Guy (1987) 'Effector pattern of basic emotions: a psychophysiological method for training actors', *Journal of Social and Biological Structures* 10: 1–19.

Cardeña, Etzel (1987) 'The magical flight: shamanism and theatre', in Ruth-Inge Heinze (ed.) *Proceedings of the Third International Conference on the Study of Shamanism and Alternate Ways of Healing*, West Indies: A-R Editions, 291–304.

——(1996) 'Just floating on the sky: A comparison of shamanic and hypnotic phenomenology', in R. Quekelberghe and D. Eigner (eds) *6th Jahrbuch für Transkulturelle Medizin und Psychotherapie*, 367–80.

——Pakianathan, I. and Spiegel, D. (1989) 'The use of evoked potentials in the classification of multiple personality subtypes', *International Journal of Clinical and Experimental Hypnosis* 37: 360.

——and Spiegel, D. (1991) 'Suggestibility, absorption, and dissociation: an integrative model of hypnosis', in John F. Schumaker (ed.) *Human Suggestibility: Advances in Theory, Research and Application*, New York: Routledge, 93–107.

Carlson, John G. and Hatfield, Elaine (1992) *The Psychology of Emotion*, Fort Worth, TX: Harcourt Brace Jovanovich.

Chekhov, Michael (1984) *To the Director and Playwright*, New York: Limelight.

Coe, William C. and Sarbin, Theodore R. (1991) 'Role theory: hypnosis from a dramaturgical and narrational perspective', in Steven Jay Lynn and Judith W. Rhue (eds) *Theories of Hypnosis: Current Models and Perspectives*, New York: Guilford, 303–23.

Duclos, Sandra E., Laird, James D., Schneider, Eric, Sexter, Melissa, Stern, Lisa and van Lighten, Oliver (1989) 'Emotion-specific effects of facial expressions and postures on emotional experience', *Journal of Personality and Social Psychology* 57: 100–8.

Ekman, Paul, Levenson, Richard W. and Friesen, Wallace V. (1983) 'Autonomic nervous system activity distinguishes among emotions', *Science* 221: 1208–10.

Eliade, M. (1972) *Shamanism: Archaic Techniques of Ecstasy*, Princeton, NJ: Bollingen.

Frank, Jerome D. (1973) *Persuasion and Healing: A Comparative Study of Psychotherapy*, Baltimore, MD: Johns Hopkins University Press.

Gosselin, Pierre, Kirouac, Gilles and Dor, François Y. (1995) 'Components and recognition of facial expression in the communication of emotion by actors', *Journal of Personality and Social Psychology* 68: 83–96.

Hanna, Judith L. (1979) *To Dance is Human*, Chicago: University of Chicago Press.

Hatfield, E., Cacioppo, J.T. and Rapson, R.L. (1994) *Emotional Contagion*, Cambridge: Cambridge University Press.

Hilgard, Josephine R. (1979) *Personality and Hypnosis*, Chicago: University of Chicago Press.

Hoffman, M.L. (1984) 'Interaction of affect and cognition in empathy', in C. E. Izard, J. Kagan and R. B. Zajonc (eds) *Emotion, Cognition and Behaviour*, Cambridge: Cambridge University Press.

Katz, R. (1982) *Boiling Energy*, Cambridge, MA: Harvard University Press.

Kirby, Michael (1972) 'On acting and not-acting', *Drama Review* 16: 3–15.

Klinger, Eric (1978) 'Modes of normal conscious flow', in Kenneth S. Pope and Jerome L. Singer (eds) *The Stream of Consciousness*, New York: Plenum.

Lanzetta, John T., Cartwright-Smith, Jeffrey and Kleck, Robert E. (1976) 'Effects of nonverbal dissimulation on emotional experience and autonomic arousal', *Journal of Personality and Social Psychology* 33: 354–70.

Lévi-Strauss, Claude (1969) *Structural Anthropology*, London: Allen Lane.

Lewis, Michael, Sullivan, Margaret W. and Michalson, Linda (1990) 'The cognitive-emotional fugue', in Carroll E. Izard, Jerome Kagan and Robert B. Zajonc (eds) *Emotions, Cognition, and Behaviour*, Cambridge: Cambridge University Press.

Miller, Mary E. and Bowers, Kenneth S. (1993) 'Hypnotic analgesia: dissociated experience or dissociated control?', *Journal of Abnormal Psychology* 102: 29–38.

Monte, Christopher F. (1991) *Behind the Mask*, Forth Worth, TX: Harcourt Brace Jovanovich.

Orne, Martin (1959) 'The nature of hypnosis: artifact and essence', *Journal of Abnormal Psychology* 58: 277–99.

Richards, Thomas (1995) *At Work with Grotowski on Physical Actions*, London: Routledge.

Schechner, Richard (1988) *Performance Theory*, New York: Routledge.

Sekuler, R., and Blake, R. (1985) *Perception*, New York: Alfred A. Knopf.

Shawn, Ted (1974) *Every Little Movement: A Book about Delsarte*, New York: Dance Horizons.

Shor, R. E. (1959) 'Hypnosis and the concept of the generalized reality-orientation', *American Journal of Psychotherapy* 13: 582–602.

Sinclair, Iain (1991) *The Shamanism of Intent*, Uppingham: Goldmark.

Spanos, N. P. (1986) 'Hypnotic behaviour: a social-psychological interpretation of amnesia, analgesia, and "trance logic"', *Behavioral and Brain Sciences* 9: 449–502.

Spiegel, David, Cutcomb, S., Ren, C. and Pribram, Karl (1985) 'Hypnotic hallucination alters evoked potentials', *Journal of Abnormal Psychology* 94: 249–55.

Tart, Charles T. (1986) *Waking up*, Boston, MA: Shambhala.

Tucker, M. (1992) *Dreaming with Open Eyes*, London: Aquarian.

Turner, V. W. (1964) 'A Ndembu doctor in practice', in Ari Kiev (ed.) *Magic, Faith and Healing*, New York: Free Press.

Warner, R. (1980) 'Deception and self-deception in shamanism and psychiatry', *International Journal of Social Psychiatry* 1: 41–52.

Weinberger, Daniel (1990) 'The construct validity of the repressive coping style', in Jerome L. Singer (ed.) *Repression and Dissociation*, Chicago: University of Chicago Press.

Zarrilli, Phillip (1993) 'What does it mean to "become the character": power, presence, and transcendence in Asian in-body disciplines of practice', in Richard Schechner and Willa Appel (eds) *By Means of Performance*, Cambridge: Cambridge University Press.

Come Back to Life

An interview with André Stitt

Simon Herbert

André Stitt's work as a performance artist usually tends to draw a reaction from an audience. Some leave elated, believing that they have seen a transformative event which reinforces the medium's potential for examining intensities in time and space; others leave disgusted, feeling that they have witnessed a spectacle of almost unbearable degradation. Neither remains untouched by the confrontation. Stitt's performances (which now number in the hundreds), first made in 1976 in his native Belfast, have spanned the last nineteen years and been presented throughout the world. His 'akshuns' involve self-abuse, aggression, tantrums and exorcisms, arrived at through pain or elation, filtered through the urges of the masculine and the dispossessed. Yet beyond a surface anger which some find so intense that it merely overloads, there lies a sophisticated meditation on the nature of social responsibility. Simply put, Stitt's 'akshuns' implicate the audience in condoning another's actions, either by default or encouragement.

This is not to say that Stitt has always remained in control of this delicate balance. In 1992 he experienced a severe breakdown when the difference between his art and his life disappeared. That he has managed to come through this and claim a new artistic strategy for himself points to the notion of redemption which always underlines even his most excessive moments. It is no coincidence that the persona he employs in his performances is the 'trickster', a half-animal, half-divine creature full of contradiction.

Simon Herbert: What do you think audiences expect when they come along to see a performance by André Stitt?

André Stitt: It seems to be the experience, and fact of my life, that risk has always been present. I was aware from an early age that I was searching for something within myself that would give purpose and credence to my existence. These were the very, very deep things that I felt as a child, and that the way in was actually to take risks.

How did that manifest itself when you were a child?

For me, it always felt like a total war going on the whole time. The way I looked at it was outside of my personal universe: there was a war going on in the city where I was born, and there was a war in the street, there was a war in the house, there was a war between all the individuals in that family. And then bringing it right down inside me, there was a war going on inside me.

You perceive yourself, in terms of your creative practice, as operating on the margins. Do you think that this definition is in any way useful?

Lately, I've been thinking more and more about this situation, compartmentalizing what artists do and what they term as disciplines. Art has always been a creative discovery of myself and the world. It's often been very confusing, because I haven't necessarily seen it strictly in 'art' terms. I've always seen it as a working process. This could come from some part of my childhood which had to do with that separation from a reality that everyone participated in, but often confused me. I actually did not know how to participate in situations. It was like people had this little rule book of how to behave and I didn't have it. At an early age Pop Art was a revelation to me and it opened up the way that I saw the world. Even before I knew about it I saw it in everyday objects. Everything looked special to me. Kids used to laugh at me when I would pick up something and say, 'Look at that.' Later, in 1976, I went to foundation school and I was painting incredibly large canvases. We are talking about 12 feet, they were really massive, big, big, heavy stretchers. I know that this was, in a way, an attempt to be the centre of attention and part of that has transferred itself into performance. But there was also a conscious attempt at changing the way that I saw art at that point. In terms of painting I became very aware of the physicality of what my body was doing with the paint, and the large quantities of paint on these big canvases and they literally came off the wall or on the ground. I was more interested in the process of thinking and feeling, and what I was doing to my body, than any finished product.

The concept of the trickster is a central element of your work. Did it become apparent to you that there were precedents in other cultures for the role that you were instinctively defining for yourself?

• André Stitt, *Second Skin/Behind the Mask*, NIPAF, Japan Foundation Forum, Tokyo, 1 March 1996. Courtesy Alex Pazmandy.

• André Stitt, *Second Skin/Behind the Mask*, NIPAF, Japan Foundation Forum, Tokyo, 1 March 1996. Courtesy of Alex Pazmandy.

1979 was the year that a lot of stuff started really to be kind of bubbling over. I very consciously decided to incorporate the trickster cycle at that point, because I noticed in my actions that each one spun off in a little cycle into the next one, and into the next one. There was no separation.

Even though each performance could deal with certain issues, there seemed to be a constant thread through them. At the same time I'm very aware that the sort of work that I'm doing now has come right back to originally how I got into it. It has flown backwards and forwards all the way, but it keeps spinning round and round. It's like a spiral. It's absolutely riddled with all those paradoxes.

During the 1980s I was intuitively responding to what was happening with Thatcherism, that whole idea of materialism and commodification. I noticed that through the 1980s a lot of performances started to get slick. They started to use an awful lot of novelty content, so that you were seeing performances as, like, 'I've got it now, here we go. It's a neon, it's a laser.' Everyone had some kind of gimmick. My performances started to get extremely complex, using lots of gimmicks. It got very complicated and probably during those years between 1982 and 1992 there was an overload of material going in. There were so many missiles being fired at an audience, metaphorically and physically. The idea was this is a macrocosm of the way I feel about the culture that I am living in and everything is comparative within this. I'm firing them out to see if they hit targets. Probably those years is why I had the most injuries in performances. They were times when, although I was intrinsically in control of the structure of the performance, I knew I was somehow going from A to B in it, in the middle of it was like all hell just broke loose. I know a lot of people got alienated by that, but I think it also dredged up something very deep within them that they were getting angry about.

Did you develop a certain amount of, probably hatred is too strong a word, but, a lack of respect for the audience because you felt that they were sat there safely?

I think that's absolutely true, to be perfectly honest. I think I was aware of that but I made excuses for my behaviour.

Do you think your behaviour needed to be excused?

To myself, because coming into the 1990s, there was something very wrong with me and in fact, I was going insane because of it. I literally did go insane, I know that now. But I was pushing too much responsibility on myself and it became very, very confused.

Your work creates a real bond between yourself and the audience, whilst simultaneously acknowledging that there's only a certain level on which you can both interact.

How can it be any other way? Because we've each got our own different personal histories, you know, and people come to performances with their own agendas and their own suppositions. It's often difficult ... in the end it turned into a freak show. I really was playing the game because it got to the point where I couldn't do it any more and I knew that suddenly it was a lie because I wasn't being honest with myself.

When you imply that your work at this time was a lie, was that because there was a certain expectation of you, and you could have become a cliché of yourself?

Yes, yes, absolutely and that's what happened in the last year or so. By 1992 I had a couple of horrific situations in performances. For instance I did one in London which I did completely in blackout. I didn't remember anything that had happened and when I came out of the blackout sometime later in the night I was suddenly told that I'd done this performance, and it was truly just shocking because that was the point where I stepped over the mark and attacked the audience. Because at that point I hated the audience, because I hated myself and what I perceived the audience had made me. They'd made me into a freak show which was never what I wanted to be. So I knew that the game was up. That's the point where I really was insane. But my insanity ... I was so confused that I kept trying to do actions ...

To find a way back in?

Yes, but it was impossible because I was insane. It was impossible. It ended up in 1992 doing a performance at the Exploding Cinema where I actually had been clean for about a week, and it was the first performance I'd done for many years absolutely 100 per cent clean. And I did this performance, basically which was about the breakdown of my marriage, about sexual problems I had and it ended up with a lot of insertions in my anus with scissors, guns – quite a brutal action. I was determined to change it back and get the raw honesty involved in it. Obviously people didn't know personally what was going on in my life at that time, they saw the outer layer, the outer context, which was looking at pornography, or whatever. But I was very confused and at that point I did try and change that but shortly after that I had a complete collapse. And so then it did change.

For a period at the end of 1992 I did a lot of drink and a lot of drugs and everything had fallen apart in my life. I couldn't go anywhere, I couldn't wash, I was totally collapsed and totally gone as a human being. Absolutely no dignity, no respect, nothing. I'd literally gone through this absolutely desperate, loneliest place, this absolute hell within myself and I just wanted to die and I knew for years I was actually almost consciously committing a slow suicide because I was almost living out this idea of the Irishman marginalized in society.

So there was a certain romanticism to it.

Yeah. And I went along with that romanticism, I mean I was heavily into characters like – not so much artists, but writers like Bukowski and Kerouac and stuff. Rock and roll and stuff and the whole deal and that's the way that I did live my life. I got to this point where nothing worked any more and I had this experience of ... I died. I am absolutely convinced that I died, there's no other way – and I've looked at it from every way – it's like I died. I was lying in the flat and I felt my whole spirit coming out of my body. This was not a hallucination. I just seemed to go down this tunnel and then suddenly there was this incredibly bright light and that's the last thing I remember and I came to a couple of days later. I just thought well that's it – I'm terrified now, I don't know what to do because something's happened there. I think I've died and come back to life but I don't understand this. But there was an absolute clarity that something had changed. At that point I actually didn't feel insane any more, I mean there was a certain clarity and my life just changed. And since that point in 1992 it's progressively got better, I've been able to key into the art that I want to do much easier.

Did you see art as having been at the root of all these problems? What was it that made you want to continue [with art]?

Because I knew that if it wasn't for performance I'd have been dead a long time ago. Art actually saved my life because it enabled me in public to get up and admit the guilt, the shame, the hurt and whatever, the most honest way I possibly could, even if it was disgusting and horrible and very frightening to look at. Art has just intuitively come back [now], there hasn't been that desperate need to push and do more and more performances. It was almost like a treadmill really. In fact the last couple of years I've only done two performances each year. What's happened is I've been able to focus very, very intensely into those two pieces each year. I've been for the first time in my life where I wanted to be in 1976 and my art is 100 per cent focused. When I was drinking and drugging, I'd be doing it before a performance because I knew that I was going to hit a point where I was totally terrified, but I wanted to go on, and of course, as any addict knows, the more that you're on this treadmill, the more drink and drugs you get, the more scared and paranoid you're going to get. So I couldn't go further each time but I knew there was a point where I wanted to get to. Now that I've reached that point – just right in there. Now that might be the sum of experiences of all these years of doing stuff which of course it is, but something else has changed as well. There's a clarity because I'm clean.

There was a point for me in your last performance, in Cardiff, where for the first time you moved outside your own internal conventions, by just sitting in a chair at the end of the live work and talking. You made your performance dysfunctional.

Exactly, and it was something that I had to really think a lot about. Performance is an illusion and I wanted to break that illusion, I wanted to take off the mask and say 'Look I'm not special, this is what's happening in my life right now, I'm a human being, don't put me on a fucking pedestal.' Because that's what people do with art. They put it in museums, they put it on a pedestal, they commodify it, they make it separate, they give power that it doesn't have – they make it so special that you can't touch it. Art is a very potent force within every human being. I believe that through art you can awaken your creativity, be responsible, and then build it into being responsible within a community. Not separated. When I started talking about that stuff at the end of the performance I was saying I am not separated from this, we are in the same community, we have to talk to each other about it.

Do you have a long-term strategy for the future?

Risk is a central part of my life. I'm not that different from other people. To grow you have to risk. You need to feel where you are headed, and part of that perception involves living by a code that you consider to be reasonable. Respect people and you respect yourself.

What about external forces such as the ageing process? Will slowing down affect the performance?

Do you mean will I be an old codger flinging around tomato ketchup? I don't think so, but who knows? Why project ahead? Make things for the here and now. If you take care of this moment you're taking care of all time.

'...and so shall you seem to have cut your nose in sunder'

Illusions of Power on the Elizabethan Stage and in the Elizabethan Market-place

Michael Mangan

INTRODUCTION: POPULAR PERFORMANCE AND 'SERIOUS ART'

In this paper I intend to explore the relationships between certain aspects of drama and popular performance in the Elizabethan and Jacobean period; in particular I shall examine the phenomenon of conjuring and illusion as it existed on the street-corner or at the fair, and on the stage. To introduce and to frame this discussion of performance, however, I first of all want to refer (paradoxically) to a novel.

Edward Marston's *The Mad Courtesan* (1992) is a historical whodunit set in Elizabethan London. It has as its central characters the members of a fictitious acting company called 'Lord Westfield's Men', which loosely resembles the historical Lord Chamberlain's or the Admiral's Men. An important subplot to the murder mystery in the novel involves an itinerant rogue and vagabond named Cornelius Gant, who travels the country with his horse Nimbus. Together these fairground entertainers perform a variety of routines and illusions, such as dances, coin-tricks, counting-tricks and slapstick routines – all featuring Nimbus in the starring role. Eventually the pair arrive in London, where Gant crowns all his previous illusions by staging a major spectacle in which Nimbus appears to fly on to the roof of St Paul's Cathedral. Gant and his horse become rivals to Westfield's Men for the custom of the town, displacing the actors first of all in the inn-yard where they are due to play, and secondly, in the hearts and imaginations of the populace of London. For a brief while, it looks as if the 'legitimate' theatre is about to lose out to the carnival juggler. Eventually, however, the novel's focalizing hero Nicholas Bracewell, the resourceful book-holder of Westfield's Men, finally routs Gant and re-establishes the licensed players in their rightful place.

What makes this story relevant to my present purposes is the exceptional clarity with which this subplot of *The Mad Courtesan* articulates traditional critical assumptions about the relationship between the street performer and the 'legitimate' stage. It does so by mobilizing a familiar set of cultural oppositions: between the playhouse and the fairground, between the aristocratically licensed actors (Lord Westfield's Men), and the legally dubious Gant, whose malevolence and dishonesty are central to his character. More specifically, the novel uses these categories to stage an opposition between art and entertainment, between high culture and popular culture, between that which is permanent and significant and that which is ephemeral and trivial, between the seriousness of true drama and the frivolity of the merely spectacular performance. Lord Westfield's Men are staging a tragedy entitled *Love's Sacrifice*, full of eloquent speeches and noble emotions, whereas Gant offers nothing but the 'crude entertainment' of the animal act. There is no doubt which of the two sides of this binary opposition is privileged. The legitimate theatre wins every time, and the paradigm is unambiguous: popular culture is to be transcended in the name of art. It is a further irony that this preference for high art over popular is inscribed in a novel which is itself an unashamed example of 'popular' genre fiction.

The oppositions between high and low art as they are articulated in Marston's novel are themselves, of course, a product of the cultural assumptions of the late twentieth century rather than of the Elizabethan/Jacobean age. They derive from a liberal consensus which affirms that it is possible to extrapolate timeless and universal values from the creative energy of a previous epoch. At its most extreme this tendency has led to the fetishization of Shakespeare as the bearer *par excellence* of such values. More recent scholarship has tended to broaden the canon of great art and great writers so that the Renaissance is no longer represented by Shakespeare alone, but also by Marlowe, Middleton, Webster, Ford and others. Yet however inclusive the canon becomes, the need remains to point to something outside itself, against which it can be measured. The popular performers of the era fulfil that function perfectly; for, of course, by their very nature none of their acts has survived. They are self-evidently ephemeral: the model is self-fulfilling.

It is this model to which I am opposed in this paper. I want to ask a series of questions about Cornelius Gant and Lord Westfield's Men. Who were the real-life illusionists of the Renaissance fairgrounds and street-corners? How, if at all, did they relate to the growing commercial theatre of the time? And in an age when witch-trials were carried out with all seriousness, when the phenomenon of demonic magic could be understood as literal truth, how were the boundaries between entertainment, stage illusion and necromancy understood? In what follows I shall look first at what evidence we have concerning the growing popularity of various kinds of conjuring performances in Renaissance culture, and show how these may be related to the representation of magic on the Elizabethan stage. I shall also explore some of the ambiguities and anxieties which that culture experienced concerning the staging of such illusions. My argument is based on a sense that it is important to focus upon those elements which unite, rather than separate, the activities of the Elizabethan street-corner illusionists and their colleagues in the new professional theatres.

JUGGLERS, GYPSIES AND ANOTHER TALKING HORSE

The Elizabethan word for what we would call a conjuror was 'juggler'. This was not simply a tumbler adept at throwing and catching balls, but a practitioner of any kind of illusion; until the eighteenth century the term 'conjuror', like the words 'wizard' and 'warlock' and their female counterpart 'witch', was reserved for a 'true' practitioner of the black arts. The Jacobean writer Samuel Rid, in his *Art of Jugling or Legerdemaine* (1612), gives a detailed history of sixteenth-century street-corner illusionists.

> Certain Egyptians banished their country (belike not for their good conditions) arrived here in England, who being excellent in quaint tricks and devices, not known here at that time among us, were esteemed and had in great admiration, for what with strangeness of their attire and garments, together with their sleights and legerdemains, they were spoke of far and near, insomuch that many of our English loiterers joined with them and in time learned their craft and cozening... These people, continuing about the country in this fashion, practising their cozening art of fast and loose and legerdemain, purchased to themselves great credit among the country people, and got much by Palmistry and telling of fortunes.
>
> (Rid 1612: sig. Bv)

The original jugglers then are 'Egyptians': gypsies and travellers, marginalized and exotic in appearance and language. They then become absorbed into the criminal subculture of the sixteenth century with 'their craft and cozening'. Keith Thomas, in his massive and seminal study *Religion and the Decline of Magic* has established the extent to which a residual paganism allowed 'cunning men' (and women) and popular magicians to make a considerable living in the sixteenth and seventeenth centuries, selling their arts of divination, making love-potions and aphrodisiacs, charming and blessing. Some of these folk-magicians clearly believed in their own magical powers. Others were self-confessed impostors (Thomas 1971: 252–300). The boundaries may frequently become blurred between the professional village magic-worker and the confidence trickster on the one hand, and the confidence trickster and the performing juggler on the other. Yet, as Rid shows, by the end of the century a distinct and recognizable performance art has emerged. And so he publishes a handbook of juggling and legerdemain, offered as a form of entertainment:

> The true Art therefore of Jugling consisteth of Legerdemain: that is the nimble conveyance and right dexterity of the hand, the which is performed diverse ways, especially three: the first and principal consisteth in hiding and conveying of balls; the second in alteration of money; the third in shuffling of cards. And he that is expert in these may show many feats and much pleasure.
>
> (Rid 1612: sig. B3)

Rid's book is one of the first magician's handbooks in English and contains a series of instructions and revelations about how professional jugglers perform their apparently miraculous illusions. There is, for example, 'A very pretty trick to make a groat or a testor to sink through a table, and to vanish out of a handkerchief very strangely'; and readers are taught how 'To consume (or rather convey) one or many balls into nothing', 'To convey money out of one hand into the other, by legerdemain', 'To throw a piece of money away, and to find it again where you please', and so on. Some of the descriptions of trickery are written in a rather hortatory tone similar to that used in the coney-catching pamphlets of Greene and others, and include familiar warnings about how to avoid being cheated at dice and cards. For the most part, however, this early *aficionado* of conjuring is sharing with the reader a naive enthusiasm for juggling as performance.

> To cut half your nose in sunder, and to heal it again presently without any salve. (This is easily done; however being nimbly done it will deceive the sight of the beholders.) Take a knife, having a round hollow gap in the middle, and lay it upon your nose, and so shall you seem to have cut your nose in sunder: provided always that in all these, you have another like knife without a gap, to be showed upon pulling out of the same, and words of enchantments to speak. Blood also, to bewray the wound, and nimble conveyance.
>
> (Rid 1612: sig. E3v)

Rid shows an almost childish delight in sleight-of-hand, and in these jokeshop-style illusions. The reader, it is implied, will want to rush off immediately and try out these party pieces.

Rid also gives examples of great illusionists – including those on which Marston's fictional Gant and Nimbus are based. Both Shakespeare (Shakespeare 1965: 50) and Jonson (Jonson 1925–53: VIII, 88), as well as other writers of the period (Nashe 1972: 275; Anon. 1844: 23–4; D'Avenant 1697: 24), allude to a famous dancing horse, a white steed called Morocco who was owned by a showman called Banks. According to Sir Walter Raleigh, 'if Banks had lived in olden times, he would have shamed all the enchanters of the world' (Christopher 1973: 24). Like the fictional Nimbus, Morocco was capable of a variety of tricks which the credulous might ascribe to magic powers. Rid describes their performance.

> Such a one is at this day in London; his master will say 'Sirra, here be diverse gentlemen, that have lost diverse things, and they hear say that thou canst tell them tidings of them where they are. If thou canst, prithee show thy cunning and tell them.' Then hurls he down a handkercher or a glove that he had taken from the parties before, and bids him give it the

right owner, which the horse presently doth. And many other feats this horse doth ... which not one among a thousand perceives how they are done, nor how he is brought to learn the same.... As for example, his master will ask him how many people there are in the room: the horse will paw with his foot so many times as there are people. And mark the eye of the horse is always on his master, and as his master moves, so goes he or stands still.... And note that the horse will paw an hundred times together, until he sees his master stir: and note also that nothing can be done, but his master must first know, and then his master knowing, the horse is ruled by him by signs.

(Rid 1612: sig. G-Gv)

As Rid reports it, the master's patter has a familiar air: it is the patter of the modern vaudeville conjuror. But Rid's scepticism is equally up-to-date. He is not fooled: he knows that the horse has no supernatural powers, but that he is responding to a set of subliminal clues from his master.

'Juggling is now become common', says Rid (1612: B2v), testifying to the popularity of these street entertainers. But what relationship did these jugglers have to the theatre which was taking place in the playhouses by the end of the sixteenth century? What interaction, if any, was there between the street-corner illusionists and the Elizabethan stage? And is it possible to consider any such relation between the Cornelius Gants of the real Elizabethan and Jacobean world, and the emerging professional theatre of the time, in terms which offer something beyond the well-worn dichotomies of 'art versus entertainment', 'literary value versus popular performance', 'the permanent versus the merely ephemeral'?

STREET JUGGLERS AND STAGE MAGICIANS

The figure of the magician was a common stock character type on the Elizabeth and Jacobean stage, and, as such, has attracted a good deal of scholarship and criticism. The main focus of writers on the subject has been on the way the magician is represented in the drama of the time, and how that relates to various other contemporary writings and beliefs about magic, drawn from both literary and documentary sources. Barbara Howard Traister's book *Heavenly Necromancers; the Magician in English Renaissance Drama* is typical:

The magician filled a symbolic role in many plays. He functioned as a man whose horizons were both limitless and limited, a self-contained paradox. The convergence of two views of the magician – one, popular and literary, perhaps most clearly expressed in the medieval romances, the other, elitist and philosophical, best studied in the writings of the Italian neoplatonists – led to an ambivalence that made the magician a potentially fascinating stage character. Brief explanation of these traditions of magic leads to an understanding of how the magician functions in individual plays and provides some background for examining his association with magical competitions, sensual delights of all sorts, and a master-of-ceremonies image.

(Traister 1984: 1–2)

She goes on to examine in detail such archetypal figures of Renaissance drama as Doctor Faustus, Friar Bungay and Prospero, drawing both on learned treatises about magic, and also on records of folk-belief in order to contextualize the kind of 'magic' they represent. The magician is thus constructed as a prototypical Renaissance figure, a representative of the new world of learning of Renaissance culture. His magic becomes a metaphor for the ambiguous state of knowledge, especially scientific knowledge, in the period. Poised between medieval and modern ways of thinking, between rationalism and superstition, the magician is both humanly flawed and exceptionally powerful in his control over the forces of nature – a potential hero or, like Icarus, a figure doomed by his pride to attempt to soar too near the sun and, overreaching himself, plummet to his destruction. He embodies, as Barbara Howard Traister puts it, 'the paradox of superhuman power that is humanly limited' (Traister 1984: 146).

This is, of course, an essentially literary perspective. It 'reads' the figure of the magician in the playtext as one might read a similar figure in a romance or an epic – and indeed, there are frequent references to figures such as Archimago in Spenser's *Faerie Queene* as influential precursors of these stage magicians. Another perspective, however, would take into account Rid's gypsies and jugglers and the practitioners of legerdemain. For the literary reading misses out an essential dimension of the stage figure of the magician – and that is his physical presence, there on the stage, in front of an audience, doing, in some form or other, conjuring tricks.

In figures like Faustus and Friar Bacon – and even in the hallowed figure of Prospero himself – the audience will indeed experience on the one hand a representation of a figure who may bring with him many of the literary associations which Traister suggests. They also, however, experience the trickster, the actor performing sleight-of-hand and staged illusions in order to surprise or delight. It may be that whereas traditional approaches have tended to stress the difference between the 'low-cultural' pleasures of the street performer, and the 'high-cultural' pleasures of the licensed player, it is more illuminating to concentrate on what these two kinds of performance have in common, to read the performances of stage magicians and street magicians intertextually, and to pay attention to the ways in which the techniques and pleasures of the fairground illusionist were imported on to the stage of the large-scale commercial playhouse. The Elizabethan professional theatre was involved in a complex evolutionary manoeuvre. On the one hand, it distinguished itself from and competed with the attractions of popular culture; on the other hand, it simultaneously absorbed them and made them a part of itself, with all the contradictions and paradoxes that this entailed. To a large extent, it *was* popular culture. Thus the 'Age of Shakespeare' was also an age in which a theatre like the Hope could be built with the express aim of fulfilling the dual function of staging both plays and bear-baiting. And those plays which dramatized the healing magic of Prospero, or the demonic magic of Faustus, also offered the popular pleasure of the fairground juggler.

Whereas literary scholarship emphasizes character ('the figure of the magician') I am more concerned to emphasize performative action. I am interested in those moments when players – whatever role they are enacting – perform illusions on stage. Plays from the middle ages onwards are full of illusions in this sense of the word. Medieval mysteries featured Moses as a star juggler; for instance, in the Towneley play of *Pharaoh*, where he changes his staff into a serpent and back again (Bevington 1975: 331), and in the York cycle *Departure of the Israelites from Egypt*. It is impossible to say how realistic, how accomplished, such tricks were. But when Hieronimo in *The Spanish Tragedy* bites out his tongue and offers it to the king; when the brazen head speaks in *Friar Bacon and Friar Bungay*; when Ariel makes the banquet disappear in *The Tempest*; when the tapers light themselves in *A Game at Chess* – all these are examples of more or less elaborate conjuring tricks to charm the audience.

In a useful early article, Louis B. Wright catalogues and analyses over fifty examples of and references to conjuring, juggling and illusions in plays before 1642 (Wright 1927). Some of the stage directions are particularly evocative. In *All for Money* an elaborately prepared stage illusion shows the character of Money 'vomiting forth' two other characters, Pleasure and Sin, a trick effected by means of 'a chair for him to sit in, and under it or near the same place there must be some hollow place for one to come up in' (Wright 1927: 273). In *Two Lamentable Tragedies*, a character is left with a hammer sticking in his head: 'When the boy goeth into the shop, Merrie striketh six blows on the head and with the seventh leaves the hammer sticking in his head:' (Wright 1927: 277). Wright draws particular attention to the use of illusion in the staging of scenes of decapitation and amputation. A famous section in Reginald Scot's *Discoverie of Witchcraft*, entitled 'To cut off one's head, and lay it in a platter, &c., which the jugglers call the decollation of John the Baptist' (Scot 1584: 13, 33), describes with diagrams just how the playhouses pulled off the trick, with a pillory-like stage section through which one actor's head could be displayed in juxtaposition with another's body.

MAGIC AS PERFORMANCE, MAGIC AS SUPERNATURAL POWER

The Elizabethan playhouse, then, was willing and able to absorb and reproduce the pleasures of the fairground juggler. Not all its practitioners found this congenial, of course: Thomas Nashe disavowed such usages in his Prologue to *Summer's Last Will and Testament*: 'Such odd trifles as mathematicians' experiments be (artificial flies to hang in the air by themselves, dancing balls, an egg-shell that shall climb to the top of a spear, fiery-breathing gourds), *poeta noster* professeth not to make' (Nashe 1972: 148). And in the Induction to *Bartholomew Fair*, Ben Jonson sneered at the vulgarity of jugglers and suchlike. In *Volpone*, however, Jonson himself includes a parody of one of the most famous illusionists of the sixteenth century. Jonson characterizes him as nothing more than a mountebank – a travelling medicine-seller whom Volpone impersonates in order to get a better look at Celia, the object of his lust. But Girolamo Scoto – 'Scoto of Mantua', as Volpone introduces him – had a much more wide-ranging reputation than that in his time. The real Scoto was a knight and a diplomat, working at the courts of, among others, the Holy Roman Emperor, Rudolf II. He was also a celebrated amateur conjuror. Reports exist of his card- and coin-tricks, in the careful notes of one bemused member of his audience, a Doctor Handsch. Handsch describes, among other tricks, standard parlour magic: officials in the courts of sixteenth-century Europe are urged to think of a card, and to take one from the pack – only to find that they have taken the very card of which they have been thinking. Nashe, in *The Unfortunate Traveller*, talks of 'Scoto, that did the juggling tricks before the Queen' (i.e. Elizabeth I) when he visited England between 1576 and 1583 (Nashe 1972: 297).

Scoto's career at one point runs into the kind of trouble that one might expect of the illusionist in an age of witch-hunters: he finds himself accused of sorcery proper. His accuser was Anna of Saxony, wife of Count Palatine John Casimir. She was charged with committing adultery with a young knight, Ulrich von Liechtenstein; in her defence she maintained that she had been bewitched by Scoto, who entered her room by magic carrying a cross bound with wire. Scoto, she claimed, ordered the wire to unravel and wrap itself round her body, binding her tightly so that she could not resist his amorous advances. Later he tired of her, she claimed, and fled with her most precious jewels, leaving her in the power of Ulrich. Not even the most credulous prosecutor seemed impressed: no charges were brought against Scoto, while Anna and her lover were imprisoned for life (Christopher 1973: 21–2). Yet the story is symptomatic of a cultural nervousness about the status of the 'juggler', the conjuror. Clearly, there is the possibility of some ambiguity here. By the same token, the story of Banks and his fabulous horse Morocco has, in one of its contemporary tellings at least, a grim ending: according to one source, which Ben Jonson repeats as truth in his *Epigrams*, the pair were both executed in Italy, burned at the stake as sorcerers (Jonson 1925–53: VIII, 88). The anecdote is unsubstantiated – yet its very existence reminds us, like the charges against Scoto, of the dangerous edge on which the performer of 'magical' tricks worked.

For the conjuror is a secular trickster pretending to be a kind of shaman or miracle-worker; making magic into performance, and performing magic in the process. Thus objects appear, vanish, reappear in unexpected places; the conjuror saws the lady in half, miraculously restoring her to wholeness again; or else he himself 'dies' in a locked chest or coffin, only to return from the underworld unharmed, having passed through the horrors. Like the shaman, jugglers and conjurors perform 'the death and resurrection show' (Taylor 1985: *passim*).

The juggler's act, moreover, is more multi-layered than the shaman's in this sense: that the latter depends on leading an audience/congregation into a secure belief (usually shared by the shaman) in the performer's 'supernatural' powers, in his or her liminality, that he or she stands on the threshold between two worlds: the natural world and the supernatural. The juggler, on the other hand, performs highly ritualized routines both to invoke and then (crucially) to disavow the supposition of supernatural influence. Henry Hay, author of 'the acknowledged classic text for conjurers, both beginning and advanced', tells the trainee magician that 'conjuring is the art – let's say the game – of entertaining by tempting a particular audience to accept, temporarily, minor infractions of natural law. If you ask them to accept permanently – to believe – you are a charlatan, a messiah, perhaps both; not a prestidigitator' (Hay 1982: 2). And this is the essential rhetorical manoeuvre which is involved in the illusionist's act: the outward appearance of magic is known to be a lie. We are asked to take pleasure, not in the belief that the performer is really possessed of magic powers, but in our own underlying certainty that he is not. The tension between belief and unbelief, between the frame of the fiction and the awareness that it is a frame, is also a major part of the rhetoric of the theatre, especially the Elizabethan theatre. As with the conjuror's trick, theatrical illusion depends upon an unstable double vision. The theatrical fiction is a product of the conjunction, and the interpenetration, of the ideal and the material: the 'ideal' fiction of the narrative 'materializes' in the bodies of real, present human beings (whom we know to be 'not really' Romeo, Hamlet or whoever), carrying physical stage props and wearing physical costumes. Such spectatorship thus involves a negotiation between two realities: in watching an actor perform a role we may become aware not only of the role but also of the actor. The Elizabethan playwrights, of course, were experts at manipulating these realities and delighted in the metatheatrical gesture. Thus the boy actor playing the female character may, at significant moments, mobilize the audience's memory of the fact that what they are watching is indeed a boy; the clown-in-character may occasionally stop the action and perform set-piece routines in his 'own' professional persona. The difference, though, is this: that the boy and the clown do not (usually) face charges of necromancy if the delicate ambiguity of representation and interpretation should break down.

With this in mind, it is small wonder that there are so few records of women performing magical tricks (Nardi 1988: 761). Quite apart from the prejudice which existed, in England at least, against women appearing as public entertainers at all, there were prevalent sexist assumptions about women's susceptibility to demonic temptation because of their inherent spiritual inferiority. Women were particularly vulnerable to imputations of sorcery, as the witch-trials of early modern Europe demonstrate. In an age which could view both childbirth and menstruation as magical in themselves, the illusion of power, of mastery (*sic*) over nature, with which a juggler flirted was a dangerous one for a woman to claim in public. One of the few existing accounts of female jugglers tells of a girl in fifteenth-century Cologne who performed a stock trick with a handkerchief, cutting it in several pieces, then showing it restored again. She was tried as a witch (Nardi 1988: 761, Christopher 1973: 16).

It would be a mistake to assume, however, that Renaissance spectators automatically harboured the suspicion that all jugglers were in league with the devil. There is nothing simple or uniform about the beliefs which were held about magic and witchcraft in the early modern period. During this time we see both credulity and scepticism, both belief in the supernatural and an urge to debunk such belief. And although there was a decline in the number of witch-trials and executions during the reign of James I (1603–25), it would be oversimplifying things to suggest that therefore there was a simple movement from medieval superstition towards a more modern rationalism in later years. Indeed the interplay between these two terms, superstition and rationalism, as between fact and fiction, could be quite complex. For example, the thirteenth-century philosopher and Franciscan friar Roger Bacon, who taught at the universities both in Paris and Oxford, became caricatured by later generations as an archetype of the sorcerer and 'necromantic mage', performing wonders 'by the operation of evil spirits' (Clulee 1988: 65). In this guise he turns up in Elizabethan prose romances, and eventually in Robert Greene's play *Friar Bacon and Friar*

Bungay. In the following speech, he describes himself as having power over the elements of earth as well as dominion over the spirits of hell:

> Bacon can by books
> Make storming Boreas thunder from his cave
> And dim fair Luna to a dark eclipse.
> The great arch-ruler, potentate of hell,
> Trembles, when Bacon bids him or his fiends
> Bow to the force of his pentageron.
> What art can work the frolic friar knows;
> And therefore will I turn my magic books
> And strain out nigromancy to the deep.
>
> (Greene 1969: 15)

The historical Bacon, however, was a convinced sceptic about much supposed supernatural magic. Writing in the thirteenth century, he explains that

> there are men who create illusions by the rapidity of the movements of their hands, or by the assumption of various voices, or by ingenious apparatus, or by performing in the dark, or by means of confederacy show to men many wonderful things which do not exist.
>
> (Christopher 1973: 16)

Indeed, much of Bacon's project as a philosopher involved an attempt to distinguish between supernatural magic (whose existence Bacon did not deny, but which he condemned because of what he believed to be its dependence on the aid of demons) and 'the legitimate performance of marvellous feats by human artifice using the secrets of nature as instruments' (Clulee 1988: 65). The historical Bacon was an early scientist with an interest in illusions and tricks, especially in optical illusions. It is likely that both of these contributed to his later reputation as a sorcerer.

This rational temper, this interest in exploring the differences between performative trickery and 'real' magic, surfaces again in the writings of the Elizabethan sceptic Reginald Scot. The title of his best-known work, *The Discoverie of Witchcraft*, might lead the reader to expect a witch-finder's manual, a latter-day version of Kramer and Sprenger's *Malleus Maleficarum*. On the contrary, however, it is a work which is largely concerned to discredit belief in supernatural magic. Scot concludes that things have got out of hand and that it is probably the fault of the media:

> The common people have been so assotted and bewitched, with whatsoever poets have feigned of witchcraft, whether in earnest, in jest, or in derision; and with whatsoever loud liars and cozeners for their pleasures herein have invented, and with whatsoever tales they have heard from old doting women, or from their mothers' maids, and with whatsoever the grandfool their ghostly father, or any other morrow mass priest had informed them; and finally with whatsoever they have swallowed up through tract of time, or through their own timorous nature or ignorant conceit, concerning these matters of hags and witches: as they have so settled their opinion and credit thereupon, that they think it heresy to doubt in any part of the matter.
>
> (Kors and Peters 1977: 328)

Like Bacon, Scot believes in the reality of witchcraft. What he doubts is its prevalence. He gathers enough examples of tricksters and trickery to feel that he must have convinced any fair-minded observer that the witchmongers were overstating their case. He asks:

> who will maintain, that common witchcrafts are not cozenages, when the great and famous witchcrafts, which had stolen credit not only from all the common people, but from men of great wisdom and authority, are discovered to be beggarly slights of cozening varlets?
>
> (Kors and Peters 1977: 330)

There was, then, a sufficiently sceptical strain in English Renaissance thought for jugglers and conjurors not to be automatically accused of witchcraft. Samuel Rid articulates the liberal view that

> when these experiments grow to superstition and impiety, they are either to be forsaken as vain or denied as false. Howbeit, if these things be done for recreation and mirth, and not to the hurt of our neighbour, nor to the profaning and abusing of God's holy name, then sure they are neither impious nor altogether unlawful, though herein or hereby a natural thing be made to seem supernatural.
>
> (Rid 1612: B2v)

In Scot's more conservative opinion, however, the

practising of such pretended magic is none the less culpable and to be punished by the law:

> Howbeit I confess, that the fear, conceit and doubt of such mischievous pretences may breed inconvenience to them that stand in awe of the same. And I wish, that even for such practices, though they never can or do take effect, the practisers be punished with all extremity; because therein is manifested a traitorous heart to the Queen, and a presumption against God.
>
> (Kors and Peters 1977: 331)

So, the street-conjuror is still not safe. The economy of Elizabethan ideology and power reinscribes the pettiest interpersonal misdemeanour as an offence against the state, against the queen and against the divine purpose, and Scot's scepticism acquits the juggler of occultism, only to condemn him anew for manifesting 'a traitorous heart to the Queen, and a presumption against God'.

Moreover, there was also a faction which would argue that the so-called legitimate stage was itself a kind of black magic. As we have seen, Samuel Rid described the early Elizabethan jugglers as marginal figures, and linked them with the Elizabethan underclass. The position of the Elizabethan professional actor was not very different in legal terms: the 1572 Act for the Punishment of Vagabonds linked actors and jugglers together quite specifically, stipulating that unless they were licensed to perform by an aristocratic patron or a magistrate, all 'common players in interludes, minstrels, jugglers, peddlers, tinkers and petty chapmen ... shall be taken, adjudged and deemed rogues, vagabonds and sturdy beggars'. And at a further extreme, among those Puritan polemicists who inveighed against the new Elizabethan commercial theatre, the belief that the illusions of the stage were just as demonically inspired as the conjurings of a sorcerer was often quite literal. William Rankins, writing in *A Mirror of Monsters*, says of the players of these theatres that

> they are sent from their great captain Satan (under whose banner they bear arms) to deceive the world, to lead the people with enticing shows to the devil, to seduce them to sin, and well-tuned strings to sound pleasing melody when people in heaps dance to the Devil.
>
> (Rankins 1587: Fol. 2v)

This is an extreme view, of course, but it makes the point: just as the conjuror, the juggler, the fairground illusionist, risks being mistaken for a 'real' wizard, so the Elizabethan actor, according to this account, also risks being taken for an agent of Satan.

There are some plays, of course, which flirt overtly with just this suspicion that the Devil may well be present in the performance. In *Doctor Faustus*, for example, Lucifer himself appears on stage; Mephistophilis is a central character, and the play contains several scenes of ritual and conjuring. The question of whether enacting a scene in which someone conjures up the devil is perhaps perilously close to actually enacting the summoning for real, clearly occurred to several contemporaries. The power of the idea is shown in the famous manuscript anecdote quoted by E. K. Chambers, concerning a performance of *Doctor Faustus* in Elizabethan Exeter:

> Certain players at Exeter acting upon the stage the tragical story of Doctor Faustus the conjurer; as a certain number of Devils kept every one his circle there, and as Faustus was busy in his magical invocations, on a sudden they were all dashed, every one harkening other in the ear; for they were all persuaded there was one devil too many amongst them; and so after a little pause desired the people to pardon them, they could go no further with this matter; the people also understanding the thing as it was, every man hastened to be first out of doors. The players (as I have heard it) contrary to their custom, spending the night in reading and in prayer got them out of town the next morning.
>
> (Chambers 1923: 423)

As is so often the case, the Puritan antitheatrical position is not simply negligible. It helps us to clarify some of the ways in which this newly influential form of art and entertainment was itself a genuine challenge to traditional ways of ordering reality. And by contemplating what the 'juggler' and the actor shared we may bring some of this challenge into sharper focus: for both of them call into question the common-sense notions of reality; both offer impossibilities as truth; both offer the spectator a tension between naive belief in the reality of what is being staged, and a more sophisticated and cooler perspective on it which knows that at one level at least it is all a trick.

It is when this tension breaks down that the meanings inherent in the performance of juggling or the 'magic' of the theatre begin to be dangerous. The Elizabethan mathematician and philosopher John Dee, who may have been a model for Faustus himself, was another famous man accused of sorcery and witchcraft. He is most often cited by scholars as a figure paradigmatic of a shift from a medieval and superstitious world-view towards a more modern one: his mathematical and proto-scientific explorations were, it is often argued, misunderstood by old-fashioned minds as mere occultism, and while he worked within a vocabulary which was still heavily imbued with superstition and magic he none the less represents an example of how 'the will to operate, stimulated by Renaissance magic, could pass into and stimulate the will to operate in genuine applied science' (Yates 1964: 150). Yet, significantly, Dee was first accused of sorcery, not because of his activities as an alchemical experimenter, nor because of his attempt to manipulate the world with arcane mathematical symbols and calculations. What first brought him under suspicion was his interest in stagecraft and student drama! For a production of Aristophanes' play *Peace* which he staged at St John's College, Cambridge, he reputedly designed a huge and lifelike mechanical scarab – so lifelike, in fact, that onlookers seriously took it to be something he had summoned up by magic (Dee 1592: 5–6, Traister 1984: 18 and Clulee 1988: 161).

CONTRACT WITH THE DEVIL/CONTRACT WITH THE AUDIENCE

I have been attempting to illustrate the complexities and ambiguities which existed in Elizabethan attitudes towards the performance of 'magical' illusion, whether on the stage or in the market-place. Slippage and interaction characterized the relationships between apparent polarities: between belief and unbelief, between the healer and the thief, between the actor and the street-entertainer, between the magic of the stage and the magic of the necromancer. I want to end with one example of the way in which the complexities of 'magical' illusion were articulated in the playhouse. I have already alluded to *Doctor Faustus* and the Exeter performance where a fear of genuine demonic presence drove the audience into a state of panic. Marlowe's play, of course, explores the moral issue of the demonic contract. Yet it deals as thoroughly with magic as illusion and performance as it does with magic as supernatural power. For the 'juggling' is an integral part of the story, and takes a variety of forms. Sometimes it operates simply as display or spectacle, 'magical' only within the terms of the fictional world. An example of this is when Faustus conjures the vision of Alexander and Darius (Marlowe 1969: 71–2). The on-stage audience experience it as the magic of supernatural power; the real-life audience experience it as the magic of performance – but agree to understand it as supernatural within the frame of the story. This is actually a play-within-a-play; the so-called magical spectacle is another form of theatre and the on-stage spectators and actual paying audience 'see' the same thing but read it differently.

Elsewhere in the play, the point of view favours the audience, who collude with the authorial voice in sharing a reality which is invisible or unavailable to some or all of the characters on-stage. In a scene set at a papal feast in the Vatican, for example (Marlowe 1969: 63), the on-stage spectators and the paying audience watch the same events but 'see' different things. Those on stage 'see' cups and food floating magically in the air, the paying audience see these objects being manipulated by bodies of actors playing the parts of Faustus, Mephistophilis and their demons. Part of the theatrical pleasure in this instance is the awareness that it is the conventions of the theatre itself which allow these two sets of spectators to see different things. Magic of a kind is staged, but the means of magic is made apparent. A third kind of Faustian illusion, however, excludes the audience from the confederacy. In two scenes, Faustus is first decapitated and then dismembered. First, Benvolio and his friends cut off Faustus's head (Marlowe 1969: 76); a few minutes later the horse-courser pulls off his leg (ibid.: 81). Arguably in the first of these and certainly in the second, both the on-stage and the off-stage audiences are meant to be surprised by the trick. In these and other examples of stage juggling, the play experiments with various different ways in which an audience might be positioned in relation to the stage illusion.

Faustus's tricks of decapitation and dismemberment foreshadow, of course, the stock-in-trade of later generations of vaudeville conjurors, who saw their assistants in half, or emerge unscathed from the box through which blades have been thrust. The essential gesture of these vaudeville conjurors is to call attention to the trick itself (or at least that part of it which they want the audience to see) and thereby to their own power. The tricks are deictic, signs which point to the conjurors themselves, with their apparent ability to flout natural law, either on the grand scale of cheating death, or on the smaller scale of making cards and coins vanish. In the playhouse the magical illusion may indeed be of this kind: many of the conjurings of Faustus, or of Greene's Friar Bacon, seem to be staged for the sake of the spectacle in its own right. On the other hand, illusion may operate as a function of the plot, a way of telling through spectacle what might otherwise, as in Greek theatre, have been told through reported narrative. Thus, even though we are used to thinking of early English theatres as essentially 'non-illusionistic' in their staging, the use of very simple illusions to further the impression of realism was common: for example, 'a little bladder of vinegar pricked' to simulate the reality of bleeding (Wright 1927: 274; Gurr 1980: 29), or as in the more extreme case of Faustus and Benvolio, a head is struck off. These, too, have their deictic function: the power to which they point is that of the stage itself, with its ability to create an alternative reality. In such moments the stage, the playhouse itself, becomes the juggler with the power to suspend the laws of nature.

Traditional literary criticism of *Doctor Faustus* has tended simply to dismiss these central sections of Marlowe's play, and indeed to question whether it was Marlowe who wrote them. Repeating the 'art versus entertainment' manoeuvre, it has suggested that at worst these scenes comprise cheap tricks for those too stupid to understand the subtle theology of the play's beginning and ending, or that at best they show thematically how Faustus himself degenerates into a mere trickster. Another way of thinking about it, however, would be to suggest that in these scenes the mode of theatre changes temporarily from the tragic into the carnivalesque, so that, through a complex sequence of 'juggling' scenes, an audience is given a variety of perspectives on magic and illusion. It is allowed to experience, and in some degree to participate in, the pleasures of those powers which Faustus will later attempt to renounce. This participation is more than merely metaphorical: the juggler's implied contract with the audience asks them to become (like Faustus himself) divided subjects. They are required to believe and disbelieve simultaneously in the magic with which they are presented, to enact an internal dialogue or 'delightful conspiracy to believe ... between the sceptical brain and the luxuriant, atavistic imagination' (Brandon 1993: 12). The juggler's contract is, to this extent, an archetypal contract of the performance event, and Cornelius Gant and Nimbus and their like are not the opposite of true theatrical art, but an integral part of it.

REFERENCES

Anon. (1844 [1611]) *Tarlton's Jests*, reprinted London: London Shakespeare Society.

Bevington, David (1975) *Medieval Drama*, Boston, MA: Houghton Mifflin.

Brandon, Ruth (1993) *The Life and Many Deaths of Harry Houdini*, London: Martin, Secker & Warburg.

Chambers, E. K. (1923) *The Elizabethan Stage*, Vol. 4, Oxford: Clarendon Press.

Christopher, Milburne (1973) *Illustrated History of Magic*, New York: Thomas Crowell.

Clulee, Nicholas (1988) *John Dee's Natural Philosophy: Between Science and Religion*, London and New York: Routledge.

Cornford, Francis (1914) *The Origin of Attic Comedy*, London: Edward Arnold.

D'Avenant, William (1697) *The Long Vacation in London*, London.

Dee, John (1592) *The Compendious Rehearsal of John Dee made unto the two Honourable Commissioners*, London.

Frazer, James (1911–15) *The Golden Bough*, 3rd edn, London: Macmillan.

Greene, Robert (1969 [1589]) *Friar Bacon and Friar Bungay*, London: Benn & Co.

Gurr, Andrew (1980) *The Shakespearean Stage, 1574–1642*, 2nd edn, Cambridge: Cambridge University Press.

Harrison, Jane (1913) *Ancient Art and Ritual*, New York: Henry Holt.

Hay, Henry (1982) *The Amateur Magician's Handbook*, 4th edn, Edison, NJ: Castle Books.

Hill, Thomas (1567) *Naturall and Artificial Conclusions*, London.

Jonson, Ben (1925–53) *Works*, ed. C. H. Herford, Percy Simpson and Evelyn Simpson, Oxford: Clarendon Press.

Kors, Alan C. and Peters, Edward (eds) (1977) *Witchcraft in Europe 1100–1700: A Documentary History*, Philadelphia, PA: University of Pennsylvania Press.

Marlowe, Christopher (1969 [1604]) *Doctor Faustus*, ed. Sylvan Barnet, New York: New American Library.

Nardi, Ralph (1988) 'The social world of magicians: gender and conjuring', *Sex Roles* 19: 759–70.

Nashe, Thomas (1972 [1594]) *The Unfortunate Traveller*, ed. J. B. Steane, Harmondsworth, Mx: Penguin.

Rankins, William (1587) *A Mirror of Monsters*, London.

Rid, Samuel (1612) *The Art of Jugling or Legerdemaine*, London.

Scot, Reginald (1584) *The Discoverie of Witchcraft*, London.

Shakespeare, William (1965 [1598]) *Love's Labor's Lost*, ed. John Arthos, New York: Signet.

Taylor, Rogan (1985) *The Death and Resurrection Show*, London: Reed.

Thomas, Keith (1971, 1978) *Religion and the Decline of Magic*, Harmondsworth, Mx: Peregrine Books.

Traister, Barbara Howard (1984) *Heavenly Necromancers; the Magician in English Renaissance Drama*, Columbia, MO: University of Missouri Press.

Wright, Louis B. (1927) 'Juggling tricks and conjury on the English stage before 1642', *Modern Philology* 24: 269–84.

Yates, Frances (1964) *Giordano Bruno and the Hermetic Tradition*, Chicago: Chicago University Press.

Study for *Miraculous Object* 14ft diameter, 1996

W.S.H*

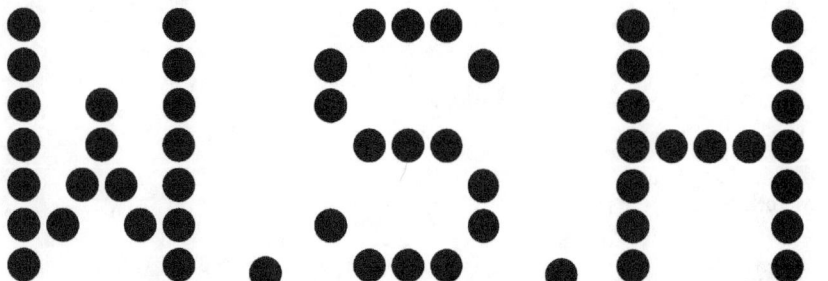

Excerpts recalled from a conversation between artist Rod Dickinson and author and ethno-botanist Terence McKenna, which took place at *The Incident*, a symposium on art and phenomena, held in Fribourg, Switzerland, June 1995.

* Weird Shit Happens

Opposite: Sighting, Chilbolton Observatory, Hampshire, 25 April 1996 (detail below)

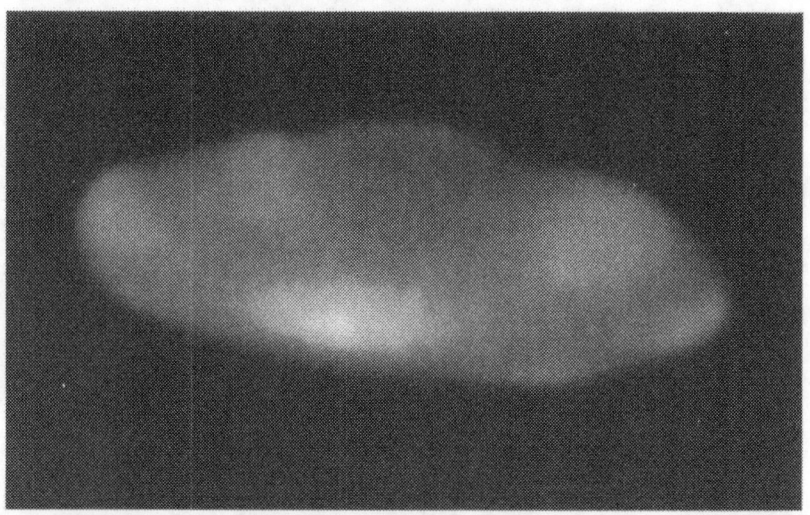

Terence McKenna: So Rod when did you first start making (crop) circles?

TM: Pretty soon after the pictograms started appearing I thought the whole thing was malarkey. I had this idea that the phenomenon was a government sponsored project to discredit all the New Agers who hang around the formations. Luring them all out on a limb with wilder and wilder statements about Gaian messages and the earth crying and so forth. Then when every nut in England has signed on, I imagined MI5 would bring on their jumpsuited crop circle team and say you people are gullible idiots, you should all find honest work because your level of credibility is now zero.

TM: Absolutely. All these phenomena; UFOs, Crop circles even the cattle mutilation in the states, are all artifice in one form or another. All this stuff, these are fluctuations in the syntactical machinery of reality. The main thing to understand is that we are imprisoned in some kind of work of art.

TM: But the question still remains: are there UFOs, Flying saucers, nuts and bolts craft, coming down, abducting hapless victims and interfering with their genitals? I say not - but there is a tradition in all times and places, of social commerce between human beings and various types of discarnate entities, or non-human intelligences. This could have been as simple as the Celtic farmer's wife leaving out a pitcher of milk for faery folk, or it could take a more elaborate form, but whatever form it takes this commerce is expressive of a very fundamental belief system that seems to be inherent in the human condition.

TM: Listen, I have no doubt that there are entities out there - I've met them, all you have to do is take DMT (Di Methyl Tryptamine). Fifteen minutes that's all it takes, give me fifteen minutes of your life and I'll give you a 20% chance of meeting alien life forms. Forget all that horseshit about UFO researchers, hypnosis and abductions. I wouldn't trust a UFO researcher with my chickens. Just give me fifteen minutes of your life...

Rod Dickinson: At the end of 1991. I made the first one out of curiosity, to see if it could be done, and to see if anyone would be convinced by it. About ten days before I'd taken a photo of a white disc like object over a circle- so I was a total believer- that first circle was a kind of conversion for me.

RD: In fact the whole phenomenon is more like a large collective work of art, involving circlemakers, investigators, the media and just about anybody who comes into contact with the circles. It's kind of mind virus- once you get involved you can't get out.

RD: Yeah, the paranormal is littered with artifice, but once you realise all these artifacts, crop circles, UFO photographs, whatever, entail an enormous amount of creative endeavour it becomes impossible to dismiss them as fakes or hoaxes. It's a perfect place for an artist to operate- I've centred my art practice on creating or interacting with these various phenomena and their attendant belief systems.

RD: It's something that has occupied artists for centuries, from Blake right through to surrealism- even early modernists like Kandinsky were influenced by occult beliefs. But as an artist practising now I feel it's less important for me to establish what kind of reality all these phenomena exist in. In many ways the poss-ibilty that much of this material has been fabricated by very human hands presents more opportunities for me. The fact is, that every phenom- enon we're discussing exists in some way, at the very least in a cultural space.

Rose English: A Perilous Profession

Lynn MacRitchie

Rose English has worked in performance since the mid-1970s. Her work touches many and varied issues but most of all it addresses theatre space itself, which she has called an arena 'like the basin of the mind itself' – atavistic, dreamlike and magical. For this issue *Performance Research* has commissioned artist's pages from Rose English which act as a sort of 'premonition' for a show, and invited Lynn MacRitchie, in the second of her articles for us, to trace Rose English's career.

> If I go through the hoop we might be able to go out of the domain of the metaphorical and into a fresh vista. We might see the place where the tangible and the intangible meet!
> (English 1992:15)

As an exercise while teaching a workshop at the Actors' Centre in London, Rose English gave each of the participants a photograph of a theatrical performer. The students had to pretend that they were this performer, and improvise an appropriate life story. One woman was particularly impressive. The photo she had been given was of a magician and his lady assistant, and she spoke of their life in convincing detail. When English questioned her afterwards about the improvisation, the woman confessed that she knew the couple in the photograph, that they were Bob Brown and Brenda, that they had visited her home and that her own son, Paul, was also a magician. He was subsequently to appear as one of the two magicians who took part in English's 1994 show *Tantamount Esperance*, giving a virtuoso display of magic tricks and exquisite illusions whilst English, playing Tantamount himself, a once famed prestidigitator, now a flawed and tragic character, mused stage front about the nature of the soul. Magical encounters may happen, it seems, both on and off the stage.

But magic – which dictionary definitions agree must involve an attempt to influence events, objects, or persons by supernatural power – is not illusion – which they define merely as a deceptive appearance, or anything that gives a false impression to the senses – and the creation of theatrical magic, although it may make use of it, is not the same thing as the art of the illusionist. In teasing out such subtle differences for rigorous examination over more than a decade, Rose English has created her own theatrical world. For her, the whole thesaurus is required to define her theatrical terms – wondrous, marvellous, miraculous, monstrous, prodigious, phenomenal, stupendous are only a beginning. Her deconstruction of the thaumaturgy – the wonderworking – of theatre has taken her audiences on a journey of philosophical discovery and in the process transformed this rigorous artist herself into a weaver of dreams.

English's achievement is all the more remarkable when it is remembered that the British fine art/performance nexus of the mid-1970s from which she emerged was one intrinsically hostile to theatricality of all kinds. As Jeff Nuttall wrote in

1979, 'The values that had been prevalent in poetry, painting, sculpture and music for fifty years had largely bypassed the mainstream of theatre. Diaghilev may have employed a painter or two, and one or two painters or poets may have turned out a play now and then ... but the theatre continued to be nineteenth century at heart' (Nuttall 1979: 18).

English initially shared this scepticism. 'I used to think that acting was lying,' she now admits, a not unremarkable view in a milieu where 'the concept of illusion was anathema, summing up everything that was despicable about theatre', and where the concept of fiction was 'very out of favour' (English 1996). In the world of performance art, the baby-boom progeny of Dada and surrealism, the art was always more valuable than the performance, the liveness of the work more highly esteemed than the particularity of its creator(s)' actions. The fact that those actions took place in that curious zone referred to as real time, i.e. they lasted as long as it took for the performer, not the audience, to achieve aesthetic satisfaction, was regarded as a guarantee of their artistic integrity. The more rigorous practitioners of live work would sometimes refuse to have their performances photographed, videotaped, or recorded in any way. Witnessing was all.

English's approach to what was in essence a debate about the status of the art object, although equally rigorous, was much more personal. Her artistic enquiry remained rooted in the terms of her own individual practice rather than embracing the givens which emerged as the growing body of live work created its own structure of reference.

Originally interested in studying theatre design, she applied to do so but was 'fortunately turned down ' (ibid.) and instead she arrived at Leeds College of Art, UK, as a Fine Art student. She found herself having to work 'in a big space like an aircraft hangar' (ibid.) while all around her her fellow students worked across all media 'being poets, musicians, making shows ... I didn't know quite how to cope with all this freedom ... I used to sit frozen at a little desk' (ibid.). Wise advice from her teacher Willy Terr who told her, 'You must just start ... ' finally got her into action.

She made things. Some of them could be worn, and included decorations made from ceramics, adornments fashioned from swans' wings, or leather and horsehair, which transformed their wearers into creatures of wonder.

> I was very conscious of the power of things, and absorbed by how objects were mediated in the world. They seemed to be both potent and redundant, depending on the focus of attention, on how their place in the world was negotiated. I was always staring mournfully at the piles of things I had made, wondering how to store them, conscious of how they cluttered up the world.
>
> (English 1996)

It was this fundamental questioning of the true nature and ultimate fate of the things she had crafted with such care, when readdressed after her experience at Leeds, where multi-media experimentation was the norm, which was to lead her into the area of live work.

After she had graduated from Leeds, and spent a subsequent unhappy year in the ceramics department at the Royal College of Art, English's first live piece was performed at Battersea Arts Centre in London in 1974. The objects she had assembled or created for *The Boy Baby* were seen by their audience for exactly one minute. Then, the porcelain horses which the two naked ballerinas had worn between their legs, the head scarves they had tied on the very tips of their chins, the swan's wings which adorned the dancer perched on a trapeze, the crinoline which graced the boy baby himself, were spirited away, to be hidden in storage, hallowed relics of a unique experience.

Her 'attachment to accoutrements' (ibid.) continued in *Quadrille*, presented at the Main Arena, Southampton Show, as part of The Performance Show, in July 1975. Six women dancers were 'shown' in an arena marked out by a rectangle formed of lines of small, white porcelain horses, wearing outfits again made by English herself. Naked apart from little tunics made from the checked lining material of horse blankets, they balanced delicately in the extraordinary shoes she had constructed for them from real horses' hooves, while at their backs curved splendid tails made from real horses' tails set in heavy leather belts fastened around their waists. *Quadrille*, which lasted about 12–14 minutes, had taken a year's labour to prepare. English began to realize that her need to display her objects in tableaux that were 'rich and potent but would not have a long duration' (ibid.) in turn required that she learn how to animate the people who were wearing and using them. She began to appreciate stagecraft.

> I benefited a lot from working with dancers. They were all students at the Place, dancers at the early stages of their careers, used to being asked to appear in many different things and able to make suggestions.
>
> (English 1996)

After a number of appearances in works by performance and theatre groups including Welfare State and Lumière and Son, English began to work in collaboration with Sally Potter and Jacky Lansley. Potter and Lansley had met as students at The Place, the London dance college which at that time accepted students not necessarily required to have any previous training in dance. Potter was one such, while Lansley had been a star student at the Royal Ballet School. Together, working as the Limited Dance Co, they were engaged in developing a style of live work which questioned the traditions of dance and theatre in an effort to produce a new type of performance experience, in which the aesthetic impact of a piece could be established purely on its own terms rather than with reference to interpretation of a story-line or a traditional dance form. The three worked together for the first time on a performance presented at Artists for Democracy in central London in 1975.

The performance, based on the nineteenth-century Irish potato famine, was put together very

• *Quadrille*, 1975, performers: L to R: Jacky Lansley, Joanna Bartholomew, Judith Katz, Helen Crocker, Sally Cranfield, Maedee Dupres. Photo: Simon English

differently from English's previous practice of long hours of solitary labour making objects. Potter and Lansley, whose dance training she recognized as having given them 'a real understanding of the nature of the body in space' (ibid.), worked swiftly and loosely 'on the floor', marking out movements with their own bodies. The work was presented outdoors: with the aid of a few props – a couple of armchairs scavenged from skips, some potatoes, lighting from one standard lamp and old black frocks for costumes, the three women and a number of collaborators including one small boy created a series of affecting tableaux, silent apart from Potter's singing of *Down by the Sally Gardens*, accompanied by herself on the violin. In a series of works created immediately afterwards in London and abroad, English, Potter and Lansley developed and refined a performance style striking in its blend of visual power and intellectual rigour.

The mid-1970s was a time when many artists, especially women artists, were engaged in questioning the fundamentals of their practice. What was art? What was its relation to politics? What was its relation to capital and labour? What was its relation to women? Was it necessary to have training in particular skills before live work could be attempted? Was a democratic approach to the making of an art work more important than the quality of the art which resulted? Was there somewhere that art could be presented free of the expectations set up by art gallery or theatre spaces?

Attempts to tackle such questions informed the structure and practice developed by the three in the making and final presentation of *Park Cafeteria* at the Serpentine Gallery, *Death and the Maiden* at Die Lantaren in Rotterdam, both 1975, *Rabies* at the Roundhouse in 1976 (in which English spoke on stage for the first time, articulating slowly in a deep, manly voice), the four-part *Berlin* presented the same year in English and Potter's London house, an ice rink and a swimming pool, and *Mounting* at the Museum of Modern Art, Oxford in 1977.

While discussion and writing formed a crucial part of the development process – the admission ticket to *Mounting* was a small book written by the artists – 'It will be sold in an art gallery. We must examine the ways in which that context will determine its meaning, its function', they wrote[*] – the performances were not driven by the requirements of a script. There were indeed speeches and dialogue, often addressing the nature of the performance and the questions and arguments raised in its making. There was music, often a solo cello or violin, or taped extracts from film soundtracks. The look of the work, however, was equally important in its overall effect, indeed its most intense and lasting impact was often as a visual spectacle.

[*] Rose English, Jacky Lansley and Sally Potter (1977) *Mounting* (Oxford: Museum of Modern Art), in conjunction with performances on 21 and 22 May.

Despite her initial misgivings, English's precious objects came out from hiding and were used again, the horse tails in *Mounting*, the swan's wings in several of the pieces. In all the works, great care was taken with location and lighting.

> They were quite epic, really, in site, in atmosphere, in what they conjured up. They had costumes, lights, sets. There was a lighting designer for *Berlin*.
>
> (English 1996)

It was as if, despite the rigour and sincerity of the political discussion which informed the pieces, their occasional use of untrained performers as collaborators, their preference for non-art or non-theatre spaces, the necessity to look wonderful remained the sole unquestioned imperative. Spectacular effects, exquisitely staged – the burning of a cradle on the ice in the second part of *Berlin*, English's leap fully clothed from a high diving-board in its swimming-pool sequence, the sight of six men perched on a marble mantelpiece above a lighted fire in its final part – won the works acclaim at the time and also prefigured the look of their next epic project, the film *The Gold Diggers*, begun in 1980, completed in 1983, on which English worked as co-writer, art director and co-editor.

Her first solo performance happened by accident. Before filming on *The Gold Diggers* began, she had accepted an invitation to appear at the

Franklin Furnace Gallery in New York in 1981. When her original collaborators withdrew, in the best show business tradition, she went on alone.

In *Adventure or Revenge*, her first solo performance, English set out the themes she has grappled with ever since. Sporting a false beard, she held forth on the nature of the theatrical persona, assisted by a trunk full of old costumes, a sword and a diaphragm. The show, briefly glimpsed at Norwich School of Art, UK then reopened on Broadway. Accompanied by tango music, it had a Jacobean-style revenge theme – the beard was stabbed to death. While satiric in tone, English's passion was clear: theatre itself had emerged as her subject.

> *Adventure or Revenge* was very exhilarating. It was exciting to have real contact with an audience. Before, I had never questioned or talked to the audience. Now, I had arrived in this scary place, a sort of arena. It was very thrilling. My reaction was exactly the opposite of what I thought it would be – I thought I would be speechless but in fact I was galvanised into what I wanted to say because the audience was there giving their attention. Afterwards I sobbed my heart out in sheer exhilaration.
>
> (English 1996)

Touring the show to New York and Toronto, she began to refine it, recording her improvised speeches, spun from 'five or six lines of writing – a haiku of a show' (ibid.), travelling with her trunk of costumes bought in a costumier's sale. She developed another piece, *Plato's Chair,* and, after touring in Canada, this became her debut as a solo artiste in London, presented in the bar of the Drill Hall in 1984. It had scenery – two white columns – a trunk of props and costumes, music from *Carmen* and a theme, the Void. It was very funny – English's emergence in London as a solo artist coincided with the rise of stand-up comedy, and she was often, wrongly, considered to be a comedienne – but it was much, much more. It dealt with concepts – the void, nothingness, death – and the way two pieces of tacky white plaster wobbling on a makeshift stage could suggest such transcendences. Funny in its particulars – who could forget English in Mickey Mouse ears, waving a contraceptive coil like an ancient talisman – it was very, very serious at heart, its philosophical subtext resonating like the space between the plaster pillars, so obviously fake, just as obviously so serious in purpose: fake for a reason. English had discovered the prop.

> I had always been entranced with the theatre, and now it became my theme. I was fascinated and perplexed by its traditions, its fusty, musty domain. I had to examine everything I found most depressing about it. I went off to Fox's and bought a great pile of doublets and hose. I had to put them on to understand what this convention was, this strange and powerful thing, why it had ever stood for anything. In *The Beloved,* I began to inhabit it.
>
> (English 1996)

• *Plato's Chair*, 1983, performer: Rose English. Photo: Genevieve Cadieux

The Beloved was presented at the Drill Hall once more, in 1985, but in the theatre. It had scenery – two bridges, rustic wood in the first half, elegant metal in the second, and 'big, black drapes' (ibid.). The theme was the word Abstract – which at one point she had the audience shout out at the tops of their voices – and English mused on this as she told tales of the touring life and drove around the deep, dark space of the stage in a real, red dodgem car. The show did in fact tour to a wide range of venues including Vienna and Rotterdam as well as the Edinburgh Festival and the Bush Theatre in London, and was also presented as part of a performance art and video installation festival at London's Tate Gallery.

The theme of theatrical illusion was first openly broached in English's next production, *Thee Thy Thou Thine* presented at the Institute of Contemporary Arts and the Bloomsbury Theatre, London in 1986. Part of her working process was then and continues to be the collection of visual images, pictures which seem to suggest something – an aura, a mood, a question – which then becomes a theme in the work. Before the making of *Thee Thy Thou Thine* she had spent much time contemplating a photograph of the ancient amphitheatre at Epidaurus, home of Greek tragedy. How could it be that theatre, born in the blazing Mediterranean light, bare of background or scenery, now existed in darkness, with light itself harnessed into the service of theatrical transformation, as the agent of concealment or revelation?

Illusion on stage, English observed, was dependent on light. In stage light, costumes, revealed as scruffy and shabby by day, came alive. Light angled on to gauze screens made objects and scenery appear and disappear. *Thee Thy Thou Thine* used all these effects. It had a full flight of stairs specially constructed, along with a backdrop and painted gauze. English appeared decked in a series of outrageous costumes – 'bodice, bustle and false eyelashes, red velvet and a bad black wig' (ibid.) – and the show had a show, *Oklahoma*, as its inspiration, and Conception as its theme. It was also the first time in this phase of her career that English chose to work with another performer, the actor Richard Wilding.

> It was about the moment of conception, the correlation between biological conception and the idea of the beginning of form. In the photos of Epidaurus the amphitheatre is like a paradigm of conception.
>
> (English 1996)

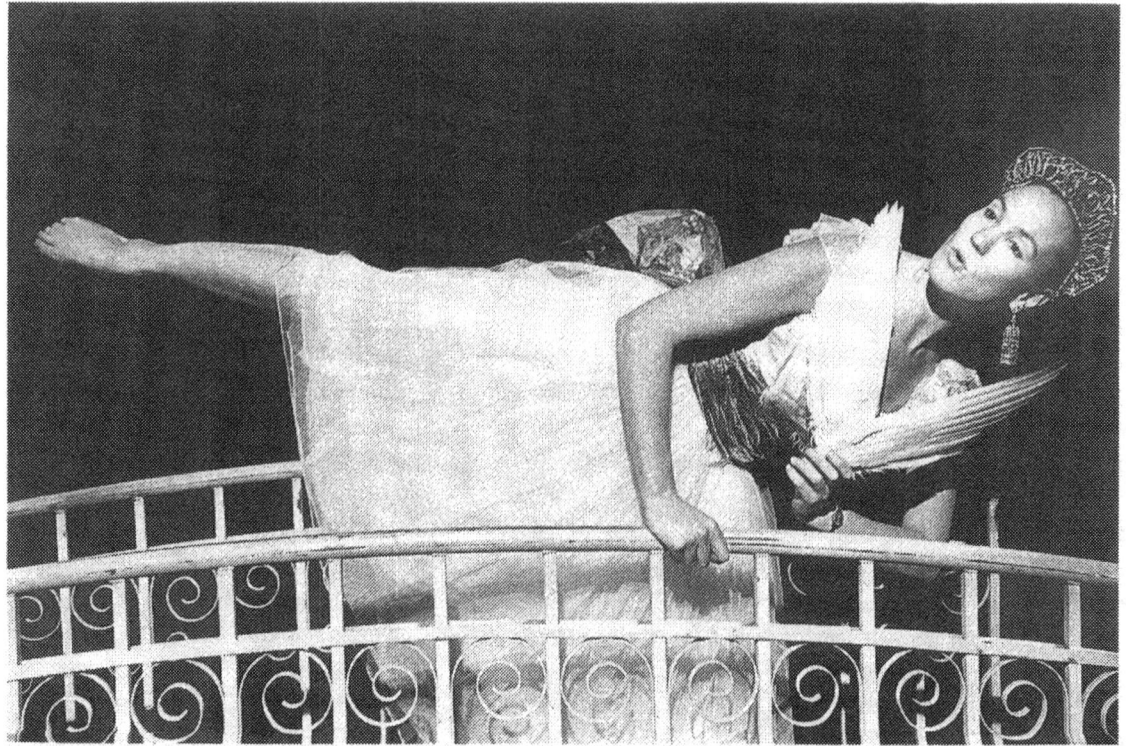

• *The Beloved*, 1985, performer: Rose English. Photo: Sarah Ainslie

The structure of the show took the form of a dialogue, based on the Platonic dialogues, which English had been studying. Using Wilding as her foil, 'He was instructed only ever to agree with me' (ibid.), themes and digressions on themes were introduced – the theatre as arena, the moment of conception, the impact of the first viewing of a technicolour movie. Wilding was addressed throughout as Curly, hero of the musical *Oklahoma*, whose image, riding through the corn 'as high as an elephant's eye', was produced in the form of a film still. It gradually emerged that English had seen only the film and an amateur production of *Oklahoma*, never the full-scale musical on stage. Tormented by experiencing only this 'Turin Shroud of *Oklahoma* by an amateur company' (ibid.) and with its technicolour image emblazoned on her memory, she strove alone to re-create, or, more accurately, to re-create the effect of, the film's Dream Ballet sequence. At the finale, as the lighting on the gauze changed, piercing the veil to reveal the flight of stairs behind, English ran up them and leapt off into the void ...

Her first use of a trained actor as performance partner was rooted in her growing respect for traditional theatrical skills.

> I wanted someone older than me on stage, someone whose presence on stage embodied his history as an actor, a history so different from my own. I had discovered my respect for this tradition, which I hadn't known before.
>
> (English 1996)

It proved to be a tradition which welcomed the outsider. Attending the Actors' Centre with Wilding, English discovered that 'not all actors come from RADA, they are not so worried about credentials' (ibid.). Many came from different backgrounds, united by the theatre's need for jacks of all trades, its mixture of on-stage and off-stage skills. She found it 'a very accepting profession, very willing to engage with people at whatever level they are, a very practical profession' (ibid.).

She explained her project to Wilding first of all by giving him copies of the dialogues of Leone di Somi on the nature of theatre, written in 1556. It turned out that he already knew them and 'was very excited by them' (ibid.). She also showed him some sheet music from *Oklahoma*, and explained that she intended to cue the piece through lights and music. Although this was unusual, Wilding was an actor who enjoyed learning new techniques. He found the challenge of working within a performance structure, where things could change every night, appealing, pointing out the different quality of concentration that would be needed from that required to deliver an unchanging performance night after night. When asked if he thought of her as an actress or an artist, English said, 'I think he thought of me as a comedienne' (ibid.).

Back at the Drill Hall for her next piece, *Moses*, in 1987, English challenged another ancient theatrical convention, the one about not working with children or dogs. Sprawled on a four-poster bed, a 7-year-old girl and a Jack Russell terrier were her companions for an exploration of the deeper meanings of *The Wizard of Oz*, a consideration of the topic of scale and some thoughts on the theme of Genesis and Hope. This time the set featured a revolve, a miniature theatre at the back of the stage, a tiny waterfall and a boat, in which girl and dog sailed off into the sunset. Rose metamorphosed from Cinderella in apron and embroidery to showgirl in full sequins and plumes: 'My first outfit from Trends' (ibid.), the theatrical costumiers who would provide spectacular costumes for subsequent works.

But it was no longer enough. Her experience of working at the Bloomsbury Theatre had had a profound effect. For the first time, English had worked in the proximity of traditional theatrical equipment, and she longed to try out its full potential. The wry detachment of the self-proclaimed amateur she had presented herself as in her earlier work, when she would draw the audience's attention not only to the obvious artificiality of stage effects but also to her own lack of the actorly professionalism needed to pull them off, was breaking down. Mere gestures towards effects, such as the 'flying' of her costume in *The Beloved*, were no longer satisfying. It was time for the real thing.

'I was dying to do something on a big scale again. I wanted to do a show for a proscenium stage' (ibid.).

That show was *Walks on Water,* presented at the Hackney Empire in the east end of London in 1988. As befitted the great variety theatre designed by Frank Matcham in 1901, it was a show with everything. It had a male chorus of twelve, the Chou Chou Ballet Company, an acrobatic double for English, flying effects, dancing, singing, several scene changes including a palace interior, a woodland glade and an underwater sequence, an illusion that failed, a waterfall that didn't and the theme of Invincibility and Infallibility. English's costumes included a cape that filled the stage, a long black plait, a shiny dress, a Principal Boy's outfit and a diamante G-string with feathery tail and headdress. As she said later, 'What more do you want for £5?' (ibid.).

The show drew on her memories of early visits to the theatre with her father, to pantomime, and to ballet. The palace interior and woodland glade with its dancing trees conjure memories of panto sets,

• *Walks on Water,* 1988, performer: Rose English. Photo: Mike Laye

and English herself appears in Principal Boy garb, slapping a fine thigh in yellow tights. The chorus are fathers, first of babes in arms, then of dancing daughters. There is a compassion here, a sadness, which slips through even as English berates her chorus boys and steals the acrobat's applause. The show began with an acrobat clinging to the bottom of the vast red velvet curtain, rising through the air with it as it was raised. It ended with English in full showgirl gear, 'flown' impersonated by her double over a waterfall at the back of the stage. 'I wanted to do it for real, to achieve the things I had been using as metaphors' (ibid.).

Throughout, however, her persona remained essentially detached, making comments to the audience, arguing with the chorus of men about the possibility of a good night out, presenting them with baby daughters to symbolize potential, insisting that they were great, great, great, great, great grandfathers. 'You see when you go that far back, everything merges together, a bit like the origins of theatre itself' (English 1992: 8). When the acrobat leaps through four flaming hoops she comments, 'Quite daring, don't you think, especially with a wig on like this' (ibid.: 15).

When the chorus come on in the second act, dressed as trees, she turns to one. 'Tell me something, Tony, what season are you in as a tree at the moment?' Tony replies, 'Spring.' 'Spring?' she rejoins. 'Tony, Spring in the middle of November. Oh, I love theatre Tony.' (ibid.:19). In a later scene she asks Tony, 'Tell me, Tony, what do you think?' 'Quite frankly,' he replies, 'we think this scene is too allegorical.' 'Oh do you indeed. Too allegorical. Frankly I tend to agree with you. Why not move back and form an avenue out of this allegory?' (ibid.: 20). And so on. At the climactic walking-on-water scene, English at first fails to achieve the feat, ending up up to her waist in a cistern of water beneath the stage. This, she explains, is because she is not in the same costume that she wore in the publicity material. Only in the full rig-out of plumes and sequins, appropriate to her role of creature of wonder, will she be able to fly, as indeed she (or in fact her double) does, over the great waterfall which appears at the back of the stage. 'I know that if I can do that my soul will fly in flight after me and I will see her leap over the void' (ibid.: 28). In these lines in the last act, before her extraordinary final soliloquy about the domain of theatre, English finally reveals the truth that, behind her joshing and commenting, her questions to the chorus and asides to the audience, for her the successful achievement of one of those clever tricks which are one of the essences of theatrical delight contains within it no less than an expression of the human spirit, fleetingly made visible in all its glory. This had been her real theme all along, of course, right from *Adventure or Revenge*, but like a true illusionist she has kept her audiences guessing, transfixed with laughter even as the hint of something very profound troubles their smiles.

English brought her persona of bullying compère, terrorizing cast and audience, to its peak with her performance in *The Double Wedding*, presented at the Royal Court Theatre, London in 1991, and set out from the start as a meditation on the theatrical experience and on the relationship between theatre and cinema. For the first time English allows some of her fellow performers, a cast of seventeen, to become characters. Working again with professional actors, she wished originally to allow them to improvise, but in rehearsals quickly realized that they were not comfortable with this approach to the work. And so she wrote a script, for the first time giving two of the characters personal names, Otto and Harry, as well as embodiments of skills; Otto and Harry are cinema cameramen. (The names in *Walks on Water* were all the real names of the performers.) The others remain named only by their personae (the Figment, the Nebulae, the Viscera) or their tasks (the Hypnotists, the Fake Adagio, the True Adagio).

Before writing *Walks on Water*, English had been one of the cast of *A Flea in her Ear* at the Old Vic. This Feydeau farce involves lots of fast exits and entrances, with no time to get back to the dressing-room between scenes, so English would sit in the wings during the sixteen-week run, studying her fellow actors as they made their entrances and exits. She hid a little notebook in her costume handbag, and also took photographs.

> I watched how my colleagues approached the task of transforming themselves, carrying out their agreement to embody a fiction, and what a complex physiological task that is, the difference between acting and performing. It was so much more difficult than I had realised. And it was all about being named, and the complexity of embodying that name.
> (English 1996)

This was a key revelation. It permitted English to experiment in her writing with the effect of identification, not just by attribute, but by the potential character suggested by a personal name. Otto and Harry have feelings, they weep and laugh. The others, too, although not yet defined with personal names, have much to say about their own professions, the show they have found themselves in, and, most of all, the terrible Hostess/Hermit who rules them with her rod of glass. At one point, the First Hypnotist sums up the Hostess' dilemma. Instead of tormenting them all with her questions, he demands, 'Why can't she for once allow herself to just be in it?' (English, 1991: 32). The full realization of the hypnotist's insight was not to come about until the next show.

As the Hostess/Hermit, English herself in a skin-tight fishtailed silver gown, hair piled up in a blonde chignon, hands in long red gloves twirling a crystal cane, had a mission. She wants to know about *The Double Wedding*, a show they had all taken part in sometime in the past, but can remember only fragmentedly. Stretching them one by one over her knee, she hypnotizes them into recollection. Desperate to understand, she demands answers, but as she bullies and cajoles them, tormenting them with her glimmering cane, her own need is made visible, her dependence on her fellow performers made clear. She needs to share their experience to understand their joint enterprise fully, to acknowledge what each of them brings to make up the whole that was *The Double Wedding*. It is worth noting, too, that again it is a ceremonial about basic human emotions – the celebration of the love between fathers and daughters in *Walks on*

Water, of a marriage in *Double Wedding* – that engages her passionate attention. The music, too, composed and performed by Ian Hill, emphasizes this quality of innocent celebration, recalling folk tunes and round dances as performed for centuries at the weddings and festivities of central or eastern Europe.

To create the *mise-en-scène* for *The Double Wedding*, English and the designer Simon Vincenzi, whom she describes as 'a philosopher of space' and who had worked with her on *Walks on Water*, went to France on a research trip which they called 'In search of excitement'. They visited the famous Lido nightclub in Paris and went backstage at the Folies Bergère, as well as to Futurascope (the futuristic cinema park), science parks and planetariums. *The Double Wedding* was to be a homage to the theatrical experience, but their research revealed aspects of that experience that they had not perhaps expected. While the Folies, in which the show included one scene consisting solely of a woman walking down a flight of stairs, her cloak spreading behind her to fill the stage, was almost innocent in its old-fashioned love of simple spectacle, English found the glitzy, almost mechanical erotic display of the Lido to be 'quite menacing' (English 1996: 39). English took great pleasure in bringing these traditions of tawdry glamour to the Royal Court, home of earnest new British writing. 'I was in heaven on that stage, in the main house, with the serious drama upstairs ... All those sequins got everywhere' (ibid.).

The stage was dressed in deepest black, richly spangled with sequins. There was a cyclorama at the back and two sets of steps and, hidden behind a spiral curtain, a tiny ice rink on which the True Adagio, in the form of Paul Askham and Sharon Jones, World Professional Ice Dance Champions,

• *The Double Wedding*, 1991, performers: Paul Askham and Sharon Jones. Photo: Hugo Glendinning

eventually showed their paces, offering the audience that moment of wonder that all the preceding discussion about naturalism, deconstruction, the differences between film and the stage, the glorious Lido Scene in which the actors, ineptly dancing in their white top hats and tails, finally fail to produce the glamorous showgirl who should have entered at the climax, had been leading up to. As their blades whirled and flashed on the ice, the two expert skaters spinning so fast in the tiny space clearly demonstrated that in the end, the skill required to achieve a moment of spectacle contains its own truth, its own ineluctability.

> *The Double Wedding* changed the way I thought about working. I was thrilled by the scenario that was set up, the opportunity of offering people treats, the chance to give them something really splendid. The previous theme had been not being able to do things, the duff aspects of tradition. But when those fleeting moments are achieved, it is something very wonderful, the moment when everyone sighs. That was what I wanted.
>
> (English 1996)

After her one-person show *My Mathematics*, 1992, in which, in dialogue with Goldie the horse, she told the tale of Rosita Clavel and her glorious but long-lost troupe of equestrians, English returned to the Royal Court stage with *Tantamount Esperance*, presented in 1994.

Right from the beginning, the show was different. This time all the parts were scripted before being cast. This time English herself played a character, the magician Tantamount Esperance, and remained in character throughout. For a time, it had even seemed likely that she would not appear at all, for she felt that 'I had got into a groove of commenting on myself. It had become too much of a device, it was expected of me. But this time I didn't want to puncture the scenario. When the show was performed, I sensed a discomfort, a dismay from the audience when I didn't do that' (ibid.). While she auditioned actors for the part of Tantamount, in the end she took the role herself. For the first time, she had, in the exasperated words of the First Hypnotist

• *Tantamount Esperance*, performer: Rose English. Photo: Hugo Glendinning (original B&W print)

in *The Double Wedding*, allowed herself 'to just be in it' (English, 1991: 32).

Tantamount is a sombre, serious piece. Designed once more by Simon Vincenzi, it is set in a mysterious space dominated by a tomb-like slab which opens to reveal blazing lights. Its cast are five immortals, met 'somewhere in splendour', as the stage directions put it, to discuss the nature of the soul. Their talk is set to the music of the tango, and all are skilled dancers. As they move around the stage, an acrobat whirls by in daring flying spirals and two magicians perform a series of exquisite illusions, while Tantamount himself, former conjuror, looks on. 'What is wizardry we wonder/ we who have never seen it ...' (English 1994: 5).

English knew from the start that she wished to work with magicians in the show, and set out to track down suitable candidates at magicians' conventions and events. She already knew of Paul Kieve from his mother, her student at the improvisation workshop, but still she kept looking for others, talking to Fay Presto and Iain Saville, the Socialist Magician, and to foreign magicians, and admiring displays of close-up work in magic competitions. All along, however, Kieve knew that she needed him. He knew that what she required was an illusionist, someone who could make people appear and disappear and hover in the air.

He could do all of that, with his collection of built illusions and experience of working in the theatre: he had been the magic consultant on Ken Hill's *Invisible Man* at Stratford East, which had transferred successfully to the West End. 'Paul understood the concept of the show and relished it' (English 1996). His magic partner in the show was Fluke, a skilled magician and contortionist, able to perform with ease the many flying effects specially developed for the show.

As was said at the beginning, illusion and magic are not the same thing. Illusionists make no claims to be able to transform just anyone, or make innocent bystanders fly through the air. Theirs is an art of deception based on physical skills developed only through long practice. The standard repertoire of illusions was mostly invented in the nineteenth century. Then, Horace Golding first sawed a lady in half, and Maskelyne lectured in a semi-scientific vein to audiences at London's Egyptian Hall. The dinner suit or tail coat still worn as a stage outfit dates from those early, quasi-academic appearances. Others claimed ancient religions as their source, with some justification since the Greek oracles had trick vessels eternally flowing with wine to impress visitors to their shrines. *Multum in Parvo*, the illusion performed in *Tantamount* in which milk is poured into different-sized vessels, is a direct descendant of this. To be able to create such effects demands the dedicated application to the craft of the task which is the lot of all who wish to realize the utmost possibilities of their profession. Like concert pianists or ballet dancers, illusionists must practise, practise, practise to achieve their effortless effects. As well as refining the skills of their hands, they must also take the greatest care in the construction of their apparatus and of the lighting and sight-lines which will reveal it to the audience.

The moment of wonder is the offspring of much labour. As Imogen Grave, one of Tantamount's fellow immortals, observes, 'Perhaps ultimately we prefer the idea of magic rather than the reality' (English 1994: 34).

As the show continues, it becomes clear that Tantamount has realized that true magic is rooted, not in the illusionists' delicious tricks, but in the realm of thought, of metaphysics. It is her command of metaphysics which gives Espiritu la Verdad the power to walk in the air 'on this cusp between light and dark' (ibid.: 5) (in a remarkable piece of horizontal flying specially developed for the show) and the power to rescue Imogen Grave. Ultimately the power of each of the five immortals is inscribed only in words, 'evoked in your image by the divinity of your name' (ibid.: 6) – Tantamount Esperance, Imogen Grave, Espiritu la Verdad, Epitome Plaisir and Vanitas Splendide. 'The names came about through watching people dance the tango. As I watched, I invented secret, tango names for them, to fit the very different personae that emerged when they danced' (English 1996).

The characters were also inspired by visual references, including a collection of pictures of magic acts and magicians, especially Horace Golding, whose beatific face inspired the look of Tantamount himself and brought about the reappearance of the trusty false beard which had been such an important part of English's very first show. The persona of the actress Eleanora Duse and the character of Cordelia in *King Lear* were also drawn upon for the particular quality of sober affection which characterizes Imogen Grave.

But the names came first. The characters were gradually revealed by contemplating the associations evoked by their names and how to embody them. Thus their creation became a meditation on the nature of acting. Tantamount is the most rounded character, troubled by the temper of his times, the seeming loss of any ability to look forward, to face the future, which makes him both sad and angry. He is also aware that the magic that he practised is tawdry compared with the power of Espiritu's wisdom. Nevertheless, he still thrills to see the skill of the young magicians, reminding him of his former self. As he observes, 'When you are in the company of conjurors, you often have the feeling that you are losing things ... you are both losing and gaining things at the same time' (English 1994: 16). In his own obsession with Imogen Grave, whom he met when she was very young, in his need to control her, he failed to notice that the tricks he was so proud to teach her she already knew. He was merely instrumental in revealing her true self, losing part of his own power in the process. Now, as they meet again, confronting each other after so many years, it is evident that she still feels affection for him. Perhaps all is not lost after all. Perhaps indeed as each character hopes, 'All will be well. All will be love again' (ibid.: 3). For the moment, Tantamount, having learned from Espiritu that 'as with all magic, the secret is that there is no secret' (ibid.: 5) has the consolation of knowing that 'If the secret is that there is no secret then this is the secret we must keep' (ibid.: 37). 'I never thought that I'd end up with spirit gum on my face' (English 1996).

In her determination to ask questions about the ancient domain of the theatre, English has herself effected a grand illusion. Her search has become a process of self-transformation, so that the probing questioner, the ruthless interrogator, has become a skilled practitioner of that which she investigated with such dedication. When performance is defined as such, instead of being used as a general noun for the doing of acting, dancing or playing music, it has an interrogative function. To perform, as in performance art, is to question the nature of process, the receipt of artistic experience. To perform in performance art is, of necessity, to keep a distance from that which is performed.

To create an illusion demands exactly the opposite approach. Only by total immersion in the process of perfecting the skills of hand and of presentation needed to achieve even the simplest effects can a moment of effortless wonder be created. English began her methodical deconstruction of the conventions of theatre from a position of scepticism. But by observing their varied methods so carefully, she came to understand and respect the processes by which their transformative effects were achieved, and, in understanding, to accept and value them. As Tantamount Esperance, she has herself submitted to the essential theatrical process of becoming a character, effecting the embodiment of an imaginary being. This being's existence as a creature of the mind leaves him free to question something much deeper than the mere mechanics of his appearance: he may seek, on behalf of all of us, to find the essence of our souls.

In *Tantamount Esperance*, assisted by her fellow magicians with their gracious tricks, English has created a theatrical world of her own, a place of sombre wonder, where meaning has been constructed from words uttered in light, surely the grandest illusion of all.

REFERENCES

English, Rose (1991) 'The Double Wedding', unpublished script.

——(1992) 'Walks on Water', in Deborah Levy (ed.) *Walks on Water*, London: Methuen New Theatrescripts, Methuen Drama.

——(1994) 'Tantamount Esperance', unpublished script.

——(1996) In interview with Lynn MacRitchie, London (June).

Nuttall, Jeff (1979) *Performance Art Memoirs*, Volume 1, London: John Calder.

éclat
sites 1–10

Caroline Bergvall's text-based performance *Eclat– Occupation des Lieux 1–10*, was commissioned as part of a series of site-specific text works entitled *Four Humours* by the Institution of Rot, London, (February-May 1996). *Four Humours* (dedicated to E.M. Cioran) featured work by Iain Sinclair, Ben Watson, Paul Buck and Caroline Bergvall. Each author was asked to draw from their own work to produce a text-based performance to animate the private spaces within the Institution of Rot. The Institution of Rot is a space (a house in north London, UK), a history (of site-specific performance installation, and sound work) and a curatorial project. Its founders are CROW (performance and installation artist) and Nick Couldry (writer and sound artist). The first performances at the Institution of Rot were in June 1993. The Institution of Rot has also performed works in Berlin (*Imperial Wardrobe*, 1995), Copenhagen (*Royal Sweatbath*, 1995), Prague (*Blind Site Deaf Words*, 1995) Fukuoka (*White City*, 1995). The following 'version' of *Eclat– Sites 1–10*, here documented for the page, was performed on May 17 1996 at the Institution of Rot on multiple audio-tapes. The sound text (on Walkmans) guided individual members of the audience on a journey through the 'actual' spaces of 109 Corbyn Street and the 'fictive' spaces of the text over a period of approximately 23 minutes. The layout and typography for this version of *Eclat* includes the 'accidental' characters that are produced in the translation from one format to another, as a means of visualising the translations that allowed the designer access in and out of the piece in its digital form.

ECLAT
OCCUPATION DES LIEUX

CAROLINE BERGVALL

1996

WEL is an occupation COME to the foreign guided a short round of observations.

Now yo. s.. now y.. don't. What not assumd .. be not hr since forver pleased are we by and large to kindly be stuck to instructs or what kind of langua would we otherwise be left with.

At any rate: The orderly fashion of starting points would have you standing please on the small X or cross we've prepared for you in the physical environment. Should more or less look like so

but bigger and yes bang on a doorstop.

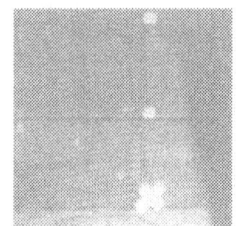

THAT (doorframe that) divider: lines up intersections between room and room: and corridor: to join & split at each such **HEREand**.
Pull in & widen up & widen up & pull in. And not there and nor here and nor there. Conflict exchange. Amassed press-ure stimuli.
Stationariness at such place brings about aphasia, loss of memory, nausea, inflammations, visionary spells, self-mutilations.
History shows and and and and and. That to transmute such symptoms into trance-like repetitions (is not the same is not the same) threatens nationalism only if accompanied by a dedicated propensity to spreading and unreasonably so.

&BREAKINGWATERÀRECULONS&ASTHOUGHWEWERENT

And in the knowledge that what is & naturally straight today will naturally be and & bent toworrow, such cumulative conjunctives have generated their own profound scholastics.
- ed.

Now: in your own time:

Slowly & lift your left & foot & bring it & forward & slowly & one step & in to the corr&idor and then: put it down. Slowly. This is fine. Just one step in any one direction is enough to indicate a move, a presence. An act of will or conviction at 'the best of times. One could say that you're leaving the threshold, clearing ground in slo'mo'. **And lift your right & foot & bring it & slowly to rest & slowly & by your left &.** This is good: **You're in the corridor:** We're on our way:

Walk at a leisurely or similar pace down the corrido.

A continuous surface is immediately interrupted or punctuated by **footsteps**.

There was a door to your immediate right.

Further down to your left another door. Leads out to a room. This is going where we are.

&

Call that a living room? THIS. is a living room. A front room. **Owdooyoodoo. Owdooyoodoo.** Cross into a rm of ths kind that we may carry & conduct ourselves as if originating from resolved
gender and normal art. Accurate, precise, seamlessly, well-adjusted. You've crossed into the.
High ceiling open fire. Name the objects arranged and negotiated.
- Wonderment domastication, don't you find.
- Ndeed.
- Biscuit?
Or make us each more certain "I'm not my own unshapely".
No big wet thing. What big wet thing. You mean this? What follows - true storage, live slice, slippery to the touch.
I'm waving a pair of.
She says "yeah why not" and also "some things best not

Wheres your pointed buster

be thought in the dark".
Ah but we did.
Next thing we know we're at the Tate encased in fomalderhyde.
Mummy! mummy mummy look! sisters? mummy looklook
sisters sisters. (Sad really). Paradoxically, stuffed like that you
need not locate your own frontal Parade to be occupied in full view.
But leave this room: your features might start drooping.
But stay here: your bone structure might dehydrate.

The choice is yours not entirely.

You've decided to follow on through. (Well done). **Leave the r....**

Back in the corridor. A long narrow strip of encased space. What app.... to b. here. Wha n.t app..rs. Stick to thplan. **Walk towards the staircase.** There's a big cracked wall doing a small Beckett to your left. A frame at th end of the by the main-door is catching your attention. You may wan t to have a l k. Then again. The staircase. Now there's a. **Lets go upstairs.**

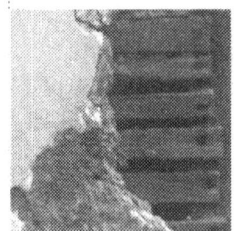

Slooowllly. One. step. at. the. time. 1and 2and 3and. *At this rate what doesn't- ed
A. staircase. is. an. elevation. device. Increases dematerialisation*. there. is. an .occupation. which. is. slow. &. open &. an. acoustic escalator. That's good, continue.
4and 5and 6and.

Well. If a straight line be the shortest distance between two points where would that leave us my dove

White walls. A regular spatial arrangement for domestic passage. Where are you not who. **You've reached the first landing.** Still. Beyond that. Who lives here. Was a sister a sister. What ap.ears to b. here. A couple of doors. Twins not twins. What you see & what you ...'t. Show caution. Ze cloth does make ze monk.

))))!(((((()))))HOI(ST)))MY)))))FAC(((!((((E)))))))OUTOF))))))DEEP((((BACGROUND

Why thanx for the top Fennigan, read useful

(sowecanseeyou)

(((((((((((Or not figur.

You're pressing the handle down slowly, giving it a small push at the same time, you're opening the door, the one facing the staircase behind you. It leads into a small ish square room. Close th door beh 'ind you. Th frosted glass of th window. Th ivy brushing on th outside.

You're walking to the middle of the room. Now you're standing in the middle of the room. Say CHEESE. CHEESE. A photograph is a moment of respite.

"There's nothing on these negatives".

Was this a surpr   ise) pendulums not spells (Bah. Was it a surpr. never still long enough to grasp your own contours. You're not here with any great precision anyway. Yes no yes no.
I'm walking towards you. Can I see myself who cannot fully see you. Or, "Nabokov had
a point whose Narcissus mistakes his own suicide for a murder". Ndeed, ndeed. As they say, whatever you do in this world, stay well-lit at all times and know your lining. Don't move. Cavities pop out with the push of a thumb. Twins not twins, **don't move.** Once in doubt, people indispensably not follow their previous arrangements.

A SOft refle a pliable ction that's how we like you.

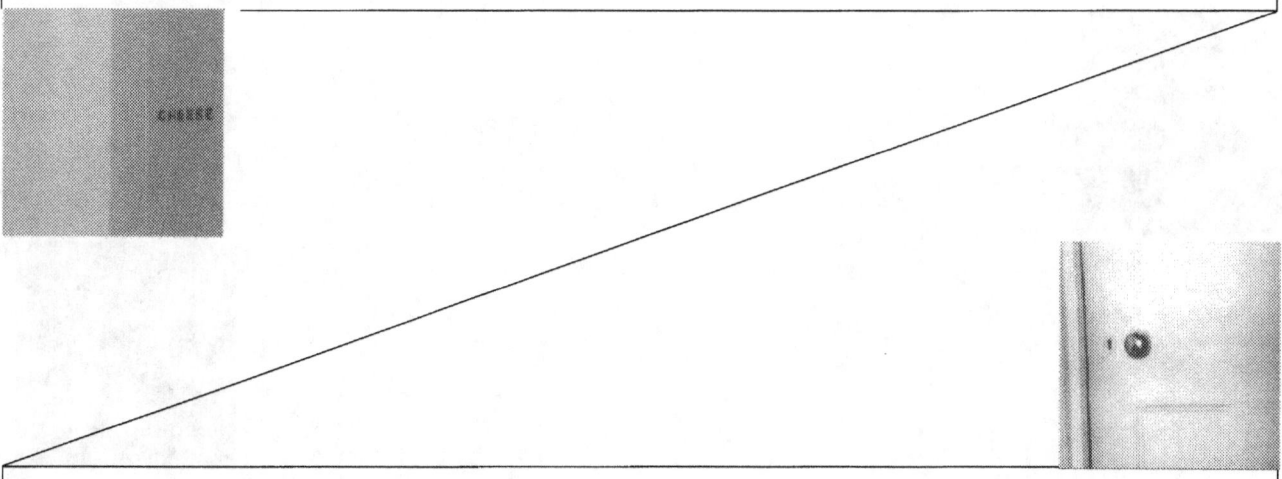

Now make your way slowl towards. that. opening. is always another. ope. leads to anoth room.

THIS once was the inner room. To occupy after much reflexivity. Still not fully. What is slow and open and occupies? Later used it was as a small storage room then a bedroom. The house into clusters various kinds of. Leaving the unchanged plaques inchangees. By and large a bedroom: is a rectangular or oblong square of contained space with sleeping ustensils. Object arrangements.
Any casual. Reconnaissoitre.
Item by item iron to flatten.
Ah but once in doubt stay well-lit. Indeed, the mass diffusion of interchangeable body parts has proven as popular as disposable vulvas.

What app..rs to. Fossilised lumps, inchoate innards, a vast amassing of human material and behavioural mishmash stocked up here somewhere.
The house develops such litteral protuberances Reorganise, reorganise that it's become currently unviable for anyone to casually set up residency. What assumed to be not h....
The image which fills like up a pouch pushes from inside the, that's what I told: my mother gets passed over. Well who's a stranger to this kind of arrangement. Mother a scratch-card.

Which reminds me: "I'm beside myself". The floreigner her accentuated gait across the rooms, whose forebearance is a wonder to stabilise, whose skirting habits carry much revelance
by way of occupancy (who interrupts a train of thought to admire someone (who bypasses their limitations (then says, theres more much more than adjustable (then says Bring out the holes, bring out the holes. And hangers. Bring out hangers. Plenty of. Who says I'm more than my own aside & asks for steadier projectors. projectiles. Things keep on. Something about the outside. A pierced nipple really is one small puncture by way of solidity, it's all so messy out and about. (And the more I wash my hands the clearer it gets).

**You can stay here awhile should you feel it occupies.
You can install œ your solid aspect on this here chair over there.
Or you can.**

Back in the other room.

It appears there's someone else. The straight point of a circle. Show caution. Stay well-lit at all. And keep moving. When you stand still, there seems to be some. nodes or something. unaccounted for. Object arrangements. Things keep on. Sticko tplan.
-And whats zis? Whats that whats zis and that and zis and this and zat and this and that.
-Whats what.
Who looks you up and down and sideways.
I CAN SEE STRAIGHT THR.... .OU.
A sister was not a mister. Was this a surprise. Yes no. It was. A sister was not a mister. Was this a surprise. Yes no it was. A sister was not a mmm. Wa this asurp Ye. Noit wa. A sist wa no mist. Yo   was. Yas.
You're wanting to comment on what app....s to b. the translucency of, what appears to, signs of rubbing off, Really it's just a very slightly negligéed state of affairs. How you walk inout of detail.
You're wanting to say I'm in a phase of appearance brings about a constant state of arousal. A constant state of. That this is a recent visitation, once occupied, it. Usually. Fleshes out.
How you constantly want to go up to someone else and. Want to go up to and h. Want to h. Constantly want to put your hand on their. There. Their Organum Genitalics: to secure (to secure, to secure).

-My pleasure, to help ourselves fluently that's the

The question asks itself pointedly: Would such an action just about reassure (probably not). Or possibly provide:
a) a clue proper question mark
b) a positive identifier question mar
c) a rush of great significance question mark

This IS a very large something or other. What isit. Just a thought.

                              no y see n w .ou don

22.2.96. agite slee. p. don figut. yEs. stick to thplan.

Walk past. Get to the door. The point is a compact line. Got to get to. open the door.
Walk past. get to the. open it. Wa & get to.
got to get to the. open it cross the threshold
get to the do.. open it cross the threshold.
close the.

Back on the landing you're back on the landing. It's the end of the yes, yes we know.

Meanwhile, back on the landing.

This good, feels fine, the landing seems wider and lighter than previously. This is nice. You're standing on the landing. It isn't giving way under your feet. This insignificant detail fills you with such a sense of embossment it is so: elating so: unbelievable so: unbelievable that you exclaim I be could happy here and quickly lift up your and pull down your and squat and press out your happening vaginals, your instinctual drive, your cultural reticence, your dutiful intelligence, your cautious elaborations, your impeccable taste in shots of urine all over the surface of this very perfect spot.

))))))))))))))s)o)m)e))))))))thing))))s))kee))pon)))(((((((((.(((((((((

(On the way up to the second landing, you're thinking that to fit oneself perfectly quite is one thing but to deploy insides out one's own extensiveness now that's now that's)

As you can see, there are another two (two) doors on the second landing. One to your left, one in front of you. To your right a large wall surface, behind you the staircase.

Intersections which might occur here are of a more intrusive kind. Wonders of artificial light. My silicons take me a long homeward way. Beyond that. Wa s a sist a mist & a tsim a tsis. yes no yes no. This 3rd arm of yours. Was a Sally a Sally. What app.... to b. .ere. That's how we like you.

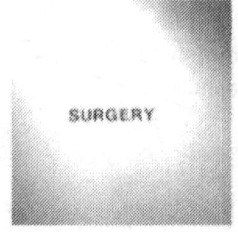

You've pushed the door to your left, the one marked surg.r. You enter te room.
Its vastness s....ises you, takes you aback. Its ornate decoration. Red deep carpets seem much at odds with the .est of the house. A wide sof. covered with a selection of cushions, not animals like cats and dogs. There's champagne in a silver cooler in a small side-crack, crystal glasses and conversations. Feathers, hats, bare shoulders. "Welcome, we were expecting you, make yourself comforta". Someone is coming towards you smiling, holding out their hand. You can't help but notice are you seeing straight through th. Everything's what it Smirnoffs.
Noting your hesitation, they gently push you towards the centre of the room, you think you're feeling the prickle of thought against your leg but there's noone here you know. You slump into one of the deeper armchairs.

Aaah th   at was a. You notice a someone sitting in another armchair facing a good one she's fiddling with her idea while engaging in conversation. Surprised, delighted you look into it grows. Was a she a she now lying on the sofaaa. Seems to be talking takes up more room laughs as clicks open a fully clit clot clited like a fat cigar, the sofa's popping out are the walls extruding the air seems hotter, tighter. She or she is pressing with her fingers and pulls the flaps apart. Coming out fast, she's conversing face down across a table her legs pushing a handful of her own up her indescribably big, her space-surround ambient organum. Is laughing and sweating. You want to. But your face is dropping out of sight and you must busy yourself looking for it. Or you want to. But her arse has come over you and is covering your face forcing itself around your mouth around your tongue. This is all doubt beyond and wonderfully opaque. You fill your throat and think of Mary, Immaculate. Your saintly unvaginal envelope, bless me as I traverse, bless me the saintly silence of your lipless. Your saintly vacated saintly vacated occupancy, bless me as I'm moved to occupy, bless me Mary as I manifestly some profound occupation. Bless me

as she unpacks I discharges. Bless me Bless me Mary never let it be said: the splendid c I mean the splendid unts are inward inwarded: sideinside in: are neither here nor there not this not that nor anything but not. Some uncool. Virginals haloed be their enduring lessening. Bless me Mary pleine de grace for to extend one's out outsides now that's now that's.

Your skin pops back to its current conventional dimensions with a slurpy sound.
In the landfill of your frock there is occupation which occupies. What app...rs t Bo be h.... crmonies of sweat 'n .isibility. A thinker once said girls make a gorgeous margin, did you believe that. I did. But really. Head on full-frontal - out - in - back - to - over - under - sideways - above - revelling - below - through - projected - projective - across - beyond now that's now that's what I'd call morphing. Adjectival distentions branched out into spectacles recombinant what I'd call.

morphing & the mis... ...companying worlds.

Sure, you can stay here you can certainly Aah that was a

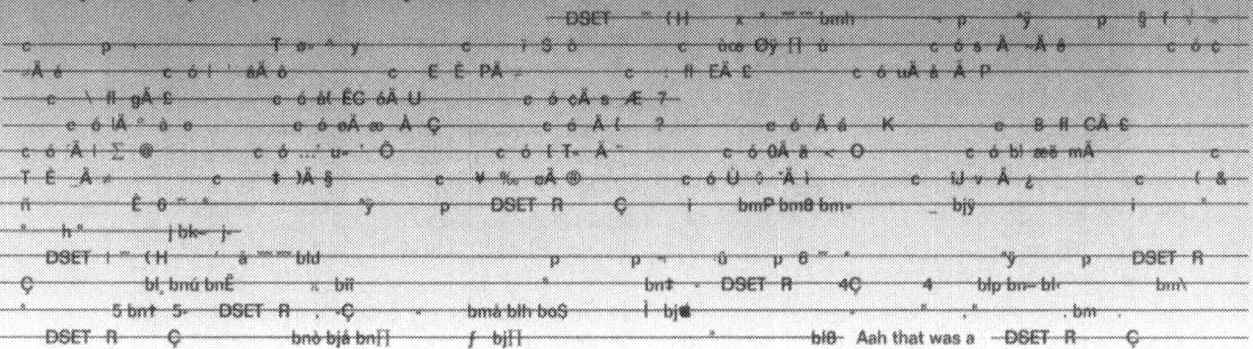

bl- bm blÃ   √ biò   bn® **never** the less DSET R Ç   bl¥ bl∫ bkË   √ bj•
"   bk‰ Aah that was a DSET R Ç   bl¿ bl∞ bl¨   ƒ bjê   "   bl‡ never the less
DSET R Ç   bkÿ blò bk·   √ bj   "   blî **never** the less DSET R ÇÄ
   bll bl® bn¨ √ biú   "   blÄ never the less DSET R Ç   blÑ blt blx
√ biË   "   bl° never the less DSET R Ç   bn¿ bnº bll   n bj.   "
bn∞ **Aah that was a** DSET R Çç   blà bl§ blá   √ bj4
       "   bm Aah that was a DSET R ÇÄ   bjD bk bk‡   √ bn∉   "   "
bmt never the less DSET R ÇÄ   bjÎ bm bi ƒ   ƒ bj   "   "   biÿ never the less
DSET R ÇÄ   bn\ bkå bnX   √ bi‡   "   bnd never the less DSET R Ç
blú bn` bjƒ   √ bjl   "   bnh Aah that was a DSET R Ç   bnl bnt bnx   √ bj
"   bnÄ never the less DSET R Ç   bnå bnÑ bnà   √ bix   "   bnê Aah that was
a DSET R Ç   bkÃ bnî bi∞   W bjl   "   bk Aah that was a DSET R Ç
bi‰ bk bjˉ   W bj®   "   bk Aah that was a DSET R Ç   bj bià bk∏   √ bk®
"   bi‡ never the less DSET R Ç   bjÄ bk$ bkh   L bk("   bi¥ Aah that was a
DSET R ÇÄ   bk8 bjÙ bk   ƒ bjL   "   bk0 never the less DSET R Ç
bi∉ ¯ bk   √ bm   "   bk' never the less DSET R Çç   , bkÑ bi'   √ bjt
"   bj‡ never the less DSET R Ç   bk4 bj bi§   º biÏ   "   bk- Aah that was a
DSET R ≤ .Ç   ∑ bj- bj‡ bi.   J P bj(P   ≤   "   ∏ bkº ∏
DSET R ÇÄ   bk biÃ bi-   n bj.   "   bkƒ *   **FNTM t ~ H**   Helvetica
Chicago   " "   **New Century Schlbk**   Palatino
Times   CUTS ak

STRONG PERFORMANCE FROM ROUTLEDGE

Performance: A Critical Introduction

Marvin Carlson, City University of New York

In the first survey to provide an overview of the modern concept of performance and how it has developed, Marvin Carlson introduces the reader to the contested interpretations of performance art.

'An essential purchase for introductory courses in performance studies and theatre history.' - *Ian Watson, Rutgers University*

May 1996: 216x138: 256pp
Hb: 0-415-13702-0: £40.00 Pb: 0-415-13703-9: £10.99

Contemporary Plays by Women of Color

An Anthology

Edited by **Kathy A. Perkins**, University of Illinois at Urbana-Champaign and
Roberta Uno, University of Massachusetts - Amherst

A collection of previously unpublished new and recent works by US women playwrights of colour. Featuring biographical notes on each writer and the production history of each play, this is a unique resource for practitioners and students.
Winner of the 1996 ATHE Award for Outstanding Book in Theatre Performance and Pedagogy.

January 1996: 246x189: 336pp: illus.18 b+w photos
Hb: 0-415-11377-6: £50.00 Pb: 0-415-11378-4: £15.99

The Intercultural Performance Reader

Edited by **Patrice Pavis**, University of Paris

Patrice Pavis gathers together key artists and scholars from around the world to provide, for the first time, a truly international overview of the new possibilities and politics of the exciting field of intercultural performance.

July 1996: 234x156: 280pp
Hb: 0-415-08153-X: £40.00 Pb: 0-415-08154-8: £12.99

Post-Colonial Drama

Theory, Practice, Politics

Helen Gilbert and **Joanne Tompkins**, both at Queensland University

Using the latest theoretical approaches, this is the first full-length study to address the ways in which performance has been instrumental in resisting the continuing effects of imperialism.

May 1996: 216x138: 360pp: illus.12 b+w photos
Hb: 0-415-09023-7: £45.00 Pb: 0-415-09024-5: £14.99

Signs of Performance

An Introduction to Twentieth-Century Theatre

Colin Counsell, University of North London

Covering the whole of 20th century theatre, from Stanislavski to Brecht and Samuel Beckett to Robert Wilson, *Signs of Performance* offers the new student working examples of theatrical analysis.

April 1996: 216x138: 256pp
Hb: 0-415-10642-7: £40.00 Pb: 0-415-10643-5: £11.99

A Sourcebook on Feminist Theatre and Performance

On and Beyond the Stage

Edited by **Carol Martin**, Tisch School of the Arts, New York University

An outstanding collection of key articles on feminist theatre and performance from The Drama Review. Includes the work of theorists Elin Diamond, Peggy Phelan and Lynda Hart and interviews with practitioners including Anna Deveare Smith and Robbie McCauley.

Worlds of Performance

October 1996: 234x156: 336pp: illus.20 b+w photos
Hb: 0-415-10644-3: £45.00 Pb: 0-415-10645-1: £14.99

Split Britches

Lesbian Practice/Feminist Performance

Edited by **Sue-Ellen Case**, University of California - Riverside

'It is such a privilege to write about creativity that has been nourished through love, intellectual brilliance and extraordinary insight into human nature. It is an invaluable contribution to the arts.' - *Ellen Stewart, La Mama Theatre*

A long awaited celebration of the theatre and writings of Lois Weaver, Peggy Shaw and Deborah Margolin, who make up this outstanding lesbian performance troup.

June 1996: 216x138: 288pp: illus.15 b+w photos
Hb: 0-415-12765-3: £40.00 Pb: 0-415-12766-1: £12.99

Routledge books are available from all good bookshops. For more information, or a FREE 1996 Performance Studies catalogue, please contact:
Cynthia Wainwright, Routledge, 11 New Fetter Lane, London EC4P 4EE. Tel: 0171 842 2032
e-mail: info.performance@routledge.com
Access Routledge On-Line:
http://www.routledge.com/routledge.html

As If Dance Was Visible

André Lepecki

ZERO; OR UNREST

They have just stopped moving; the lights are fading out; applause will soon follow.* And then they'll leave, taking the dance with them, taking it behind the four walls of the stage, taking the dance under their skins.

> *A different version of this article appeared in *Etcetera*, journal of the Flemish Theater Institute, February 1996. For the (considerable) revision of the ideas exposed on that first draft I am indebted to the generous critiques and comments of Annemarie Bean, Mark Franko, Richard Green and Myriam van Imshoot.

Until the next time. And as we, the audience, leave the theatre – still energized by the dance that is now no longer present, that is already cooling in our bodies – a fresh new sediment of experience spreads out in our memory, claiming its space as a new past. Until there is remembering. For some of us in the audience this remembering means: until there is writing, as the moment arrives of writing on the dance that just was, of revisiting dance's mnemonic space, of locating and probing its precarious site. This moment of revisiting and restaging the dance in the scene of writing and in the scene of memory is what will interest me in this essay. A mnemonic endeavour for which success is guaranteed only by the means of mimesis, when the writer accepts that the translation of what no longer moves into the movement of writing depends upon a play between eye, hand, and the theatre of memory.

In this sense, writing is *putting in motion* – an odd reviving of the dance, its repetition, its restaging. Only this time the dancing bodies are purely imaginary. But were they ever *not* imaginary, those moving bodies of dancers now resting in some hotel room? Is it possible to affirm unconditionally that their presence on the stage was purely physical? And if we decide to answer no to this question, what implications must we draw regarding representation – both in dance and in the writing of dance? Peggy Phelan, in her remarkable essay 'Thirteen ways of looking at choreographing writing', cogently outlines the theoretical set-up in play here. She argues:

> [i]n all forms of representations of the body – from portrait photograph to historical dance reconstructions – the body in question seems to make an appearance, then it definitely disappears, and is then re-presented. History and writing are constituted from and by that disappearance. Moreover, this disappearance suspends the proprietary relation between body and being. In its journey from disappearance to representation, the body does not 'belong' to the subject who wears it, who dances in and through it.
>
> (Phelan 1995: 204)

In her approach to an ontology of dance performance Phelan recuperates certain aspects of Martin Heidegger's metaphysics of presence.* Following from and expanding Phelan's approach, the tension resulting from this

> *Compare Phelan's quote with Heidegger's: 'The apparent is that which from time to time emerges and vanishes, the ephemeral and unstable over against being as the permanent' (Heidegger 1987: 98).

continuous oscillation – from dissociation to overlapping of the physical and imaginary dancing bodies – not only informs historical dance reconstructions, but also constitutes the necessary condition for any dance to come successfully into being (i.e. to be a 'good' dance piece) as well as for any writing to address a dance piece successfully (i.e. to be a 'good' review). For this tension and this oscillation have a rhythm – one already choreographic.

THEATRES

The humming of a spinning hard drive as soundtrack and the lighting of flickering electrons crashing against the surface of the computer screen as moving 'bodies' set up writing in an altogether different theatre than that of dance. But the moment when those sedimented images of dancing bodies metamorphose into writing is one already informed by a choreographic motion. This motion is not simply that of fingers running nervously on the keyboard, trying to catch up with the dancer's steps by the means of scribbled notes, loose recollections, sensations lining up as if one could believe for a moment that indeed the dance could be realigned again in the shape of words. Rather, this motion is highly supplemented by the means of mnemonic associations, mimesis, displacement and projection, all contributing to compose an imaginary room for the dance to move again; and in this mimetic/mnemonic theatre of writing, in the resulting tension between materiality and spectrality, the dance is put into motion again, surfacing as an image between desire and repression – a spectre of what we think it was probably there on the stage once; just now, last night, a year ago.

Thus the theatre of writing and the scene of dancing are not altogether as different as we thought they were. The writer trusts that she can recapture what she thinks she saw being danced on stage, just as the choreographer trusts she can recapture and organize in her piece that precarious, precise, improvised gesture she thinks she saw in a rehearsal. This unstable oscillation between writing and dance, mediated by an uncertain pendular motion between the recollection of movements that are no more and words that are yet to be, already gestures towards choreography. The choreographic flow in the realm of signification. A diacritical ghost dance.

FIRST POSITION

Dance as an art of erasure; as opposed to dance as an art of presence and inscription. To think of dance as that which vanishes as opposed to that which is present. I am aware of the boring hues of this discussion, the terms of which have by now become widespread.* I intend to reconsider the ethical implications of these positions once we acknowledge that the dance is profoundly informed, constituted, built upon mo(ve)ments that exceed the economy of the 'purely physical' – (e)motions disturbing the law of commonsensically dulled eyes and commonsensically dulled feelings. I am theorizing here that *both dance and writing* are already implicated in the organic system of historically inscribed sensorial practices. Which means that as writers, as dancers and as writers on dances there is something to be gained in investigating the possibilities for a writing and a choreographic project that rearticulates the intricate relationships between nervous systems, sensorial organs and the linguistic/epistemic apparati as constitutive of political, aesthetic, physical, phantasmatic and theoretical cultures. This gain is that of understanding choreography (the syntactic logic of organizing movements within time) as an activity that surpasses the boundaries of the visual; to see dance as an incantation, already haunted by spectres (of meaning, of recognition, of sounds, of promises). Such gain is an ethical one – it acknowledges the Other as organizing our (aesthetic) experience, as staging and marking the boundaries between what is and what should be.

* For a recent discussion see van Kerhoeven (1995: *passim*).

The ironic result of such theoretical refinement (if it is, indeed, a refinement) is that as the understanding of dance-as-erasure becomes more and more widespread, and as it points to ideological organizations of the eye, it relaunches the old project of dance criticism as a form of archival duty. The over-investment in the blindness of description is reinforced by what seemed to undermine it. 'If dance vanishes as it is danced, as poststructural theories of the dance now tell me,' says the happy descriptive critic, 'then my moral duty as a critic is to prevent this dying by the means of my indelible writing.' In this version of dance writing, the critic is a kind of optimistic semiotician spinning wild in teleological delusion. His 'ethical' drive participates of an history of hygiene: nothing will be corrupted by the passing of time.*

* For a discussion on the descriptive versus interpretive debate in dance criticism, see Carroll (1987) and Copeland (1993).

The obvious problem with the belief that writing can be a way of capturing and freezing dance (and dance's signification) in the linear flow of time is that the word is an entity as fluid as the dancing image it dreams to capture. It is in acknowledging this instability of the dance *and* this instability of the word that we would have to reconsider the possibilities of *writing on dance* as another art of erasure.

This rethinking can be proposed as a form of anatomical problem: what are the relationships between the writer's eye, mind, hand (whether the writer is a critic, a reviewer, or a scholar), and the self-effacing dancing body? To answer this question we must leave our cosy havens of meaning, our eye's lazy habits, the security of our skins, and open up some doors outside our everyday and linear time and see what moves back there.

RE/COGNITION

> The weak walls of our ROOM, of our everyday and linear time, will not save us.... Important events stand behind the doors; it is enough to open them.
>
> (Kantor 1993: 142)

Anna Halprin, who was a teacher of Trisha Brown, Yvonne Rainer and Simone Forti, reformulated her approach to choreography by comprehending and theorizing the implications of dance's predicament as an art of erasure, as an art of traces. Halprin stated: 'I remember thinking that dance was in disadvantage in relation to sculpture in that the spectator could spend as much as he required to examine a sculpture, walk around it, and so forth – but a dance movement – because it happened in time – vanished as soon as it was executed' (Sayre 1989: 117).

Halprin's insight had an obvious impact on contemporary dance practices (it virtually made history). In order to control what she perceived as the vanishing nature of dance, the dying of dance, Anna Halprin introduced repetition in her work. Repetition has a long history in western art, but Halprin's use of such an aesthetic device had a particular purpose aimed at reinforcing the persistence of the dancing image in time, and therefore in the spectator's memory. Through re-cognition the spectator could reinvest the vanishing form with an illusion of permanence. By the means of such insistent repetition / recognition Halprin staged Heidegger's early conceptualizations of the presence of image as a constant reiteration of itself through time. Her student Trisha Brown turned this pedagogical moment into masterpieces: *Glacial Decoy* (1979) and *Set and Reset* (1983). Henry Sayre appropriately comments on these two works:

> If in *Glacial Decoy*... the dancers continually vanish away into the wings, such is the condition of our own perceptual relation to even those movements we can see, or rather have just already seen. The moment one of Brown's dancers disappears from view, we are forced to recognize that the dance itself – what was until a moment ago present before our eyes – has also disappeared. Dance is defined as a vanishing act.
>
> (Sayre 1989: 140–1)

But this disappearance in Trisha Brown's work is more complex than Sayre makes it. Its paradox is that the repetition that informs it constitutes the same act which guarantees that the vanishing dance be always available for re-presentation and for its reproduction. But isn't this paradox precisely the bulk of the hard work of being a dancer, of being a choreographer: constant repetition, that is to say, in French *répétition*, a continous rehearsing? This endless striving to recapture a perfect moment, a perfect pose, spin, intention, that we believe can be realized again from its own disappearance?

It is in this revisiting that the choreographic reiteration of the vanishing moment becomes a special sort of repetition. The vanishing traces of the dance lead us to the Derridean definition of trace as difference (where the trace leads us not to a stable referent, but to a fluid, endless chain of different traces) rather than to the Freudian return of the repressed (where the subject is trapped in a pathological fixed re-enactment of the unresolved trauma). Instead of a certain fixity in repetition, an arresting return, dance rehearses a historical motility within time. On this precise point, historian Mark Franko suggests, in a manner similar to Peggy Phelan's, that the 'disappearance presence of the trace' is the 'being of performance' (Franko 1995b: 206). But Franko adds something else to the definition, in a somewhat Marxist move: the trace in performance may well be unrepeatable 'but not for that reason [is it] culturally irrecuperable' (ibid.). The very fact that there is memory and that there is rehearsal makes the traces of dance 'enduringly worldly' (ibid.).

This sense of endurance and worldly recuperation is referred to by the Polish director Tadeusz Kantor writing on the theatrical space as that which one keeps 'reconstructing again and again / and that keeps dying again and again' (Kantor 1993: 143). To this labour the project of writing on dance must gesture, for it provokes a radical questioning of dance's place, of where dance 'takes place'. It is Martha Graham's question, one that also launches a shock-wave on any writing on dance.

SECOND PROPOSITION

The questions, as of now: where are the sites for dance to rest once it is over? Where does the dance go to? And how is it set in motion again, in the mimetic remembering of writing? The question of destiny, of destination, of the purpose of the dance, of its path and of its faith, is one and the same question as that of the economy of the gaze, that blindness of the eye that beholds the dance as 'purely physical'. These questions take us further back into memory, at least some thirty years before Anna Halprin's theorization and rehearsal of the dancing trace in the 1960s. So, back to the past, to 1937, not to Martha Graham dancing in her studio in New York City, but to Martha Graham writing on the dance. She writes: 'To understand dance for what it is, it is necessary we know from whence it comes and where it goes' (Graham 1966: 83).

Graham's sentence is extraordinary in every sense of the word. I reread it over and over again before moving on to the next section. Maybe you could do the same ...

STAINS, AS IN DESTINY

Where does the dance come from and where does the dance go to? This is the question that haunts signification and the project of writing dance, of writing on dance. For this travelling implicates sites of departure and of arrival that are not evident and, moreover, that try not to leave evidences (of their location, of their particular movements). Which space does dance fill in this journey of uncertain origins and ends? If it is indeed a space, a place, it must be uncharted – a space not belonging to the realm of representation, but that *allows* representation. A room. Moreover, a dark room, a *camera obscura*, that black box which allowed the enlightened eye to put the world into perspective, that room upon which the eye withheld the possibility of representation *but that is always outside representation proper*. This space between departure and destination is that which allows dance to become, that which gives dance understandability. Such space that is uneventful in order for the event to be staged, can never be contained; for this dark room not only is full of moving inhabitants but is in itself moving, always in tension. Such is the room of theatre, as Kantor described it: 'the room cannot be real, i.e. exist in our time: this room is in our memory, in our recollection of the past. This is the room we keep constructing again and again and that keeps dying again and again' (Kantor 1993: 143). Such room, where allusions to appearances are allowed to emerge, is ontologically unstable in the realm of discourse and in the law of signification. It is always in motion, always dying, but always being reconstituted, worked through, oscillating between presence and memory, physicality and trace – as matter, as the dance should be.

Kantor concludes the previous citation by suggesting that this temporality is informed by a rhythm, which is to say, the room moves: 'This pulsating rhythm must be maintained because it delineates the real structure of our memory' (Kantor 1993: 143). To understand and cope with the economy and the poetics of this appearance and disappearance as mnemonic rhythm constitutes the problematic kernel of dance criticism (and of choreography); for this oscillation constitutes the element that holds the possibility of stating: I am dancing, I am seeing dance, I can see dance, I am writing about dance.

Now one must ask: why is it that Kantor has to say that the room he always builds only to see it die again, *does not exist in our time but exists in our memory*? If the room does not exist in our time because it is in our memory, what is the time of memory then? Does memory entail the same temporality as that of presence (of our presence as spectators, as critics, as dancers in performance)?

REPETITION REPETITION REPETITION

> But an equally important need for complexity hinges on asking how much of dance practice materializes as visible, or should be understood in visual terms alone.
> (Franko 1995a: xiii)

What happens in between steps, in between touches, in between half-motions of undefined intentions? Such is the space of apparitions, of ghosts, of illusion in representation. It is while choreographing also this 'in betweenness' that dance happens more successfully. The choreographic play of invisibilities challenges the critical fetishism of thinking, writing and seeing dance as that which pertains only to the visual. When choreographer Meg Stuart speaks of her work by saying that her choreography is informed by her understanding that 'life happens in between' this statement has to be read not only as an allegory of the movements the dancers will repeat – but as a praxis that organizes the emotive power of her work. That which is not apparent moves as well.

This space in between is where the flow of choreography oscillates, the space the dance moves into, escaping from the linear time of everyday life to the pulsing time of memory. This is where the ethical encounter with the Other becomes choreographic: it collapses with Graham's ontology of the dance as travelling, and with a certain description of the unconscious as a rhythmical structure. Jacques Lacan writes that 'the unconscious is what closes up again as soon as it has opened, in accordance with a temporal pulsation' (Lacan 1981: 143). Since Lacan, the unconscious is the discourse of the Other, we can return to Martha Graham's answer to her own question on dance's origins and of dance's end. Note how, for Graham, this movement of dance is one happening between memories and in between memories:

> To understand dance for what it is, it is necessary we know from whence it comes and where it goes. It comes from depths of man's inner nature, the unconscious, where memory dwells. As such it inhabits the dancer. It goes into the experience of man, the spectator, awakening similar memories.
> (Graham 1966: 83–4)

In other words, dance as elusive presence organizes recognition (of the Other) as its very promise of becoming.

But ... is this all? Is this all there is to it at the end; in the end? This return to the Freudian postulate of an unconscious to unconscious communication? The answer, of course, is yes. But only in one level. A yes with a yet – with the caution of any project that gestures towards ethics, towards reconsidering the laws that regulate the always tense *pas de deux* between eye and hand, performance and writing, presence and its spectres. Let us not forget that if ethics is an encounter with the Other, what prevents that encounter is precisely a closure of the unconscious, our closure to the discourse of the Other. Lacan sees the 'closure of the unconscious [to the Other] as the act of missing the right meeting just at the right moment' (Lacan 1981: 145). It is this missing, this not understanding, not being able to see, hear, feel, that initiates repetition of the traumatic, thus fixing the subjects in a moment of loss. It is in this sense that Graham indicates an ethical movement through the rhythmic travelling of dance between its origins and its ends. This travelling revisits, but it also transcends and reformulates the shape of time.

Hence, in order to track down what invades the unstable, vagrant, nomadic space of choreography-in-writing, of choreography and writing, one must pay careful notice to (must pay homage to, must invoke, problematize, dance and write on) those suspended moments, where gestures, sounds, landscapes are not (yet) visible as dance but point to the choreographic tension between physicality and imagination. One must pay attention to the spectres in the dance. It is not only that those moments of interruption are the ones where we are most likely to find the presence of the phantasm. But mostly because those moments of interruption, of suspension between matter and memory, or, to use again Peggy Phelan's words, between what 'seems to make an appearance' and its apparent disappearance, those moments open up doors, slash the narrow boundaries of the descriptive eye, cut the vulgarity of interpretation and description, expand the self into the non-timely realm of the room of dancing memories – so that our spectating bodies and our spectating minds can pulsate in the rhythm of theatre, the oscillating rhythm of degeneration and reproduction, where we write with the dancers a shared rehearsal and participate in a dance of intelligence.

REFERENCES

Carroll, Noël (1987) 'Trois propositions pour une critique de la danse contemporaine', in M. Febvre (ed.) *La Danse au Défi*, Montreal: Les Editions Parachute.

Copeland, Roger (1993) 'Dance criticism and the descriptive bias', *Dance Theatre Journal* (Spring–Summer): 26–31.

Franko, Mark (1995a) *Dancing Modernism/Performing Politics*, Bloomington and Indianapolis, IN: Indiana University Press.

—— (1995b) 'Mimique', in E. W. Goellner and J. S. Murphy (eds) *Bodies of the Text: Dance as Theory, Literature as Dance*, New Brunswick, NJ: Rutgers University Press.

Graham, Martha (1966) *Martha Graham*, Princeton, NJ: Princeton University Press.

Heidegger, Martin (1987) *An Introduction to Metaphysics*, New Haven, CT and London: Yale University Press.

Kantor, Tadeusz (1993) 'The room. Maybe a new phase 1980', in M. Kobialka (ed.) *A Journey Through Other Spaces*, Berkeley and Los Angeles, CA: University of California Press.

Kerhoeven, M. van (ed.) (1995) 'On memory', *Theaterschrift* 8, Brussels: Kaaitheatre *et al.*

Lacan, Jacques (1981) *The Four Fundamental Concepts of Psycho-Analysis*, trans. Alan Sheridan, New York and London: W. W. Norton.

Phelan, Peggy (1995) 'Thirteen ways of looking at choreographing writing', in Susan L. Foster (ed.) *Choreographing History*, Bloomington and Indiana, IN: Indiana University Press.

Sayre, Henry M. (1989) *The Object of Performance*, Chicago and London: University of Chicago Press.

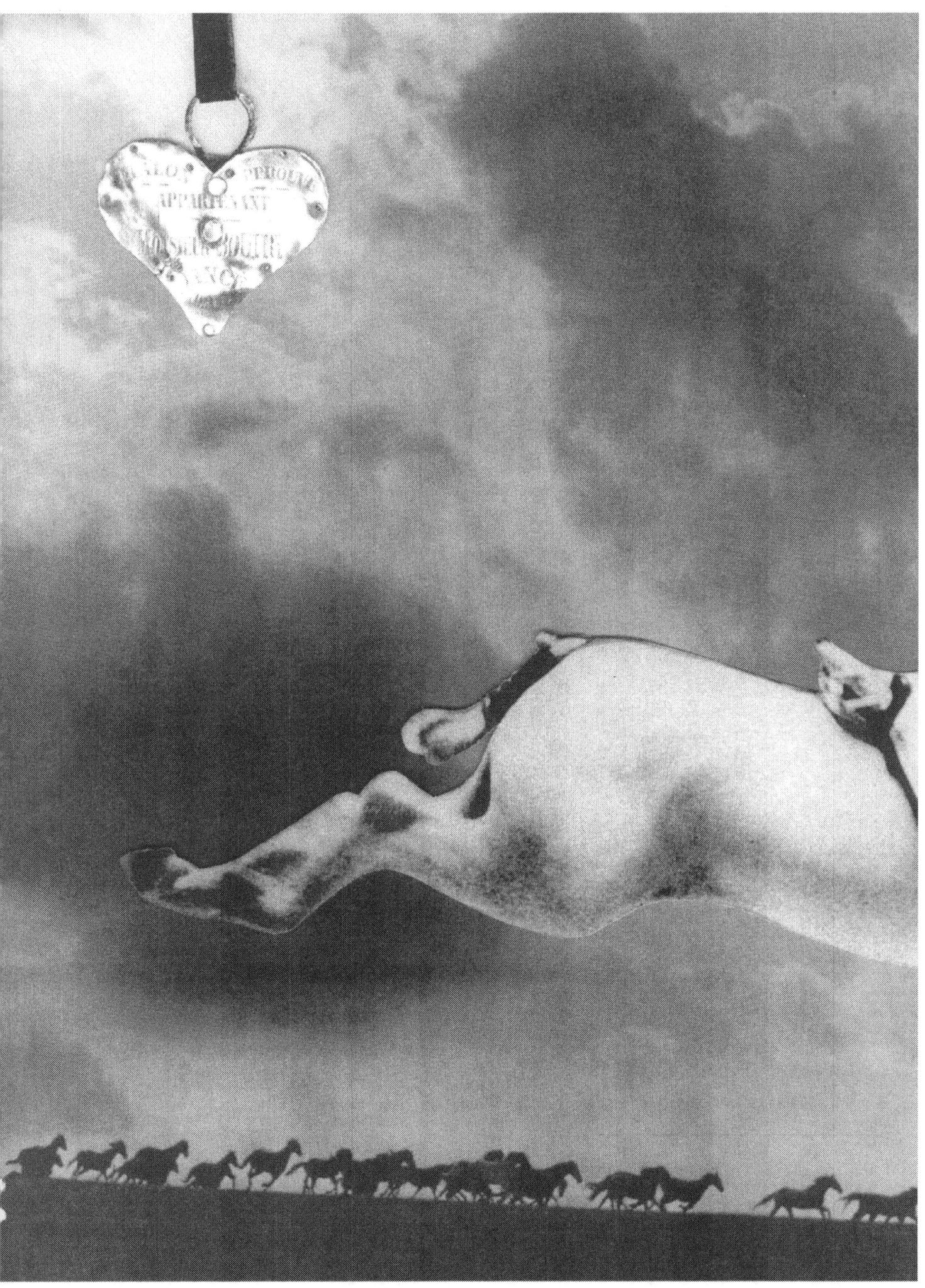

Hotel Pro Forma

Exposing Reality as a Visual Illusion

Erik Exe Christoffersen

The Danish theatre company Hotel Pro Forma is based in Copenhagen and under its director Kirsten Dehlholm has been making large-scale visual theatre events since 1986. Hotel Pro Forma is a hotel-like factory hall on Amager just outside Copenhagen where the theatre has its workshop, archives, costumes, depot, a kitchen and a library and meeting-room. Engaging in a nomadic dramaturgy between the moving theatre and the static exhibition, between role and fate, the theatre of Hotel Pro Forma is an exhibition that borrows aesthetics from the world of theatre and a theatre that uses the aesthetics of the exhibition in order to stage the gaze of the audience.

THE HOTEL

As implied by its name, Hotel Pro Forma is a theatre company whose point of departure is form and the formal. It is a theatre with no stage, no specific members and no repertory. But it is always in motion. It is the hotel as a *stage*. A temporary home in that foreign borderland where one is liberated from the pressure of social and psychological questions. The borderland is a *displacement* which is always off-balance, due to cultural shifts and discontinuities. In such borderlands the individual's culture, background and history dissolve. What is left is a figure, standing in an unknown context. Hotel Pro Forma is a nomadic stage in a land of possibilities, where one can lose one's sense of direction, context, social position and identity.

Hotel Pro Forma works with a coherent, recurring concept, which has been developed and tested through constantly changing forms and points of departure. The company's creative development, or change from one performance to another, is interesting not only as a historical development but also as a total oeuvre.

Hotel Pro Forma's restless scanning of various materials and shapes has one common theme – formal or existential boundaries. This means that a number of questions emerge. What is a staged representation? What kind of knowledge can be presented or represented? How is the process organized? What is the creative process, the relationship between producer, actor, set designer and spectator? Where does the process start? In this way it is the rediscovery of theatrical forms which is crucial. In her attempt to answer such questions Kirsten Dehlholm has attempted to redefine the actor, the use of text in theatre, the theatre space, the relationship between spectator and actor, dramaturgy and the identity of the artist.

Hotel Pro Forma has created a double staging: partly of the performance and the space, partly of the concept of theatre. The stage is no longer a clearly defined place, but a metaphor which can be established anywhere, even in a traditional theatre. This does not mean that everything is theatre but that the boundaries of the institution of theatre have been moved to new areas, framing not only the individual performances but the work as a whole in a constant delineation between art and non-art, theatre and non-theatre. A staging of the theatre concept where the theatre's framework, the building, the institution and the perception are all dislocated or displaced, could also be called a retheatricalization or ritualization of theatre, which seeks a basic form through reductionism or minimalism. This runs contrary to a traditional theatre, where the issue of credibility is connected with the actor's ability to enter into a spirit, where the actor represents and plays a part. With Hotel Pro Forma credibility is an inherent part of the concept. In order to achieve credibility it is necessary to create a precise form which catches the audience's sense of orientation and perception without leading to a strict interpretation. The place of enunciation is the 'hotel' as a metaphor, a stage, a temporary home in the unknown. It is a way of staging a void, which can open up for potential opportunities a haven in which one can play with identities, motives and dimensions.

BETWEEN BAROQUE AND ROMANTIC

Performances in non-theatre spaces – in a public swimming-bath, in an old railway station or on the roof of a supermarket – are familiar forms of artistic displacement. Here the background, the space, or the situation 'plays' along and influences 'the figure' or the way in which 'the figure' is experienced. The framework of the theatre visualizes itself as a stage-set. The relationship between figure and background or text and context is revisualized in Hotel Pro Forma. This creates uncertainty or disorientation in different ways. Placing something in unfamiliar surroundings, in a new context, may create an unusual way of seeing reality and a new form of understanding. The figure or the background changes character. The well-defined borders between them are dissolved. In the end, the relationship between work and framework, between theatre and non-theatre, is brought up for discussion, and eventually the relationship between life and death. The two worlds begin to merge in a peculiar way.

Hotel Pro Forma's first performance *Terra Australis Incognita* (1986) played in the hall of the National Museum in Copenhagen. It dealt with the idea of an unknown southern continent, shaped by the imagination and pictured somewhere between the heat of the equator and the ice of the North Pole. The need to discover new worlds was conceived in order to complement the well-known, the familiar. The audience had a bird's-eye view of the

• Hotel Pro Forma, *Why Does Night Come, Mother?*, 1988. Courtesy of Roberto Fortuna.

performance. The floor, which was the stage, was painted as a hierogram (a secret holy scripture) without any depth perspective. This initial use of the 'bird's-eye view' was further developed in *Why Does Night Come, Mother* (1988). The viewpoint of the audience was vertical instead of horizontal. It was first performed in the five-storey town-hall building in Århus, with the audience on the upper floors, around an inner well that cuts through the building. The audience looked down on to the performers on the floor, which served as the stage. It seemed as though gravity had been removed. The performers appeared to float in a void between life and death. In a fine example of double staging, the actors´ movements on the white floor became signs, patterns, icons with secret meanings. At the same time the placing of the spectators signified a staging of their viewpoint and sense of direction. As a sense of direction was lost, due to its dependence on the horizon and gravity, the disintegration of space set in and this made it possible for the audience to interpret the scene freely. It was like looking into a grave in which the dead were floating, as though they wanted to ascend towards the gaze of the spectators.

The 'figure – background' relationship is well known in psychology and geometry. An example is the ambivalent picture of the young woman/ toothless crone. One and the same picture, changing according to how the eye plays with the figure – background relationship. It is also well known that proportions, dimensions, colours and so on are decisive in the experience of the figure-background relationship. This is a basic principle in the so-called 'puzzle pictures' or visual illusions, which aim to trick the observer with their hidden writing. The same principle is used in '3-D' pictures, in which the two-dimensional image is changed to a completely different three-dimensional picture, when the observer represses the usual urge of the eye to focus. The sensory work (which could be called the *double view*) of the Rorschach test, in which a person observing form, colour, or rhythm in an image 'finds' a personal and unexpected meaning, provides a further example.

• Hotel Pro Forma, *Why Does Night Come, Mother?*, 1988. Courtesy of Roberto Fortuna.

In *Carpe Carpe Carpe* (1989), performed in a shipyard hall, a figure–background relation is created between children and texts, through complicated poems which the children have learned by heart, but which they do not understand. Consequently these texts are recited without interpretation. With the children as ´background´ the texts are given a new meaning and a new textuality as sound images, just as the children themselves are made more prominent by the adult quality of the text.

The Ship Called Bridge (1991) was created in connection with a carnival week in a small provincial town and performed on the roof of a warehouse in the town centre. Approximately 700 citizens participated in various activities: archery, motor-cycling, aerobic teams, dog-training and so on. These well-known but not usually visible activities were taken out of their original context on to the roof, where they were performed at unusual hours – at night, for instance – and combined in new ways, contrasting with each other and/or supplementing each other. The consequence was that these apparently purposeless activities took on a whole new meaning. They became mythical actions, like secret rites, choreographies and patterns or pictures revealing the hidden strangeness and mystery of the neighbouring activity. The actions and activities were associated with a new code so that they could be read or seen from a different viewpoint. The dramaturgical technique lay in *montage*, which removed things from their original context and transplanted them into a new context.

Central to Hotel Pro Forma's practice is a formal engagement with shapes and sense of direction or orientation which, among other things, is inspired by the principle of the earliest museums, the *Wunderkammer* or the 'cabinet of curiosities'. Here no distinction was made between nature and art. Items were collected and exhibited in a very peculiar order: minerals, fossils, animal skeletons, ethnographical items, crafts, sculptures, paintings and wonderful natural formations were all placed together. The idea was that there was a relationship between nature and art, the traces of which could be found when things were taken out of their usual functional contexts and placed together in new ways.

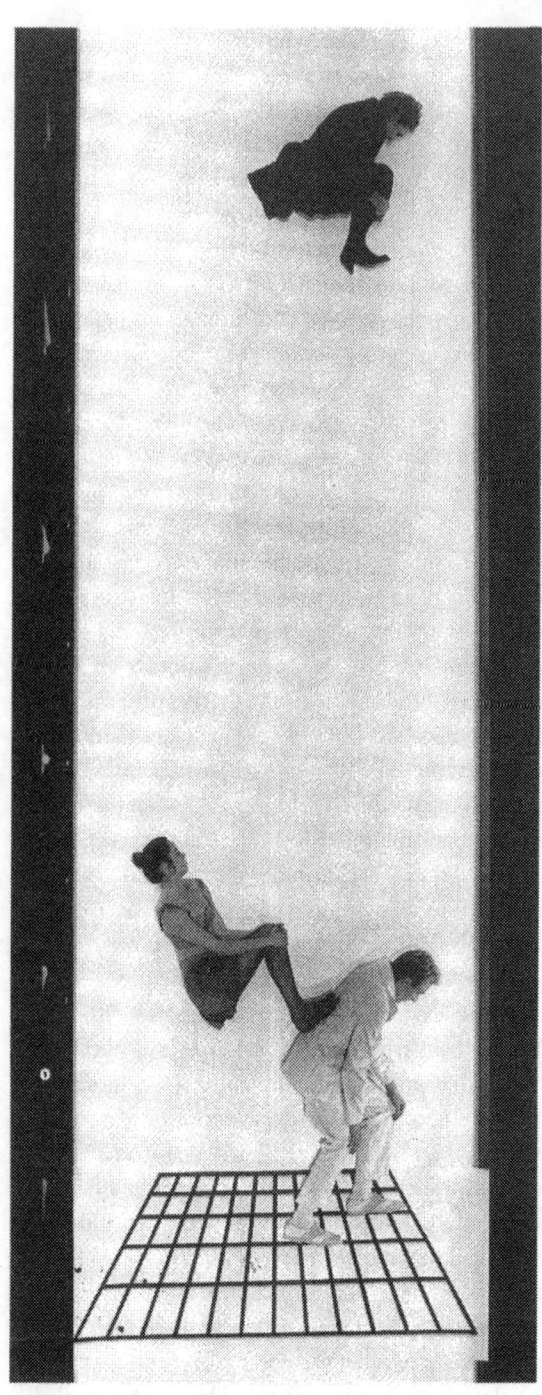

• Hotel Pro Forma, *Why Does Night Come, Mother?*, 1988. Courtesy of Roberto Fortuna.

Fact – arte – fact (1991) was a performance and an exhibition at the State Museum for Art in Copenhagen. It was an 'art treasure' which brought together human beings and strange objects, both displaced from their point of origin, without any explanatory text, but presented in a way that made the tableaux illuminate and contrast with each other. The performance dissected life and dissolved creation in an anatomical theatre which asked the questions: What is life? How is life created? How does life disintegrate? Can life be copied?

The performers were five pairs of identical twins – ranging from 7 to 67 years of age – presented or exhibited as supernatural phenomena, wonders, or creatures who touch the themes of authenticity or artificiality (genetic engineering), the unique or the copied. Typically one might associate twins with something sacred, divine, mythical in relation to creation itself, but also as something scary, disastrous – the double or the shadow from Hans Christian Andersen or Dostoevsky. The twins are both exhibited objects and living miracles. During the performance the audience was divided into two groups, walking in either direction in parallel rooms, able to see only half of the performance but able to hear it all.

The Shadow's Quadrant (1992) also used the vertical viewpoint, the 'bird´s-eye view'. The spectators were placed on balconies on two levels looking down on to a baroque garden characterized by geometrical constructions and mathematical patterns, which formed the principles of encounters or evasions. Twelve characters and two musicians populated the scene, all using different qualities of movement, which resulted in an authentic and specifically baroque choreography.

The text was concerned with four faculties which the gods steal from human beings: sleep, pain, memory and voice. Themes like geometry, passion, staging and 'the artificial' or 'the beautiful' were utilized to form an epic play about identity, fate, possibilities and shadows. Like a court audience the spectators become observers, the 'cognoscenti'. They can embrace the play with its knots, its staging of live components, each with his or her own specific allegorical characteristic: the one-legged man, the archer on stilts, the lame person, the hunchback, the singer, the dancer and so on.

Operation: Orfeo (1993) used the idea of an optical space able to function, due to the lighting, as a two-dimensional expanse, a flat wall, or a three-dimensional space, a deep staircase. The legend of Orpheus provided a familiar framework. In this performance opera, visual art, dance and architecture met in one great limbo, in which individual art forms are autonomous and appear simultaneously, merged without repeating each other and without linear narrative. *Operation: Orfeo* was installed itself in the classical Royal Theatre, Copenhagen. However, it was not a return to the institution of theatre as such but a staging of the theatre space which was being used as a form. The space has its own specific architecture with certain qualities and principles including a determined linear perspective.

Using a large white frame in front of a shiny white staircase with half-metre risers meant that the frontal viewpoint of the audience gave the impression of a never-ending staircase. The performers – a chorus, a solo dancer and a solo singer – were all situated on the staircase and appeared alternatively as individuals, a singing pattern, a relief, or a shadowland. The singers carried out a number of minimal actions, gestures, or movements while the dancer slowly glided down the staircase and later ascended again. They were all dressed in greyish black costumes and crowns reminiscent of imperial Japan or China.

The performance, like the legend of Orpheus, dealt with the transitory state between darkness and light, between life and death. This threshold was to be found in the construction of the set, where the contours of the staircase disappeared under certain lighting, making the figures seem as if they were floating on the wall, defying gravity. In a different light the contours of the staircase were sharp and the figures consequently grounded in the pictorial frame. The audience was partly sucked into this floating state and partly held by gravity. The visual composition of the performance was strictly graphic, arranged in accordance with geometrical changes rather than with narrative development. It was a precise range of pictures, like a story-board, forming a movement. Not a story but a movement.

In this sense the scenic concept was very similar to the tradition of classical Chinese or Japanese theatre. The set flats of Kabuki are movable in the same cinematic way, in relation to the precise physical actions of the figures. The entire performance reached its climax with green laser beams being transmitted from the staircase into the smoke-filled audience space. This created an undulating surface slowly rising like a floating sheet towards the ceiling, making the spectators sink to the bottom. The spectators were now travelling in limbo themselves, with an ocean of smoke above them as a borderland between this world and the kingdom of the dead.

The use of negation as a distinctive feature of Hotel Pro Forma´s working method is here very clear. The immediate starting-point is not the

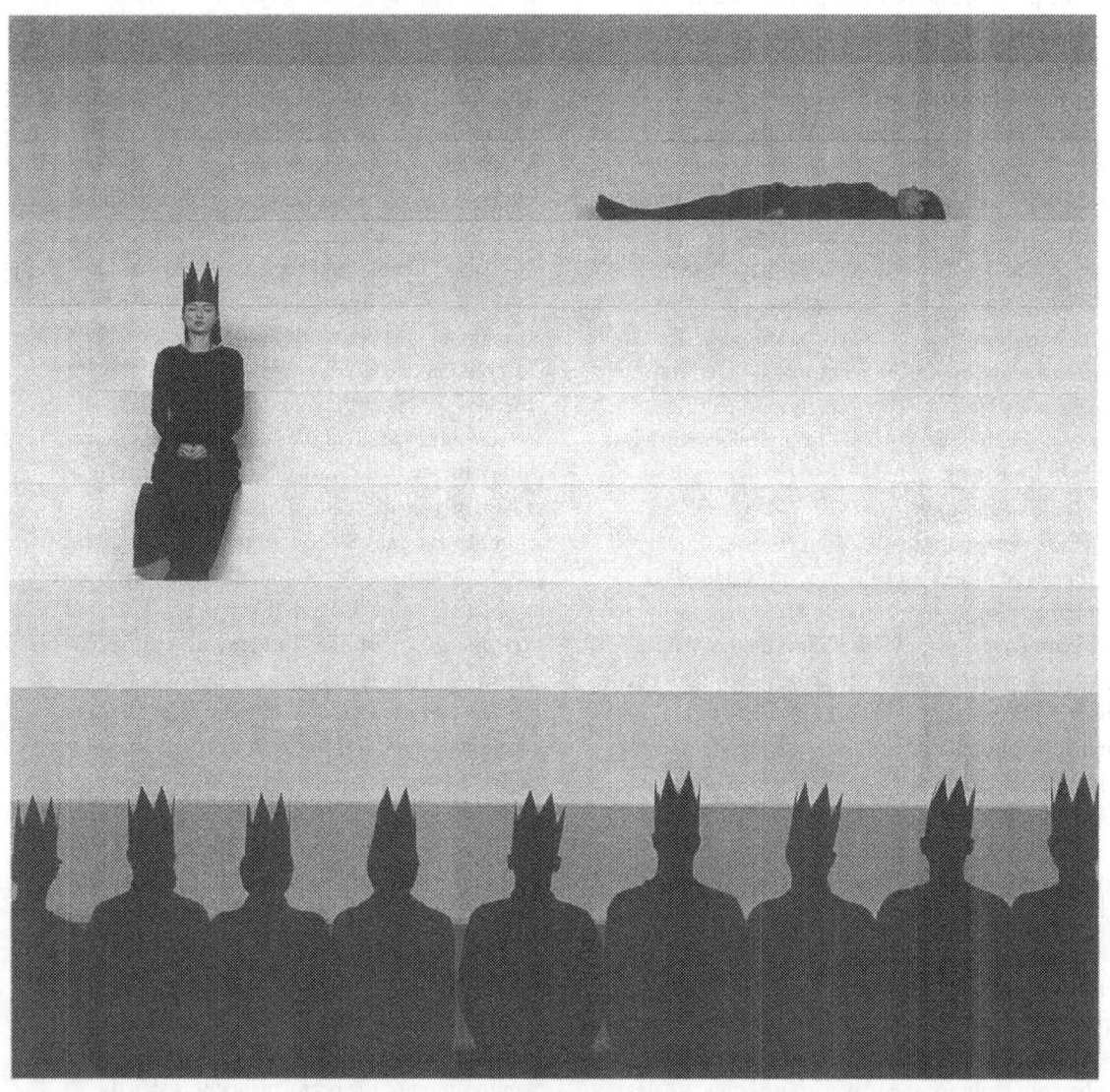

• Hotel Pro Forma, *Operation: Orfeo*, 1993. Courtesy of Roberto Fortuna.

desire to express something in particular, interpreting a legend or creating a specific subject-matter. On the contrary, the basis is the forms which are being compared and contrasted. These create a semantic void which the spectators can fill with their own meanings and readings by letting themselves be sucked into a concrete physical space created by the frame, the staircase, the movements of the chorus, the shifts of the light, the text and the music. There are no limits. There is only a limbo in which the possibility for the creation of new meanings may arise.

The play with the limits of the visual originates in the *trompe-l'œil*, and particularly the visual deception of the Baroque, in which the picture plane extends the architecture of the room, framing the sensed 'reality'. Such a technique consists of creating two different levels of reality in the picture. When one of them is depicted as fiction, something painted on a canvas and thus flat, the viewer is led

• Hotel Pro Forma, *Operation: Orfeo*, 1993. Courtesy of Roberto Fortuna.

to see the other level as three-dimensional reality. It is a fiction within a fiction, a play within a play. The level outside the fiction is identified as reality, even though it is a layer in the construction. *Trompe-l'œil* provides a reading of the relationship between art and the frame, and thus what is on the other side of the frame – a 'reality' which, on closer examination, turns out to be yet another fiction. When playing at the limits of art uncertainty is created about what is art and what is reality. *Trompe-l'œil* points to the fact that limits exist while at the same time being a fiction and a passage to another fiction. *Trompe-l'œil* provides a reading of the deception of the 'borderland' and the play of illusions.

A study of strangeness, *The Picture of Snow White* (1994) was performed at Kanonhallen (Copenhagen) and extended the theme of the format or the relation between figure and background. Eight dwarfs and two twins, two soldiers, an opera singer and a young woman were used as natural 'objects' situated in a borderland where the relation between figure and background is problematic, though not abnormal.

The twins reflected themselves in a mirror, both doubling themselves and developing a kind of narcissistic gaze. Quite the opposite happened to the dwarfs who were never reflected in their surroundings but were always observed by others. Actual dwarfs and twins were included in the performance, their differences, their mental and physical presence, their peculiarities, enabling them to represent 'the other'. They were used to being

• Hotel Pro Forma, *The Picture of Snow White*, 1994. Courtesy of Roberto Fortuna.

looked at as part of their existential being (like strangers, different races, celebrities, the disabled and so on); it was this quality of 'being' which was exhibited.

The performance however, was not a simple 'exhibition' of these dwarfs and twins. Its point was that 'the other' is a mirror, which in reality shows only yourself, and therefore the dwarfs and twins functioned as a mirror to an audience whose voyeurism was displayed. The performance dealt with the idea of being a 'format' (size/ measurement) and being a spectator. The actors' own thoughts about identity, fate and existence were very central. Dehlholm has persistently opposed the obvious interpretation of the story as a process of individuation concerning the integration of evil, innocent and emotional qualities (as we know, the colours of Snow White are black, white and red). In some senses the story was deconstructed by looking at the individual elements as exhibits: the individual dwarfs, the individual number, an object and a text; all of them single fragments which were only sporadically allowed to interact. Attention was focused on individual stories ('fates'), edited and played on a tape recorder. The actor-characters´ own lives were brought to the foreground and the fairy tale receded into the background. Usually it is the exact opposite in a performance. The private fate of the actor is more or less an unknown background to the fictive part.

The dwarfs were introduced one by one through an action or an object, with their own stories as

• Hotel Pro Forma, *The Picture of Snow White*, 1994. Courtesy of Roberto Fortuna.

recorded speech. The common feature of these stories is 'format' (size, what can be measured) as point of identity orientation. The stories of fate here become form or format and the played part becomes a copy. The continuing small stories or characteristics become universal. The dwarfs are formally different but turn into archetypes. They become metaphorical characters because they touch the 'childlike' and 'sacred' elements of the audience.

In contrast to the dwarfs' thoughts on physical size and their perspectives on the surrounding world, Snow White's way of orientating herself was more psychological. The actress told her own story, an identity parallel to that of Snow White's. The two hunters tell how they were trained to have an almost mathematical attitude to killing. They have been taught to separate life from death mechanically. The Queen and her reflection (the twins) describe their mutual relationship and their desperate need to find a difference between them. Letting the performers tell of their own worlds creates for the audience a kind of identificatory space, which changes the stories to statements about the human condition. This play between 'dwarf/child' and 'big/adult' was the focal point of the performance. Here an almost ritual play between identification and distance was established. Between figure and background, between normal and abnormal, between big and small, between mirror and reflection. It is the identity between fate and role: the geometry of existence as the enigma of format and reflection.

The enigma of beauty: Who is the most beautiful? How do we drift towards beauty? The Queen wishes to have her identity as the most beautiful woman confirmed by the mirror. She seeks the absolute, unchangeable answer to her identity. Only in the world of art does beauty exist as something unchangeable, fixed and immortal. Everything else in life is mortal, degradable, losing beauty. Only the dwarfs are able to let go of absolute beauty. The Queen is not, and as a consequence she murders Snow White. In the performance the dwarfs were subject to constant observation by the spectators, while Snow White took on the Queen's urge to see the immortality of her own beauty. In this crossing between mobility and constancy the performance ended, like a visual illusion. In some sense the mystery or ambivalence of life was represented in this deep, unnerving, unbearable, beautiful sound of silence.

The ambiguity and sensorial deception that helped stage the world optic of the Baroque is expressed in the theatre metaphor: *teatrum mundi*. The concept captures the unreal and the invisible in the cultural pattern. The face is a mask, behind which hides another mask in an infinite recession. The same thing goes for space, which apparently can be limited only in perspective and which turns out to be a side scene hiding a new room in a labyrinthine order. Acting is a play for the eyes, an optical illusion in which only differences and outlines create a limited reality. *Teatrum mundi,* then, points to the fact that reality is not a given and can be experienced only through the staging of the theatre. The world is, so to speak, framed like a theatre.

Dust (Wau!) Støv (1995) was staged as a baroque-drama, a *teatrum mundi*, with two actors and various voices; for instance, twins and dwarfs. In a special, rhythmic, chanting way various texts, omens, proverbs and horror stories were recited; for example: 'If one goes away and has said goodbye, one must not turn around and look back, it brings bad luck on the journey'; 'If for fun, one puts a child outside a window and pulls it in through another window, the child will never grow bigger'; 'A witch can be recognized by always looking people straight in the eyes'.

The lovers in the performance, He and She, sang and spoke a text written by Christina Hesselholdt. The two lovers could be Hamlet and Ophelia, Othello and Desdemona, Romeo and Juliet, seeking to interpret their experiences and sensations in relation to the world which they themselves create and are a part of. Shakespeare is the unsurpassed master of creating a scene for the play of illusions and sense illusions. Is the phantom in *Hamlet* a real one or a sense illusion? Is the love of Othello and Desdemona false or real? Are the twins in *Twelfth Night* delusions or reflections of each other? Everywhere Shakespeare creates doubt, because he incorporates a theatre metaphor, a game, reflecting the story. This reflection is once again reflected in the performance situation, becoming a hall of mirrors – reflection upon reflection in an infinite process.

The audience for *Dust (Wau!) Støv* was placed in the cinema at the Copenhagen Planetarium, where the stage is a 1,000-square-metres arched dome reaching from floor to ceiling. The performance consisted of 70 mm omnimax film and ordinary film as well as texts projected on to the screen. There were taped voices and two actors, showing up in different places behind the big screen in small rooms outlined by light, in which they both spoke and sang. At the same time a film was being shown

• Hotel Pro Forma, Planetarium project, *Dust (Wau!) Støv*, 1995. Courtesy of Roberto Fortuna.

on the rest of the screen. Sometimes abstract pictures, patterns and movements, sometimes recognizable pictures such as a chair, a veil, a room, or a shoe being enlarged. The two characters were in a changing picture universe, a theatrical frame around human existence. The performance had nine parts – the nine lives of the cat. The text explored the idea of being shaped: moving from the body as prison, the home, the hug, death, lust, the storm, the blue, between ocean and sky, to the heavy sleep, which threatened to paralyse her: 'It seems as if my one hand becomes enormous. I cannot move, let alone lift it. The hand is an anchor, tying me to the bed. I have to struggle to get loose. I have to struggle to get loose.' The 'I' of the text struggles between form and formlessness in a boundless universe. Confronted with dissolution the performance all the time sought the formed, the limited, the safe. But over and over again the limit turned out to be fiction. Certainty is given only in the shape of omens and lessons.

The stage is a theatre (a world of illusions), in which signs, omens, questions and phrases both help to create this world and, conversely, make it possible to understand it. The baroque drama has to involve the audience in this infinite process of interpretation. The audience is situated at the origin of the theatre, the pre-expressive stage, the beginning, when nothing is what it may later become. The audience is placed in the room of creation. The place where interpretation can be moved. The audience is part of the physically sensuous illusion of the theatre and practically surrounded by this world theatre both visually and acoustically.

For the audience the sudden sensation in the stomach feels as if one is riding in a lift, or as if the figures are moving even though one knows that they are standing still. It is like a dream. And one wakes up in a previous dream. Or is one still in another person's dream? Someone once said to me: 'You have not awoken to a waking condition, but to a previous dream. This dream is within somebody else and so forth, infinitely ...'

The audience was staged physically not from a bird's-eye view but from a wide-angle worm's-eye view. But the view of the audience was changed by means of optical illusion. That was probably the most unique function and surprise of the performance: that the body (the stomach, the sense of equilibrium) believed this *trompe-l'œil*, which could make one just as sick as a real roller-coaster. Sense illusions work in defiance of our conscious ability to understand what is happening.

On the stage, for instance, two performers were seen, illuminated through the big film screen which showed a measuring device for longitude and latitude. If the eye focused on the vertical axis the horizontal axis moved. However, if the eye focused on the horizontal axis the vertical one moved and the two illuminated figures moved with it, as if they were standing in a lift. After a short while the spectators felt as if they too were moving upwards. And it was almost impossible to stop this sense illusion.

Dust (Wau!) Støv explored this double field of art as a sensuous object, which must be seen from some viewpoint in order to become art. Hotel Pro Forma's work on the construction of the authentic exhibits sensation itself as real and unreal, as between physical and metaphysical, between reality and sense illusions. At the same time it exhibits the place from where we sense as a place in movement. Sensation becomes a relative phenomenon, which we try to systematize to avoid bad luck, illness and death, in the same way as we try to systematize rules for beauty, art and the divine. Without yet having succeeded.

In a way it is also about art as representation. In Hotel Pro Forma there is a wish for a pure art, representing nothing else but itself. An art which touches the senses without trying to determine meaning. An art, in the words of Antonin Artaud, that is 'cruel' in touching life before language. The theatre metaphor creates a hall of mirrors, where figure and ground no longer let themselves be deciphered, and where no one knows where the original is. Here it is the dissolution of the audience (to dust) that one looks in the eye, like Orpheus who turned to Eurydice and saw himself as a picture, dissolving and disappearing.

NOMADIC DRAMATURGY

The dramaturgy of Hotel Pro Forma seeks or re-creates reality as comparison, juxtaposition and isolation, uncovering, wrapping and exhibition of early and spatial shapes: not through the continuity of the story but through discontinuity. It is not a dramaturgy of the line but of the jump, not one story but parallel stories between baroque tendencies towards stagings of space and romantic longing for the indestructibility and formalization of time as beauty. It is the dramaturgy of restlessness or of the nomad somewhere between movement and being, format and identity. As a nomadic theatre it has chosen to be in motion and, thus, sees reality from different points of view, contrary to the settled, who sees the world from home and, thus, structures the world with the home as the centre. The nomad has no such centre, but perceives the world as differences, distances, proportions, points of view and therefore develops a phenomenal sense of direction and an ability to find his or her way in the visible and invisible spatiality, in proportion to light and darkness, depth structure and flat, movement and stagnation, distance and nearness, figure and ground. Nomads do not allow themselves to get confused by 'optical illusions' or sense illusions (*trompe-l'œil*) as a natural effect of, for instance, the *fata morganas* of the desert or of the snowscape. The illusion is part of reality.

• Hotel Pro Forma, Planetarium project, *Dust (Wau!) Støv*, 1995. Courtesy of Roberto Fortuna.

The Ear of Man Hath Not Seen

Nicholas Till

Reflections on performances of Varèse's *Déserts* with accompanying film by Bill Viola (Ensemble Modern, Queen Elizabeth Hall, February 1996) and Schubert's *Winterreise* staged by Christian Boltanski and Jean Kalman (Opéra-Comique at the Lyric Theatre, Hammersmith, March 1996)

> The eye of man hath not heard, the ear of man hath not seen, man's hand is not able to taste, his tongue to conceive, nor his heart to report what my dream was.
> (*A Midsummer Night's Dream*, Act IV, scene i)

Does Bottom convey confusion or wisdom? Do we sneer at his synaesthetic muddle? Or perhaps, as would romantics and symbolists, do we share his regret? Or do we, like the neo-classical or modernist critic, approve of those bounds to perception and communication?

We could simply point out that Bottom is wrong. Our primary experience of the world is synaesthetic, and artists know well how the senses colour and inflect one another. Stravinsky once reported that to experience his music set to dance was 'to hear the music with one's own eyes' (Taper 1987: 258). How would we know what to feel when gazing at the shapes and shadows of the film and TV screen were it not for the suggestive promptings of sound and music?

Artists have often argued for the greater plenitude of experience offered by the arts in combination. For Wagner that plenitude had once existed in Greek drama, and the art form most impoverished by the subsequent fragmentation of art into separate disciplines was, for Wagner, music. What music lacked could be restored only by reuniting it with narrative, movement and spectacle in the *Gesamtkunstwerk*. Wagnerian music dramas were to their creator 'acts of music made visible' (Willsdon 1996: 61).

Who could blame either Brecht or modernists such as Greenberg and Adorno for their violent reaction against the Wagnerian wedding of music and spectacle after the experience of both fascism and Hollywood? It may well be that institutional arguments for maintaining the specificity of art forms need challenging. But the modernist insistence upon the integrity of media, or Brecht's demand that where media are combined they must retain their critical autonomy in relation to each other, is moral and political.

These arguments are founded upon false premises, however. For regarded phenomenologically music is primarily synaesthetic: an embodied mode of production, as Roland Barthes never ceased to remind us, communicated visually as well as aurally. Only a culture that had suppressed the originating embodiment of music could argue for the morality of preserving its autonomy as pure sound, or suggest that music's supposed lack needs to be supplemented by spectacle or discourse.

If 'the ear hath not seen' it is because it has been trained not to do so. In western culture every effort is made to deny the physical embodiment of music (and hence also the social context of its production and reception). Wagner banished his orchestral musicians to their own Nibelheim under a hooded pit at Bayreuth. And when it is unavoidably visible the western classical orchestra is represented as a smooth-running machine. Its working parts are regimented in anonymous uniforms, powered by a conductor, an appellation which reminds us of the role's dual function as guide for the performers and transmitter of the originating impulse of the absent composer (represented by the musical score, ever visible like the word of God upon the church lectern).

More recently classical performers have adopted a token rhetoric of informality. But their studied casualness of platform manner simply affirms that, since we are supposed to be listening and not looking, we should ignore the non-musical evidence of the performer's presence in favour of the music being performed. It took John Cage to recognize that the 'theatricality' of a horn-player draining the dribble from his valves might be as interesting as the melody he had just played (Cage 1965: 50) and thence to foreground the physical rituals of performance in so many of his works.

The disembodiment of music is justified intellectually by the aesthetics of absolute music, or music as pure form – an ethereal emanation of the spirit, free of matter, as Goethe and Hegel perceived it (Vergo 1994: 131). For those who promote an exclusively aesthetic attitude to art, music becomes in this guise the paradigmatic art form.

The 'idea of absolute music' (Dalhaus 1989) is an ideology of absolute music. If music is to be commodified it must be freed from the limitations of time and space imposed by physical performance so that it can be circulated more widely in the form of printed or, in this century, recorded music. Disembodied and torn away from its social context, printed music on the page reifies music, privileging its formal properties. Where eighteenth-century theorists examined the 'affect' of music on the listener, nineteenth-century musicologists developed a language of abstract structural analysis. Performance is repositioned as a predicate: interpretation. Or more often it is spectacularized in the eroticization of the performer's extra-musical attributes. In the age of recorded music fetishized performance becomes a supplement for music's self-inflicted lack. Jacques Attali, in his critique of the political economy of music, sees this process as 'illustrative of the evolution of our entire society: deritualize a social form, generalize its consumption, then see to it that it is stockpiled until it loses its meaning' (Attali 1985: 5).

And so we find ourselves back with the medieval neo-Pythagorian Boethius, who argued that *musica instrumentalis*, music produced by human beings, is but an ephemeral echo of the eternal, cosmic music of the spheres; *parole* to the *langue* of the musical score that stands behind and before it, as Saussure so misleadingly suggested (Durant 1984: 74).

Was Roland Barthes's regret for the decline of *musica practica*, music known to us through physical engagement as performers rather than as passive consumers (Barthes 1977: 149–54), anything other than sentimental? In their response to music by Varèse and Schubert, Bill Viola and Christian Boltanski suggest a different solution for the erasure of meaning brought about by the spectacularization of music: the recuperation of meaning through visual commentary.

Edgar Varèse's *Déserts* was written between 1950 and 1955. Varèse was pioneer in a number of areas of twentieth-century music: the exploration of rhythm and timbre; the use of non-musical instruments; and experiments in electro-acoustic music. *Déserts* is a late work which combines instrumental performance and taped electronic music.

Varèse's preoccupation with the density, texture and spatial extension of sound was experienced by many musicians in the middle years of this century as a 'liberation of sound' even more radical than Schoenberg's more notorious 'emancipation of dissonance' (Quellette 1973: 47). Yet although Varèse renewed awareness of the material physicality and spatial extension of music, revealing what he described as a 'third dimension' in music (ibid.: 84) his experiments remain predominantly acoustic. Retaining a mentalist concept of music, he borrowed a phrase from the musicologist Hoène Wronsky to describe music as 'the corporealization of the intelligence in sound' (ibid.: 17).

Déserts evokes not simply physical wildernesses, but also the boundless inner spaces of the human mind. Varèse had always been interested in the relationship between film and sound, working on projects with both Miro and Léger, and he hoped that *Déserts* might be accompanied by a film, which was never made. Enter Bill Viola, who has repeatedly explored visual images of the desert as a metaphor for states of human consciousness, and who brings a musical sensibility to the structure and texture of his video works.

Viola's work is, in his own words, synaesthetic, reaching for a blurring of sensory experience through which a more holistic relation of inner and outer world may be intimated (Viola 1995: 164). Viola's film *Déserts* is sensitive to the formal structure of Varèse's score, which alternates between austere instrumental passages in which humanly produced sound strains to emerge from the silence, and electronically treated echoes of distant industrial machinery. Viola disclaims any intention to 'illustrate' Varèse's music (ibid.: 263). But cutting in conjunction with Varèse's score between parched images of nature straining to materialize from video snow and burr and a developing sequence in which a solitary human figure sits at table in an empty room, he creates a narrative in which the dualisms of inside/outside, mind/world are finally transcended when the floor of the room dissolves to become a deep pool of water into which the room's occupant plunges.

Despite Viola's intention of creating a parallel mosaic of evocative images to Varèse's score, it remains almost impossible for us to maintain the fiction of complementary events. With the performers in darkness to allow Viola's images to be visible, the music is forced back into the Wagnerian subliminal. As Lawrence Kramer has suggested of the relationship of sound to image in film, 'music connects us to the spectacle on screen by invoking a dimension of depth, of interiority', serving as an essential supplement for the lack of space and texture in the film image (Kramer 1995: 112). Viola's film sucks sound into its own spatial vacuum so completely that the materiality of Varèse's music is negated. Moreover, it becomes increasingly difficult not to privilege the visual as soon as a narrative element is introduced, as Viola does here.

By contrast Christian Boltanski brings a post-modernist disjunction of forms to his staging of Schubert's *Winterreise*. Here the structure of Schubert's cycle is a sequence of discrete songs linked by an implied narrative – the winter journey of the title. The lover leaves his faithless mistress and journeys away from the city which has rejected him. In fact, it is no sort of journey, but an obsessive circling around the lost loved one. The once benign natural world is now alienated, presenting itself to the wanderer as a series of signs pointing inexorably back to the moments of happiness. The poet wanderer's only escape is to take control of the relentless signifying process in song itself.

Boltanski places his singer and pianist at the centre of the stage, and gathers around them a series of acts and events which make no attempt to acknowledge the structure of Schubert's formal sequence of songs, and illustrates its outer narrative only in the sporadic projection of a view through a moving railway carriage window of a featureless landscape. Randomly, two men and a girl carry out a series of tasks. Suitcases are carried on and off; the girl is bundled down a trap in the floor. The suitcases proliferate until the stage is full. They are opened, and clothes and possessions tumble out.

Boltanski's reflections on memory, displacement and identity inevitably recall images of the Holocaust. Boltanski has recognized that the romantic quest represented in the German *lied* is also the quest for metaphysical certainty in which nineteenth-century German artists were so absorbed, a dislocation at two removes of the need for a transcendent cultural identity outside the contingencies of history and geography. Boltanski intimates that the totalizing forms of political, social and cultural expression to which that need gave rise resulted in the fascist state and its far more violent dislocations of identity and memory.

Boltanski provides a perceptive historical commentary upon Schubert's romantic journey. But the complexities of the relationship between singer and song, text and role, time present and time narrated are ignored in the process. 'What, then, is this body which sings the *lied* ?' asked Barthes in another of his reflections on music (Barthes 1986: 289), the very question which had led Rimbaud to formulate one of the key statements of the alienated modern consciousness: 'A song [is seldom] a thought sung and comprehended by the singer. For I is someone else' ['Je est un autre'] (Rimbaud 1966: 305). The romantic song problematizes the construction of subjectivities. The narrative position switches, sometimes within one song, between the singing voice of the subject, characters within the narrative, the person addressed, and the implied voice of author/composer. By adding a visual commentary to the performance of *Winterreise*, Boltanski underestimates the inherent complexities of song. Remaining intact in the midst of Boltanski's fragmentary discourse around the songs they are performing, singer and pianist are endowed with a spurious integrity in which embodiment is reinscribed as unproblematic subjectivity.

Against the spectacularization of music and the emptying of meaning we should reaffirm the connection between embodiment and meaning. Musical meaning resides neither in intention nor interpretation, nor does it precede or circumnavigate embodied performance. We need not be compromised by nostalgia for the metaphysics of presence, or fear the dispersal of desire in the quest for meaning, if we remind ourselves that musical performance is a richly complex discursive field in its own right.

REFERENCES

Attali, Jacques (1985) *Noise, the Political Economy of Music*, Manchester: Manchester University Press.

Barthes, Roland (1977) 'Music practice', in *Image Music Text*, trans. Stephen Heath, London: Fontana.

——(1986) 'The romantic song', in *The Responsibility of Forms: critical essays on music, art and representation*, Oxford: Basil Blackwell.

Cage, John (1965) 'Interview', *TDR* 10 (2): 50–72.

Dalhaus, Carl (1989) *The Idea of Absolute Music*, trans. Roger Lustig, Chicago and London: University of Chicago Press.

Durant, Alan (1984) *Conditions of Music*, London: Macmillan.

Kramer, Lawrence (1995) *Classical Music and Postmodern Knowledge*, Berkeley, CA and London: University of California Press.

Quellette, Fernard (1973) *Edgar Varèse*, London: Calder & Boyars.

Rimbaud, Arthur (1966) *Complete Works: selected letters of Rimbaud*, trans. Wallace Fowlie, Chicago and London: University of Chicago Press.

Taper, Bernard (1987) *Balanchine, a Biography*, Berkeley: University of California Press.

Vergo, Peter (1994) 'Music and the visual arts', in Keith Hartley *et al.* (eds) *The Romantic Spirit in German Art*, London: South Bank Centre.

Viola, Bill (1995) *Reasons for Knocking at an Empty House: Writings 1973–1994*, London: Thames & Hudson.

Willsdon, Clare A. P. (1996) 'Klimt's Beethoven frieze: Goethe, *Templekunst* and the fulfilment of wishes', *Art and History* 19: 1.

Five Microlectures

Matthew Goulish

The following five 'microlectures' were delivered by Matthew Goulish of Chicago-based theatre company Goat Island on the morning of 13 April 1996 as part of 'Performance Writing: An Interdisciplinary Symposium' held at Dartington, UK and organised by Writing Research Associates in association with Dartington College of Arts. Further information on Performance Writing is available at the following web-site: http://www.ex.ac.uk/Dartington/Performance_Writing/perf_writing.home.html

INTRODUCTORY REMARKS

I will not be discussing performance writing – at least not directly. Instead, through the exploration of related concepts, I will try to approach performance writing through a kind of indirect process of encirclement. This method perhaps reflects my position in Goat Island as a performer and a

• *How Dear to Me the Hour When Daylight Dies*, Goat Island, 1996. Photo: Alan Crumlish.

collaborator, and not specifically a writer. It also hopefully reflects in part the process of Goat Island – a process which values the considered response no more than and no less than the seemingly unrelated distraction or the simple mistake.

In his poem *The Golden Boat* the Bengali writer Rabindranath Tagore tells the story of a poor field labourer who at harvest time loads all his crops on to a boat, and then asks the boat's driver if he himself may also board. But now filled with his crops, the boat has no more room for him, and the farmer sits alone in his empty field as the boat sails away up the river. 'I have nothing,' he says, 'the golden boat has taken all.'

Please think of these microlectures as this farmer's crops, and be reassured that the golden boat of time will carry each one away in less than five minutes.

MICROLECTURE 1: A MISUNDERSTANDING

A few years ago, a producer whose name was Rollo made a special trip to see a performance of Goat Island's piece *It's Shifting, Hank* (1993) Afterwards he wanted to give us his reaction, and I was elected to talk to him. I can summarize the conversation now as follows:

> Rollo said: 'What is the reason for all this repetition?'
> And I said: 'What repetition?'

Although at the moment I had no idea what he meant, I did sense that a significant insight lay somewhere at the heart of our misunderstanding.

Take, for example, the process of memorizing an alphabet. Is the act of recitation repetitious? One says one letter, and then another, and then another. But if all the letters are different, one could say there is no repetition. It is only at the point where a letter returns, and we recognize its return, that familiarity has occurred. But is even that a repetition? Perhaps the letter returns changed by time and events, altered by the nature of the intervening letters. At this point, can we say that there has been an occurrence of music?

To state the problem: what some see as a single moment repeating, others see as a non-repeating series of similar moments. The difference in perception indicates not only how closely one is prepared to examine any given moment, but also a basic difference in philosophy. As John Cage said in his 'Lecture on nothing', 'Repetition is only repetition if we feel that we own it' (1968). To restate the problem: does one see the repeating/non-repeating moment as occurring *inside of* or *outside of* a language? Because with his invocation of *ownership*, Cage perhaps refers not only to possession, but also to understanding, recognition, and especially familiarity. An authority on dance, whom we may refer to as an informed viewer, upon seeing a dancer perform two similar moves, may conclude, 'The dancer repeated the step.' One who is ignorant of dance and claims no ownership of its language, whom we may refer to as an ecstatic viewer, at this same moment might say, 'The dancer performed two similar movements – the first in one place in the room, the second a little later in a different place in the room.' The differences observed by the second viewer might seem so insignificant to the first viewer that he chose to ignore them altogether, concentrating instead on the larger patterns which conform to the language of dance which he feels he owns.

At this point we must question the dancer's intention. A creative artist, just like a creative audience member, may function as informed or as ecstatic, or may switch back and forth at varying moments of the performance. But if the artist's intention is to step outside of the language to the extent that such an action is possible, and to function creatively as an ecstatic over a sustained period of time, then no difference between two moments is insignificant. Stepping outside of familiar languages requires an attempt not only to generate a new language, but also to reinvent the very notion of familiarity.

The Scottish composer James MacMillan once described his style as the repetition of ideas of deliberate limitation. Through the course of the composition these elements either remain constant or gradually, integrally transform, depending on their nature. MacMillan, a spiritual composer, has related this process, in content and structure, to religious ritual. For the purposes of this series of microlectures, I will relate it to a different ritual, maybe a meta-ritual, between the performance and the audience. Processes of repetition and differentiation, of microelements combining and recombining to generate familiarities, lead us into a ritual of the possible occurrence of learning.

MICROLECTURE 2: LEARNING TO READ

In her novel *Summer Rain*, Marguerite Duras told the story of Ernesto, the oldest of the children of a suburban family of Italian immigrants living in France (1992: 6–10, 138). Ernesto left the school in the middle of his first lesson and refused ever to return. Later a series of events transpired in which he learned how to read.

Ernesto must have been between 12 and 20 years old. Just as he didn't know how to read, so he didn't know his own age.

In the space under the ground floor of a nearby house, a kind of shed that the people who lived there left open for the children – there, by the central heating pipes under some rubble, the smallest of the brothers found the book. He took it to Ernesto, who looked at it for a long time. It was a very thick book bound in black leather, and a hole had been burned right through it by what must have been some terribly powerful implement like a blowtorch or a red-hot iron bar. The hole was perfectly circular, and around it the rest of the book was unscathed, so it must have been possible to read what remained of each page. The children had never seen a book so cruelly treated before. The youngest brothers and sisters cried.

In the days that followed, Ernesto entered a period of silence. He would stay in the shed all afternoon, alone with the burned book.

At that point in his life Ernesto was supposed not to be able to read, but he said he'd read some of the burned book. Just like that, he said, without thinking about it, without even knowing what he was doing. And then he stopped bothering with whether he was really reading or not, or even what reading was – whether it was this or something else. At first, he said, he'd tried like this: he took the shape of a word and arbitrarily gave it a provisional meaning. Then he gave the next word another meaning, but in terms of the assumed provisional meaning of the first word. And he went on like that until the whole sentence yielded some sense. In this way he came to see that reading was a kind of continuous unfolding within his own body of a story invented by himself. And thus it seemed to him that the book was about a king who reigned in a country far away. The king was a foreigner, a very long time ago, and he spoke of chasing the wind.

Ernesto told his brothers and sisters, who said to him:

'How could you have read it, stupid, when you don't know how?'

Ernesto agreed: he didn't know how he could have read the book without knowing how to read.

He took the book to a teacher who had university degrees and a definite age: 38. The teacher said that it was a story about a king.

MICROLECTURE 3: W

This fragment of Duras's *Summer Rain* concerns our problem of learning and repetition in two ways. First, it blurs the distinction between the ecstatic and the informed: Ernesto's private invented story yields the 'correct' meaning as confirmed by the teacher, but it also yields something more – the sense that the words not only mean, but also live, and effect an irreversible change on the reader. Second, the story introduces a conduit between the words and their meaning. The conduit is the body – Ernesto's body, as he comes to see reading as 'a continuous unfolding within his own body' – and also the body of the book itself, burned, damaged, and scarred. Our dialectics of repetition and non-repetition, of ecstatic and informed have begun to be replaced by a different set of concepts yielding even more possibilities: the encounter between reader and book – the interaction of the internal differences of reader and book – through a discovered ritual of learning, initiates a momentary becoming, as reader becomes book and book becomes reader – and afterwards the internal differences have changed both, through an unfolding.

I remember as a child forming a personal relationship with the alphabet one letter at a time. I had twenty-six flashcards, and one by one I'd memorize the name of the letter on each card. A B C formed the simple first triad, D E F the almost as simple second. G was the first letter of my last name, although for some reason it always reminded me of my father. Since the most dynamic and flashy characters seemed crowded at the end, I'd work backwards at times from Z Y and X – a triad so exotic its members rarely, I was told, appeared in words at all. As a memorization device for each letter presented itself, the seemingly infinite catalogue of symbols grew smaller and more manageable, and began to collect meanings, my own invented meanings as well as those apparently shared by the rest of English-speaking America.

Over the course of my learning, a pattern emerged. The names of the letters always resembled their sounds as they occurred in a word. The letter T was called T because it made a T sound, as in CAT or HAT. The letters Q and U almost always appeared together and made Q and U sounds as in QUIET or QUIT. But suddenly I encountered the problem of W.

This letter not only defied explanation, but it also presented myriad contradictions. Why was it called W? It made the sound *wah*, not the sound W. W wasn't even a sound, it was a description of the way the letter looked. If we were going to call this one W, why not call it instead *double v*? Why not call it *M upside-down*? For that matter why not call X *two crossed lines*, or O *circle*? W contradicted the pattern. Furthermore, it was the *only* letter which contradicted the pattern. Thus I found it impossible to remember.

As I stared at the flashcard W, I knew that a problem had arisen for which logic and reason provided no solution. Three choices presented themselves. I could rename W in an attempt to bring it more in line with the other letters. This was the pedantic option. I could initiate a lifelong boycott of W, and all words containing it, to protest the inconsistency. This was the rebellious option.

The third choice was the most practical, but also the most frightening. I could accept W, and change myself. I could alter my notion of the alphabet. After all, what value is there in relentless consistency? Isn't the alphabet more interesting with one letter that refuses to conform to the pattern of the other twenty-five? I could go on building words, and one day even sentences and paragraphs, using W as though it were just another letter, but all the time remembering its difference. An unfolding took place inside my body. I knew then that the third choice was the road that lay ahead for me, and also I had some inkling of its consequences. I must become W.

MICROLECTURE 4: PROLIFERATION AND SUFFERING

What we call learning is a process through which signs change, subject becomes object, and truth unseparates from the reality to which it refers. What we call learning may arise through a process of repetition. What we call repetition presents an instability of differences. What we call repetition presents a permeability of identities. The individual meets the collective. A repetition that touches its limit may constitute a learning. A repetition that surpasses its limit may produce a proliferation. Proliferations always threaten order. Proliferations we find in the worlds of plants, insects, geology, the subatomic universe, the sea. But among the world of humans in the twentieth century, the exemplary limitlessness has been the capacity for cruelty, for destruction, for the proliferation of suffering.

Masuji Ibuse wrote in his non-fiction novel *Black Rain* of how Mrs Iwataki searched Hiroshima for her husband, 8 August 1945, two days after the atomic blast. Mrs Iwataki's recollection:

> I went straight to the hospital.
>
> Actually it was the national elementary school building, and when a sergeant who seemed to be acting as an orderly took us into the classroom we found that every inch of the floor was covered with the injured. I had no idea where my husband was. The soldier who looked like an orderly called, 'Medical Reservist Iwataki! Where are you?' So I called out too, 'Hiroshi! Are you here, Hiroshi?' Something seemed to grip my chest. It was difficult to breathe. There was no reply.
>
> Then I saw a hand raised feebly. His face was swollen to twice its normal size, and his right ear was covered with gauze.
>
> One thing struck me as strange – when one patient groaned all the others would start groaning at the same time. It was an uncanny sound. Perhaps I shouldn't say it. But it was for all the world like a chorus of frogs starting up in a paddy field.
>
> (Ibuse and Bester 1971: 255, 259)

MICROLECTURE 5: MULTIPLICITY

Between repetition and proliferation, there remains a third phenomenon. It is perhaps the most pertinent phenomenon to my misunderstanding with Rollo, as stated in the first microlecture of this series. I will try to approach it through three examples.

Example No. 1: in 1963, American composer Morton Feldman wrote a piece of music which he dedicated to his friend and fellow composer Christian Wolff. The composition might be described as two or three instruments playing two or three notes very softly for two or three hours. When listening to it, some hear repetition, others hear difference – a phenomenon possible only through the composition's severe limitations. Christian Wolff, when asked why Feldman had dedicated the piece to him, had this to say about it:

> I think what Feldman had in mind was – he'd been to Cambridge twice when I was there. The first time he met me, he came into my room. I was staying in one of the Harvard dormitories, in an old-fashioned building, old-fashioned room with a very high ceiling. And I was sitting at a desk with books all around, and my nose – I'm short-sighted – my nose very close to the paper. And he came in, and he saw me there. And then we had a very nice time. I had organized a concert on which his music was played. And then, perhaps five, six, or seven years later, again there was a concert. And Feldman again decided to come up. In those days Feldman very rarely left New York. It was very unusual for him to go anywhere. This was quite special. And my address was once again this very same place. And he knocked on my door, and there I was in exactly the same situation he had seen me in five or six years before.

Example No. 2: if we picture our lives taking place on a calendar – a desk calendar, the kind with one date on each page, and all the pages stacked up – if we picture each day of our lives taking place on the surface of one of these pages – and we drill out and remove a core sample of this calendar at any particular moment – for example, the moment when one wakes up in the morning and gets out of bed – then we line up all these moments in a row – one could see oneself in a kind of film, each frame of which shows a different picture of one getting out of bed in the morning. In this way, one could say, 'I am always waking up. I am always getting out of bed. Every time it's different. This is my life.'

Example No. 3: this reminds me of one of the *Tales of the Hasidim* as retold by Martin Buber (1991). A man moved to a room in a house in a new city. On his first night, he heard wedding music and the sounds of celebration from the house next door. 'How wonderful,' he thought, 'the daughter of this house is getting married.' Because it was the custom in the small town he had come from for the wedding to take place in the house of the bride's family. But the next night, he again heard wedding music and celebration. This time, he thought, 'How strange. But there must be two daughters in this house, each married a day apart.' However, the pattern continued, and he heard wedding music and celebration each day for the week. Finally his curiosity overcame him, and he knocked on the door and asked the man, 'How many daughters live here anyway?' 'No daughters live here,' said the owner. 'Then how has it come to pass that a wedding has taken place here every night this week?' The owner explained, 'We rent this place out for wedding parties, and we do an excellent business.' The man returned to his room next door. That night, he heard wedding music and celebration again coming from the house. 'How wonderful,' he thought, 'to live in this world of weddings.'

What is a moment? A moment consists of a small action in a small amount of time in a particular place. The moment exists inseparable from the action, the time and the place. It is that action at that time, for that amount of time, in that place. Some philosophers might call a moment like this Being (with a capital B). What happens then when a moment repeats or non-repeats? A recognizable pattern of time/place/action quality emerges in a perceivable proximity, with clearly shifting detail. Maybe we can now say something new has appeared: the moment has multiplied – and through its multiplicitness, it has begun to accumulate meaning, or history – an alphabetical history, a musical history. It repeats, and it does not, in conformity with its own qualities of multiplicity. In this way, the many moments become one, and the one moment becomes many.

REFERENCES
Buber, Martin (1991) *Tales of the Hasidim: The Later Masters*, New York: Schocken.
Cage, John (1968) 'Lecture on nothing', in *Silence*, London: Marion Boyars.
Duras, Marguerite (1992) *Summer Rain*, trans. Barbara Bray, London: Macmillan.
Feldman, Morton (1986 [1963]) *For Christian Wolff* (score), London: Universal Edition.
Ibuse, Masui and Bester, John (1971) *Black Rain*, London: Secker & Warburg.
Lechte, John (1994) *Fifty Contemporary Thinkers, from Structuralism to Postmodernity*, London: Routledge, pp. 102-4.
MacMillan, James (1991) *Three Dawn Rituals* (score), London: Schott.

Book Reviews

The Twentieth Century Performance Reader Michael Huxley and Noel Witts (eds)
421 pp., London and New York: Routledge
1996. £14.99.
ISBN 0 415 11162 8 7

Twentieth-Century Theatre: A Sourcebook
Richard Drain (ed.)
387 pp., London and New York: Routledge
1996. £14.99.
ISBN 0 415 09620 0

Art into Theatre: Performance Interviews and Documents
Nick Kaye
281 pp., Harwood Academic Publishers
1996.
ISBN 3 7186 5789 9

Each of these books is a collection of texts related to twentieth-century performance and while they include many of the same artists the editorial approach of each is very different. They share a commitment to the voice of the artist, and like other recent collections of new and archival material – for instance, Mariellen Sandford's recent *Happenings and Other Acts* or Catherine Ugwu's *Let's Get it On: the politics of black performance* – they are books which bring performance criticism to meet the writings of artists themselves.

Each also implies a politics of reading and writing. In the introduction to their performance reader, Michael Huxley and Noel Witts talk of the ways in which 'the ideas of one era often come to haunt another' through the records which artists leave in print. Current performance practice may be haunted by the ideas of dead artists but it is also haunted by its equivocal relationship to the ephemeral. Since these anthologies are concerned with essentially ephemeral media and since many important artists have published very little, the variety of writings is extraordinarily diverse. Prologues and prefaces, poetic addresses to the reader, letters and notebooks, fragments of diaries, and in Nick Kaye's case extensive interviews, artists' drawings and scores, appear alongside essays and polemics. The editors invite us to make connections between entries and to read across excerpts and in doing so they ask the reader to reflect actively upon the nature of what it is to perform.

Richard Drain's collection of around ninety essays, letters and working notes is by twentieth-century practitioners who have addressed theatre and chosen to challenge its boundaries. He begins with André Antoine and ends with Guillermo Gomez Peña; in between John McGrath, Carolee Schneemann, Bertolt Brecht, Adolph Appia, Vesta Tilley, Wole Soyinka, Judy Chicago, Augusto Boal, Hélène Cixous, Ntozake Shange and Edward Bond share space in five parts or 'dimensions': the modernist, the political, the popular, the inner and the global. Each section is arranged chronologically and introduced by Drain. The haunting of one era by another is ever present and it is tempting to match fragments; for instance, Tristan Tzara's commentary on his *Handkerchief of Clouds* (1925):

> There are only three characters who keep their identity throughout the whole play. The six commentators play seventeen different roles. They make up and change costumes on stage. Their names are the same on stage as they are in life.... The settings are not there to give the illusion of reality, but to establish where the action takes place. An on-screen enlargement of a picture postcard goes with each act.

This seems to invite a response from Robert Wilson's speech introducing Freud (1969): 'I see it simply as a collage of different realities occurring simultaneously like being aware of several visual factors and how they combine into a picture before your eyes at any given moment.'

Richard Drain's talent as an editor lies in combining eclecticism with narrative drive. He leads and tantalizes his reader, especially in his judicious use of fragments of text, with excerpts like Valeska Gert's memoir of the 1920s: 'I performed theatre. I longed for the dance; I danced, I longed for the theatre.' Drain has a highly personal sense of history and a politics of performance which is soundly based in the intentions of the artist and his introductions are peppered with imageic comments: 'Dada strews tin tacks on the highway of art, and both legitimacy and status end up badly punctured. It points the alternative way, across open country, where disruptive activities become theatre, and theatre becomes a disruptive activity.'

If Drain's is of the from/to variety of anthology Huxley and Witts eschew chronology and plump for the democracy of the alphabet in their collection, saying, 'We wish to avoid spurious intimations that artists, simply by following each other chronologically, develop the idea of performance, or even worse, are part of a cultural "evolution".' While the tone evinced here implies a polemics of performance, their collection too is eclectic, including among others Laurie Anderson, Sally Banes, Peter Brook, Doris Humphrey, Philip Glass, Robert Wilson, Wole Soyinka and Tadeusz Kantor. They argue in their introduction for a new approach to the classification of performance. While Richard Drain has no problems with the term 'theatre', using it as a frame and as a location for the work while subjecting it to criticism, Huxley and Witts engage with 'performance' itself, saying that there have been few attempts to address 'performance as a discipline in its own right'.

Richard Drain's historical reading of twentieth-century theatre relies heavily on the early European avant-garde, that other side of modernism: disruptive, diaristic, boundary-crossing and performative, which is linked to the development of performance and conceptual art,[1] but he also brings other important views into play. Ntozake Shange's 1979 essay 'Unrecovered losses/ black theatre traditions' links contemporary African-American theatre to slave narratives and performance forms derived from African traditions of dance and music. It prefigures many of the arguments put forward more recently by critics like Coco Fusco, Joseph Roach and bell hooks which call for a critique of prevailing views of the history of the avant-garde and for more inclusive forms of criticism which can account for the migration of forms in different ways. Drain also includes an essay by Kwesi Owusu from 1986 on the Notting Hill Carnival which evokes the history of the fairground and the playing-space as vital places of popular transgressive creativity. He ends with Guillermo Gomez Peña's 'The border as performance laboratory' in which Gomez Peña acknowledges the importance of acting in that large, public yet colonized territory which is the art world and invokes into its space the artists of the borders, and in doing so allows the politics of identity to meet the politics of form. Drain's decision to deal with theatre history necessitates dealing with historical drives and movements. While these ideas are traces which 'ghost' his choice of pieces – reading Peña's essay we go back and read Tristan Tzara's flirtatious love affair with primitivism in quite a different way – they are decisively present.

In dismissing history almost anecdotally Huxley and Witts lose the opportunity to engage with it in a productive way. While I agree with them that simplistic chronologies can be misleading, there is a strong sense in which they seem to be saying in their preface that history does not matter. I think they mean something else – possibly that history is uncertain and all moments contain contradictions – but the arrangement of their book gives them little opportunity to engage with these ideas. What they gain from their approach is a looser, more lateral reading of performance, one which returns the task of making connections to the reader. They also include critical essays which represent significant moments of critical insight into performance. Critics Raymond Williams, Sally Banes, John Martin and Roselee Goldberg are represented and extend ideas set up in the introductory essay. Huxley and Witts stand back as editors, refusing to take a stance but allowing, through their very clear cross-referencing – every excerpt is followed by indications for further reading within and without the book – the manner of reading across ideas and statements which they wish to encourage.

The strength of each of these books really lies in its selections, and these are excellent. The books can be cross-read to great advantage – for instance, where Huxley and Witts have an interview with Pina Bausch, Bausch does not appear *per se* in

Richard Drain's book, but her predecessor Valeska Gert is included. Similarly they include John Cage, who is referenced in Drain through Alan Kaprow and Peter Schumann. Each includes a different mix, a take on the influences on and predecessors of contemporary performance. Both books are important sources of archive material for students, teachers and artists themselves. They provide a contextual network of writings through which to read new work.

Nick Kaye's beautifully produced and thoughtful book of interviews and performance documents is timely. It feels like an art book, and has some very good colour reproductions of artists' scores and line drawings, notes and plans by Anthony Howell, Dennis Oppenheim, Brith Gof, Carolee Schneemann and John Cage, among others. Kaye engages with the ephemeral quality of performance through including texts by artists he has interviewed over the past fifteen years. He includes some of the significant figures of European and American performance; he has, for instance, multiple entries on John Cage, together with fragments of scores, essays and notes, and interviews with Barry Le Va, Carolee Schneemann, Michael Kirby and Richard Foreman. He includes alongside these a number of important British artists: Anthony Howell, Julian Maynard Smith and Stuart Brisley among them. He is an illuminating interviewer and his introductory essay is excellent and extremely specific. He understands the often mutually exclusive (and even dismissive) worlds of visual art and theatre and is able to bring them into a productive relationship in his criticism. As an editor he consciously neither chooses the 'single, overbearing narrative voice' nor pretends to 'a neutrality the process of editing sometimes stands behind'. Instead he places himself in a partial and partisan relationship to the work whose 'developing logics' he discusses. I have been reading Nick Kaye's writings on performance for some years and this essay is one of his best. He has the confidence to bring into play his personal position and values in ways which give his editorial practice vitality and a sense of dialogue – he curates this collection as much as he edits it.

These books share a commitment to engaging with artists' work through representing the voice of the artist. In the emerging discipline of Performance Studies, where the need for academic critics to make their own mark can result in highly definitive statements, the impetus to edit and curate the artist's work for the page can be seen as less important. In much recent writing on performance it is the voice of critic as performer which is dominant. The sense that the page itself is a ludic space and that the work of art is a springboard for elegant and sometimes even impudent textual play can be thrilling, but within those terms artists are often marginalized. These three books mark a turn away from this and towards engaging with the artists' work in direct and appropriate ways.

Witts and Huxley talk of helping to define a field with their collection. They are wrong, happily. None of these editors defines a field; instead they explore it and illuminate parts of it in the company of artists they have seen, read, respected, admired, and sometimes worked and argued with. Conversations with the living and the dead, engagement with the passions and ideas which fuel and inform the disciplines of performance today are evoked here and, to paraphrase the closing words of Nick Kaye's introductory essay, it follows that at this point this review should reach a natural close and give way to the discussions themselves.

Claire MacDonald

Note

1 For an excellent discussion of the 'other side' of modernism and its relationship to conceptual and performance art see Michael Newman's 'Revising modernism, representing postmodernism: critical discourses of the visual arts' (*ICA Documents 4*, London: ICA, 1986).

Atlas Anti-Classics: Shorter Works of the Anti-Tradition '4 Dada Suicides: Arthur Cravan, Jacques Rigaut, Julien Torma and Jacques Vache': selected texts, introduced by Roger Conover, Terry Hale and Paul Lenti, trans. Terry Hale, Paul Lenti, Iain White
267 pp. London: Atlas Press 1995. £9.99.
ISBN 0 947757 74 0

Atlas Archive Series: Documents of the Avant-Garde 'The Book of Masks' essays Remy de Gourmont: author's texts selected by Andrew Mangravite, trans. Andrew Mangravite, Iain White, Terry Hale and others
304 pp. London: Atlas Press 1994. £13.99.
ISBN 0 947757 81 3

Encyclopaedia Acephalica: two collections, edited by Georges Bataille and by Robert

Lebel and Isabelle Waldberg: assembled and introduced by Alastair Brotchie, biographies by Dominiqe Lecoq, trans. Iain White

173 pp. London: Atlas Press 1995. £12.99.
ISBN 0 947745 87 2

An Anecdoted Topography of Chance: Daniel Spoerri, in collaboration with Robert Filliou, Emmett Williams, Dieter Rot and Topor, trans. Malcolm Green

241 pp. London: Atlas Press 1995. £13.99.
ISBN 0 947757 88 0

> To stand in this moment, in a city in history, thinking of a lost man who was great. And if he is great, what is his greatness? If he is great, why is he lost? Thinking, rather, of his traces among us who hardly know his name.
>
> (Rukeyser 1972: 3)

The opening to Muriel Rukeyser's extraordinary work *The Traces of Thomas Hariot*. Throughout it she shows that Hariot – friend of Walter Raleigh, Francis Drake, and Christopher Marlowe – is, demonstratively, a crucially influential, rather than merely a 'minor', Elizabethan figure. Yet he is almost unknown now, and all we have left are literally traces – from which Rukeyser constructs a detailed and highly charged portrait.

Wading, even waking, among the Best of Schubert and boxed set James Herbert yardage, it's sometimes all too easy to forget that anything else is out there.

Emerging artists and students on performance courses are often frustrated by a lack of available reference and primary resources. Books, and recordings, published in small editions (sometimes just 500 or fewer) – let alone one-off undocumented performances – are cited but unavailable. Work which has been accorded 'seminal' status exists as 'cloister whispers', larded over with a slippage of de-positioned emphases. Go and check your local library, or even your university library, and see what I mean. Where exactly does a young performance writer get a reference copy of Kathy Acker's early *The Life and Times of the Black Tarantula*, or of *White Subway* by Burroughs – should they want to? Where is information about performances by Carlyle Reedy? What was the extent of Henry Flynt's involvement with Fluxshoe? If we have anything at all it is increasingly a digest of archive materials represented by a critical theorist. Not bad in itself, but worrying in the absence of the primary resources. What gets taught, tends to be what can be researched by an average student without too much difficulty. This traps an underfunded network into acceptance of canons policed by cautious publishers and so on. If we aren't to be continually resubjected to the whims, and sometimes wilful misinformation, of revisionist historians, then surely more primary materials are needed. The recent publications by Atlas[1] are extremely welcome in this respect alone.

Atlas began their Archive series to 'examine and publish previously unavailable material relating to issues, or neglected groups, within the avant-garde "anti-tradition" of the last 100 years'. Take, as one example, Jacques Vache. Maurice Nadeau in *The History of Surrealism* points to a meeting that André Breton had with Vache at a field hospital in Nantes, 1916, as 'a decisive encounter [which] was to influence his [Breton's] life' (Nadeau 1973: 56). Yet Vache was otherwise left shrouded in mystique with legendary status merely attributed. Thanks to Atlas, their editors and translators, we now have verso pressings of Vache's letters. And in them we begin to glimpse why Breton was so impressed by this early mail artist – 'he used to entertain himself by painting and drawing a series of postcards for which he devised strange captions' (244):

> Modernity is also both constant and murdered each night – We ignore Mallarmé, without hatred – but then he's dead – But we don't recognise Apollinaire any more, or Cocteau – because – we suspect them of making art too consciously, of slicing romanticism with telephone wire and not knowing the dynamos. The stars are still disconnected! – it's boring – and then sometimes they speak so seriously! A man who believes is a curiosity.
>
> (227)

4 Dada Suicides provides lengthy introductions to Vache, alongside Jacques Rigaut, Julien Torma and Arthur Cravan. It's provocative, rather than passive, showing that many of these hidden (his)stories are still unravelling. There is considerable doubt shed on Cravan's presumed disappearance, for example. It's a companion volume to the first of the Archive series, *Dada Berlin*, an annotated version of Richard Huelsenbeck's 'classic' *Dada Almanac* of 1920. Also a link, to some small extent, between the latter and a sizeable collection of French symbolist and decadent writing of the 1890s, *The Book of Masks*, which contextualizes selections by forty-four writers of that previous *fin-de-siècle* period. As one would expect, such a trawl throws up some 'big' names such as Gide, Huysman,

Mallarmé, Rimbaud, Claudel, Lautréamont; the best surprises though, for me, are Rachide (one of only two women present throughout four largish collections – a lack which Atlas could profitably address in a future project) and Gustave Kahn. I knew neither previously, and that's exactly the value of this book; serving as a working introduction to a strangely coherent, and demonstratively influential, body of thought and practice. It's a point of access then, and some of it never previously translated.

But, whilst I understand the alternative to naturalism that symbolism explored and began to open up, much of the prose in this book sits too close, for my comfort, to male fantasies born out of an over-literary denial, a kind of curtain peeping at the world (not even *flâneurial*) – but you can take that as a purely personal prejudice. For all that, an important book. It's something of an indictment of the debilitating culture of ideas in the UK – where obscurity is aligned with difficulty and suspicion – that, whilst Atlas's books sell well, they do so mostly in the United States.

Perhaps this is a good moment then to recommend not only the generally high editorial content of these books, but their quality production values. These are handsome and very affordable books – both to have and to hold.

Archive 3 presents texts either written by, or else written by those in contact with (through the Acéphale group), Georges Bataille. These are pieces as encyclopaedia or dictionary entries, in many cases supplemented by photographic 'evidence'. Alastair Brotchie points out, in an excellent introduction, that Bataille's principal, and lifelong, obsessions surface here. In that sense this book forms a workable and delightful entry point into Bataille's thought, and into the underbelly of modernism – close to the surrealist stream. Selective taxonomic cross-breeding, and resultant estranging hybrids, rather than gestures towards meta-narrative. Entries from the *Critical Dictionary* include those on – Dust, Eye, Factory Chimney, Hygiene, Mouth, Spittle, and Threshold. You can tell, simply from the titles of such entries, I hope, something of the quirky range which is given presence to. Writing brimful with philosophical slippage, heterogeneous humour; a kind of psychotropic vaudeville.

Just as essential is Archive 4, a revised and re-annotated edition of Daniel Spoerri's *An Anecdoted Topography of Chance*, one of my all-time favourite publications and rightly considered an 'artist book' classic. The version I've known, until now, is the Something Else Press edition of 1966 (the second in the series, this is the fourth major version). Longevity was, I suspect, not a foremost consideration of Spoerri's when beginning to 'set out here to see what the objects on a section of this table . . . might suggest to me, what they might spontaneously awaken in me in describing them: the way Sherlock Holmes, starting out with a single object, could solve a crime; or historians, after centuries, were able to reconstitute a whole epoch from the most famous fixation in history, Pompeii' (23). Nevertheless, thirty years down the track, time has given an additional resonance to the whole project. If you want to engage with Fluxus, then this is as good as it gets.

Briefly, the book presents eighty numbered 'things' (from a 'piece of White Bread', via 'Worm-eaten joined wooden box' and 'Sample of Olfran after-shave lotion', to a 'Cigarette Burn') as 'found' on a table in his hotel room. They are described in a discursive, anecdotal fashion (60):

> 14. Package of Twining's Chinese tea which I bought for a change of aroma, although I still have some Orange Pekoe left. I wanted smoked tea and they sold me this package pretending it was, which it wasn't.

Such entries have been further annotated by his co-writer Robert Filliou, Emmett Williams and Dieter Rot in gradually thickening versions since 1962. Tiny caption illustrations have been drawn along the way by Topor. Then of course there are processes of translation – from Spoerri and Filliou's French into Williams's English, and Dieter Rot's German, then back into English via Malcolm Green for this deluxe Atlas compendium edition. Translation too from one typeface, page size and overall layout into another typeface, a different page size and so on. The book(s) resist(s) closure, both individually and collectively, and ideally anyone could add their own anecdotes and annotations. Much of the Fluxus project was concerned with social production, by friends working with 'poor' materials, to tease the distances between boundaries of 'art' and 'everyday life' (although such a supposed binary actually strikes me as an oversimplified formulation). Surely the extension of this idea, through de Certeau's articulation that 'space is practised place' (De Certeau 1984: 117), into a cultural paradigm for 'performance', forms one of the central discourses of twentieth-century western cultures? This is a crucial document in that onward discourse. With an *Oulipo & Ouxpos* collection recently available and several others, including *Vienna Actionists*, in the pipeline the Atlas Archive series is a must.

cris cheek

Note

1 All Atlas Books are available through Airlift (++44 (0) 181 443 5333)

References

De Certeau, Michel (1984) *The Practice of Everyday Life*, Berkeley, CA: University of California Press.
Nadeau, Maurice (1973) *The History of Surrealism*, Harmondsworth, Mx: Pelican.
Rukeyser, Muriel (1972) *The Traces of Thomas Hariot*, London: Victor Gollancz.

Ecologies of Theater

Bonnie Marranca

289 pp., Baltimore MD, and London: Johns Hopkins University Press/PAJ Books, 1996. £13.00 (paperback); £32.00 (hardback). ISBN 0-8018-5273-0/0-8018-5273-2

Collected writings (particularly writings such as these which have already appeared over the years in a variety of journals) invite the reader to become personally acquainted with the writer's voice, to savour its plurality rather than its argument, to recall, perhaps, some features of a long-standing relationship. I therefore allow myself to remember here Bonnie Marranca's first book, *The Theater of Images*, appearing in 1977, and the sensuous taste it left in my mind of theatre-making beyond Aristotelian modes. I recall, too, the first issue of the *Performing Arts Journal*, of the year before, 1976, and in particular its very first article: 'Louis Aragon's open letter to André Breton on Robert Wilson's "Deafman Glance"' – an aged French poet writing to a dead confrère about a young American's theatre work. It has always seemed to me that the publication by Bonnie Marranca and Gautam Dasgupta of that letter in a journal funded partly out of their wedding gifts the previous summer and put together on the floor of their New York apartment was indicative of Marranca's project – her struggle over twenty years to sustain one of the West's leading theatre journals, her sense of history and of the provenance of art forms, her engagement in contemporary performance. In England at that time we were already talking of ecology and of theatre, reflecting upon possible contiguities, but the terrain of ecology, it seemed to us, was fast being appropriated by New Age writers, and it has taken twenty years and such a writer as Marranca, to draw together the languages of natural history, landscapes, social history and performance into the rhetorical question she asks herself: 'What is theater but the history of figures in a landscape, the earth itself a history, older than humankind?' It is, moreover, a question she, together with Heiner Müller, asks in some urgency, for it opens out towards an end of human history, an end of a species, in which the ecological theme subsumes all political issues.

Ecologies of Theater is a collection of Marranca's writings, recorded conversations and talks made since her last collection, *Theatrewritings*, published in 1984. Here, in writing that has little truck with current jargon or the need for critical peer reference, and which is charged with her commitment to a sense of modernism, is her belief in the organic interrelationship of the natural, social and spiritual worlds: a celebration of John Cage; her fascination with the work of Robert Wilson; a lecture to the American academic community and its theatre departments; her journey with Müller through despoiled shores in an essay echoing Artaud's last writings on Van Gogh; her analysis and care for the work of Irene Fornes, Rachel Rosenthal and Meredith Monk. There is her reply to the advocates of interculturalism, her reflections upon Karen Blixen, introductory essays to gardening and the Hudson Valley, an exquisite little acceptance speech of the George Natham Award for Dramatic Criticism in 1985, and all the way through this collection there is her whispered and beloved conversation with Gertrude Stein.

For Marranca is first and foremost a writer, as was Stein, a writer of her own thinking, and both, it seems to me, have in their own ways, helped forge one of this century's most significant tectonic plates – the one that is shifting slowly through human consciousness, both of itself and its technological surround – namely, the change in perception from the Euclidean depth analysis of the Renaissance, which, for so long, has formed ways of seeing, thinking, narrating and representing, to the complex plane analysis first intimated, in the visual arts by Cézanne in those hinterlands between the viewer and Mont St Victoire. From cubism to Duchamp to Stein, from Tzara to Breton to Pollock, from Kaprow's reading of Pollock's work to Live Art, from Schwitters to Rauschenberg and beyond, to name but a few of the traces in the visual arts alone, there has been a very clear and perceptible movement to bring to the surface from the hidden depths (and depth is a human construct) of perspective and teleology, the objects of our attention – with no concomitant loss of density, with no diminution of reference, but situated in a very different, perhaps even liberated, landscape. What Braque referred to as '*Une Certitude*', what Artaud later described as a '*principe d'actualité*', has been taken up in a world that is no longer anthropocentric, but biocentric, admitting to a multiplicity of languages and species, the equal value and rights of beings and things, a non-hierarchic and fractal landscape.

Marranca stands within, articulates, this emerging landscape, as it is now taking shape across the image-making processes of the western world. She is, of course, well aware of its modernist history, not only in the visual arts (she founded a short-lived magazine called *LIVE*, devoted to Performance Art, between the years 1979 and 1982), but also in this century's western theatre (acknowledging, rightly it seems to me, its debt to Japanese culture). From such a sense of place, she is at work identifying ecosystems as they fold into cultural and social systems, carrying with them issues of ethics and spirituality.

Marranca steadfastly maintains that it is an ecology of theatre and not an ecology of performance that is her concern. In the reconfiguration of theatre currently taking place, it is the concept of performance which is being foregrounded. Critically, educationally, artistically, even managerially, it wields considerable symbiotic power.

But Performance, Marranca suspects, has been colonized by the social sciences. Every gesture seen as a social intervention. 'There are no longer agreed-upon critical standards or art values for addressing any work.' Her own position, on the other hand, is decidedly within 'theatron' – a place for viewing. Indeed, for her, 'Thinking is a kind of spectatorship', and more than once she reminds us of the proximity of theatre to theory. That this affords her the space to discriminate is clear; it also allows her to hold a strong sense of tradition, observing lineages, noting roots. It is a lack of theatrical consciousness and tradition that she senses both within the current rise of the notion of Performance, and in the espousal of interculturalism.

> What is wonderful about writing is its ability to reimagine worlds in endless possibilities, and what is more remarkable, even dangerous, about theater is its ability to demonstrate the potentiality of future worlds in their very possibility of being acted by human beings living now.

Her writing is never less than passionate and visionary. Often it has the rhythms and exclamations of speaking. Where would you find a critic declaring: 'Oh, things could be appreciated . . .'? Some, though not I, might baulk at its emphases, as it exhales to assert this and that. And certainly it is true that when she writes of those closest to her – Stein, Cage, Müller and Blixen – her writing, particularly at its more elegiac moments, breathes more naturally, is inspirational. But she is a most serious thinker at all times, and the quality of what she writes demands our attention as she weaves her text through the ecologies she perceives:

> Among the ecologies of theater, I began to think of the promise of culture as horticulture and myself as a naturalist, so to speak. Theater appeared as an endangered species. This way of thinking seemed to me to point to an all-encompassing humanism that would embrace biological, social, ecological, and political issues in the study of an art form in relation to its environment, its culture, in other words, its livingness. In this context, critical writing is not merely an activity but a way of life, an attitude toward living. It is the same verb, to cultivate, that gives definition both to cultivation of the land and of the human body. And sometimes in history knowledge grows on trees.'

Peter Hulton

Archive Review

Cricoteka: Centre for the Documentation of the work of Tadeusz Kantor, 31-002 Krakow, Ul. Kanonicza 5, Poland. Entrance to the museum/archive is free. Cricoteka is open Monday to Friday from 10.00 – 14.00; and in July and August Tuesday to Sunday 10.00–14.00. A Web site is to be established later this year.

Situated in the heart of Krakow's Stare Miasto (Old Town) near to the Rynek Główny, the magnificent medieval town square, where for centuries market stalls have sold flowers, cloth and woodcarvings, is Ulicia Kanonicza, one of the oldest streets in Krakow. At number 5 Ulicia Kanonicza, in a fifteenth-century building still owned by the church, is the Gallery-Museum Cricoteka, the archive of Tadeusz Kantor and his world-famous theatre ensemble Cricot 2.

> Tadeusz Kantor created the Cricoteka as a Living Archive of his theatrical work so that his own ideas would be preserved, not in a dead library system, but in the minds and imagination of future generations. In accordance with the Artist's wish, a unique collection of objects, and theatrical machines from Cricot 2 performances, theoretical writings, drawings and plans, films and video records and thousands of reviews in many languages as well as dozens of special issues of periodicals and books – the fruit of many years' wandering by Tadeusz Kantor and his troupe – have found their home in the Gallery-Museum at 5 Kanonicza Street in Krakow.
>
> (Plesniarowicz 1996)

Cricoteka is the combination of the name Cricot (itself a French-sounding anagram of the Polish term *to cyrk* – 'it's a circus') and *teka*, which in modern Polish means a collection of archival material, drawings or papers, and also the place which houses the collection. However, the Greek origin of the word is *theke*, meaning a place of concealment. Kantor's choice of words like everything else he did was deliberate and significant. Indeed, Krzysztof Plesniarowicz, the charming and enthusiastic curator of the museum, who is also a erudite scholar of Kantor's work, has written:

> The name of the theatre museum and archive is a perfect expression of the basic ideas of Kantor's art. Firstly, of the double meaning, the metaphysical concept of the circus ('it's a circus': a formula of the poor Fairground Booth, as Kantor called his theatre). Secondly, the principle of antithesis, of raising by abasing, of expressing life by invoking death, of a 'poor' reality by the degradation of the symbol, of the *sacrum* by the *profanum* (the anagram 'Cricot'). Thirdly, the method of 'concealment', of 'wrapping', or the emballage, one of the most interesting and original features of the paintings, happenings, and of Kantor's theatre ('Teka').
>
> (Plesniarowicz 1996)

Kantor was very aware of preserving his objects and ideas. He felt the Polish tendency had been to destroy or to discard everything, then attempt to reclaim it twenty years later. He was anxious to establish a museum before his death; to preserve the ideas in one space:

> When man and his work cease to exist, there remains the memory, a message sent forth to the future, to the coming generation ... memory is a condition of development which in turn is the essence of the life. All our crises are caused by failure to respect memory.
>
> (Kantor 1986)

What exists now at Ulicia Kanonicza certainly respects memory and also enables research and promotes a greater understanding of Kantor's work for future generations. Indeed it is difficult to imagine a more useful archive for the scholar or enthusiast of Kantor and Cricot 2. Everything is assembled here, not only the primary sources; Kantor's manifestoes, scenarios, theatrical reflections, drawings and plans, but also all the film and video documentation known to have been made, thousands of photographs and reviews and a library of published and unpublished work (in many languages), together with numerous theses, effectively forming a complete manifestation of the Kantor/ Cricot 2 bibliography.

The gap between a proposal and its realization, between intention and reality, is often wide and so it was with interest that I read Kantor's manifesto for the Cricoteka within the Cricoteka. If only more artistic and educational aspirations could be so accurately realized.

Archives' as a museum:
The Archives' function as a museum is fundamental and necessary. The museum preserves works, experiences, ideas. It guarantees the continuity of the development of culture. The Centre serves these purposes, preserving the theatrical and artistic achievements of Tadeusz Kantor and his TROUPE.

Archives' functions:
collecting complete documentary materials

a) collecting photographic materials from performances
b) collecting reviews, articles, catalogues, programmes, prints, posters, books and publications edited by Polish and foreign centres associated with Cricot 2 Theatre's activities
c) classifying, listing, photocopying, providing commentaries for materials
d) collecting materials recorded on audio tapes, video tapes, films and slides; recording performances, rehearsals, interviews, lectures, press conferences
e) organization of all kinds of recordings: radio, TV, film
f) its own recordings of all sort of meetings, lectures and conferences
g) collecting theoretical texts of Tadeusz Kantor, essays, scripts and stage designs

The scholarly nature of archives:
A detailed selection of documentary materials serves, above all, scholarly and didactic purposes. The experience of Tadeusz Kantor and his troupe (covering more than 20 years), contained in the stages in the development of idea, should be handed down to subsequent generations of theatrical art, theatrology and visual arts.
(Kantor 1986)

What is particularly striking about this archive, however, is the care, diligence and enthusiasm of the permanent staff. In addition to his native Polish, Krysztof Plesniarowicz is also fluent in English and French and can speak 'a little' German. The three other members of the Cricoteka team, two archivists and an administrator, are also able to assist in English and French. As a visitor one is made to feel welcome, given a desk and encouraged to delve into the material; a specific enquiry into a detail of Cricot past is immediately taken up with interest and the relevant sources indicated. It would be a joy to do research here and to live in the beautiful and vibrant city of Krakow. And clearly many people do; it seems that at any one time there are usually two or three postgraduate students conducting research in the archive, most often from France, Germany or the USA.

As well as being an immensely valuable research archive the Cricoteka also functions as a museum and exhibition space and welcomes the art or theatre enthusiast and the Kantor fan or follower as much as the scholar. It is quite possible to drop in and watch a video screening of *Wielepole, Wielepole*, one morning or roam the crypts and take in the current exhibition. The exhibitions change frequently depending on the demand for artefacts (objects, drawings, photographs, etc.) by other museums and curators. Major exhibitions on Kantor and Cricot 2 have been mounted in Paris and Brussels, exhausting the Cricoteka of most of its collection, but when that happens there are wonderful photographic exhibitions that can be mounted. During my recent visit the photographs of Maurizio Buscarino were on show. Buscarino followed Kantor's work from *The Dead Class* onwards and accurately captured fleeting qualities of all the productions during live performances and without recourse to studio or posed 'shoots'.

Also, it is now possible to visit Kantor's last studio, several streets away on Maly Rynek. This has been preserved as it was on the evening of Kantor's death, with a copy of Milan Kundera's *Unbearable Lightness of Being* (in French) still beside the bed, an unfinished painting on the easel and Kantor's suitcases and other objects of wandering scattered around the bedroom/studio. It is an eerie feeling to stand alone in this studio looking out across the old town through the small attic window, and to reflect on Kantor's last hours. I imagined him struggling up the several flights of steep steps after excusing himself from the rehearsals of *Today is my Birthday*. Did his thoughts remain in the theatre, or turn to his painting, or to his writing (a notebook remains open on his desk)? For a man so preoccupied with death, the creation of a theatre of death and the legacy of his work, one can't help but wonder what his last thoughts and actions were.

The actors of Cricot 2 tried to continue without Kantor after his death; but his active participation in every performance was essential and as necessary as the conductor of an orchestra. He did actually structure the rhythm of the performance through his interventions, manipulation and presence; it was not an empty theatrical device. The first time the actors performed *The Dead Class* without Kantor it lasted twenty minutes longer. However, Kantor did not score or notate how his performances should be delivered in terms of speed, rhythm or tempo, and so the archive does not contain any notation with regard to this sculpting of time that made the 'Theatre of Death' so very much alive. Another sense of loss and emptiness confronts you when you witness one of the famous 'Bio-Objects'. These are the artistic objects/sculptures (far more than props) which, as Kantor said, possessed a peculiarity: 'Its own living organs – the actors'. How does a museum present what was a relationship – the actor and the object, the Bio-Object – when only the object is left? Krzysztof Plesniarowicz has written:

> The interchangeability of the function of the actor and the object made evident the conflict of intellect and matter. However, it also imparted a mechanical character to the stage existence of the Bio-Object. The 'Chaired' person, united with the vehicle (cart, bicycle), with the mannequin or an object (a suitcase, desk) was not only imprisoned in the form of a Bio-Object but was impelled to free himself rhythmically from the ties with that object and take up again the function of a living organ.
> (Plesniarowicz 1996)

Now, as curator of the museum he is perplexed as to how to re-animate the relationship. How to present the Bio-Objects not as artifact, stage requisite or redundant prop but as one part of a dynamic relationship. The struggle of the actor with this encumbrance and against this imprisonment of the object created in fact one of the lasting memories of a Kantor production. The Bio-Objects now rest immobile in the cellars of Kanonicza creating an eerie feeling of a torture chamber, devices that clearly had a purpose, retaining the propensity to act, dormant but not dead.

Similarly the costumes, which have all been preserved and collected, retain a sense of purpose. Conceived by Kantor as something far beyond dressing or decoration, more like a mask, they have a uniformity of decay and the bitter poignancy of dereliction. As in a mask exhibition, one stands in awe at the detail of construction and one's mind speculates upon their use, the animation, the actor inside. Although having the worn and distressed look of a skin shed by a snake these costumes still suggest that their grey, crushed and crumpled outer bark might still be haunted from the hollow within – especially when you turn the other way. In a strange way the fully clothed mannequins that so populated Kantor's productions are less threatening, seemingly still and serene, their wandering having ceased at last.

As a stage designer Kantor was interested in clothing and costume and in particular the notion of layers; layers upon layers, like a palimpsest, the clothing retaining both memories and history:

> ... nomadic people ... roaming outside society in a ceaseless wandering without any aim or a home formed by their madness and passion for packaging their bodies in coats, saddle blankets, canvas, *sunken in the complicated anatomy of clothing, in the arcana of bundles, bags, packages*, thongs, strings ...
> (Plesniarowicz 1994: 23)

Emballage was an extension of collage ('an onomatopoeic replica of collage'), a multi-layered collage where layers, material, wrapping and packaging (envelopes and sacks) concealed elements of the composition and obliged the looker to look at the 'other side'. This concept of emballage clearly extended to many aspects of Kantor's scenic design (wardrobes revealing dead soldiers on the march) and even the construction of characters on stage complete with emblematic costume, mannequin, appendages and located within a Bio-Object. All these elements, the material basis of Kantor's craft together with all his theoretical writings, manifestoes and texts, are assembled within the Cricoteka, the only 'thing' that is missing is that which cannot be replaced or reproduced, Kantor and his actors/ animators.

Richard Gough

References

Kantor, Tadeusz (1986) *Cricot 2 Theatre Information*, Krakow.

Plesniarowicz, K. (1994) *The Dead Memory Machine: Tadeusz Kantor's Theatre of Death*, Krakow: Cricoteka.

Plesniarowicz, K. (1996) *Theatre in Poland*, No. 1, January.

Performance Research: On Illusion
Notes on Contributors

THE EDITORS

Ric Allsopp is a joint editor of *Performance Research* and issue editor for On Illusion. He is co-founder of Writing Research Associates, an international partnership organizing, promoting and publishing performance. He is currently a research fellow at Dartington College of Arts. He has been a research associate with the Centre for Performance Research, Cardiff since 1986, and has been associated with the School for New Dance Development, Amsterdam since 1990.

Richard Gough is general editor of *Performance Research* and currently senior research fellow in the Department of Theatre, Film and Television Studies at the University of Wales, Aberystwyth. He is Artistic Director of the Centre of Performance Research (CPR), the successor of Cardiff Laboratory Theatre, of which he was a founder member. He edited *The Secret Art of the Performer* (London: Routledge, 1990) and has curated and organized numerous conference and workshop events over the last twenty years as well as directing and lecturing internationally.

Claire MacDonald is a joint editor of *Performance Research*. She is a writer and critic and is currently completing a book on feminism and performance art for Routledge. She was head of Theatre and Dartington College of Arts 1987–9 and is now senior lecturer and research fellow in theatre at De Montfort University in Leicester, UK. She was a founder member of Impact Theatre and Insomniac Theatre companies and has written performance texts and librettos for many productions, including, most recently, the script for the music theatre piece *Beulah Land* (London, ICA, 1994).

CONTRIBUTORS

Annemarie Bean is the co-editor, along with James V. Hatch and Brooks Namara, of *Inside the Minstrel Mask: Readings in Nineteenth-Century Blackface Minstrelsy* (Wesleyan University Press/University Press of New England, 1996). She writes on and teaches classes in issues of race, gender and performance and is currently working on her dissertation for the Department of Performance Studies, New York University.

Caroline Bergvall is a writer and Director of Performance Writing at Dartington College of Arts, UK. She was awarded The Showroom Live Art Commission 1993 for her choral piece *Strange Passage* (Equipage, 1993). Collaborative text-sound pieces have been presented at Ars Sonora '92, the Spanish Radio Art festival and Hearing is Believing, Video Positive '95. Her texts have been widely published in experimental poetry presses and magazines in North America and Britain.

Etzel Cardeña did graduate studies in stage directing and has a PhD in Personality Psychology. He has worked professionally as an actor and director, has published on shamanism and performance, and his publications on dissociation and hypnosis have garnered awards from professional societies.

cris cheek is a performance writer, sound composer (with Slant), poet, freelance broadcaster and curator. Co-founder of Chisenhale Dance Space, co-founder of shinkansen and co-director of Sound & Language; currently editing Language Alive books, the Sound & Language CD label (including his own recent spoken word recording *Skin upon Skin*) and producing occasional events in London and East Anglia.

Rod Dickinson is an artist who lives and works in London. His art practice includes creating large-scale crop circle formations. He has most recently exhibited at the Cabinet gallery, London, the Malibu Art Ranch, California and the fields of Wiltshire.

Rose English makes shows. She is Senior Research Fellow in the Theatre Department at Wimbledon School of Art and she and her company, Walks on Water, are resident at The Circus Space in London. She is currently working on three new productions.

Erik Exe Christoffersen lectures in the Department of Dramaturgy at the University of Aarhus in Denmark. He has written books and articles on Odin Teatret and ISTA (International School of Theatre Anthropology), *The Actors Way* (London: Routledge, 1993) and made a video for RAI 2 (1991) *On the Way Through Theatre: Odin Teatret 1964–1990*.

Martha Fleming is a visual artist and writer who makes sitework and insallations and text/image projects for publication. She was born in Toronto, lived 15 years in Montreal, and is now resident in London. Her work in collaboration with Lyne Lapointe has been produced in New York, London, Montreal, Bath, Sao Paulo and other places and she publishes internationally.

Goat Island are a performance group based in Chicago, Illinois. Goat Island have toured internationally giving workshops and performances since 1989. From January–July 1996 they were artists-in-residence at the Centre for Contemporary Art in Glasgow, UK, where they developed their new show *How Dear to Me the Hour When Daylight Dies* (1996).

Matthew Goulish is a founding member (with Lin Hixson) of the Goat Island performance group.

Simon Herbert is co-director of the visual arts commissioning agency Locus+. He is also an artist who has presented performances in Europe and Canada, as well as a regular contributor to arts journals and catalogues.

Peter Hulton is Director of the Arts Documentation Unit, Exeter, UK, publishing Arts Archives, a multimedia archive of arts practice, and is currently Honorary Research Fellow in Drama at the University of Exeter.

Hans-Peter Litscher was born in Switzerland in 1955. From 1976–8 he studied at the Jacques LeCoq School in Paris. Since 1983 he has made a number of works including the spoken opera *Island of the Dead* (1984–9) and *Caduta Massi*, a 'hommage' to film maker Stephan Mahler's unrealized project on Giovanni Segantini, painter of mountains, who died in 1989 shortly before he could realize his dream of erecting a giant panorama of the Engadiner Alps, complete with ozone-rich Alpine air conditioning, under the Eiffel Tower in Paris, France. At present Hans-Peter Litscher is making a documentary on the Polish trick-cyclist Wanda Tura, and her Palazo del Ciclismo Intergalattico.

André Lepecki is a dance critic and writer, based in New York. He is a contributor to Ballet International/Tanz Aktuell and to the literary supplement of the Portuguese daily *Publico*. Since 1992 he has collaborated with Meg Stuart on dramaturgy and set design.

Lynn MacRitchie is a writer and critic based in London. She writes regularly for the *Financial Times* and *The Guardian* newspapers and is London correspondent of *Art in America*. She is a former editor of *Performance* magazine.

Michael Mangan is Senior Lecturer in Drama at Loughborough University. He has taught in the UK, the USA and Poland, and has published several books and articles on Renaissance and contemporary theatre, of which the most recent, *A Preface to Shakespeare's Comedies*, was published by Longman in 1996. He has also worked professionally as a playwright, director and dramaturg.

Andrew Quick is Lecturer in Theatre Studies at Lancaster University. He has written on Forced Entertainment and the sublime in *Contemporary Theatre Review* and is currently preparing a book on the politics of experimentation.

Nicholas Till is Lecturer in Theatre Studies and Senior Course tutor on the MA in Theatre Design/Scenography, at Wimbledon School of Art, London. He has written and directed a number of music-theatre works, and is currently working with composer Andrew Lovett on a community opera for the city of Peterborough, UK. He is the author of *Mozart and the Enlightenment: Truth, Virtue and Beauty in Mozart's Operas* (Faber & Faber, 1992).

Nicholas Zurbrugg is Professor of English and Cultural Studies in the School of Humanities, DeMontfort University, Leicester, UK. The author of *Beckett and Proust* (1988) and *The Parameters of Postmodernism* (1993), he guest edited The Multimedia Text issue of *Art and Design* (1995).

For Product Safety Concerns and Information please contact our EU
representative GPSR@taylorandfrancis.com
Taylor & Francis Verlag GmbH, Kaufingerstraße 24, 80331 München, Germany

www.ingramcontent.com/pod-product-compliance
Lightning Source LLC
Chambersburg PA
CBHW080811010526
44113CB00013B/2360

9780415162104